Communication Forms and Communicative Practices

Language and Text Studies

Edited by
Alexander Brock and Annette Schiller

Volume 15

PETER LANG
EDITION

Alexander Brock / Peter Schildhauer (eds.)

Communication Forms and Communicative Practices

New Perspectives on Communication Forms, Affordances and What Users Make of Them

PETER LANG
EDITION

Bibliographic Information published by the Deutsche Nationalbibliothek
The Deutsche Nationalbibliothek lists this publication in the Deutsche Nationalbibliografie; detailed bibliographic data is available in the internet at http://dnb.d-nb.de.

Library of Congress Cataloging-in-Publication Data
A CIP catalog record for this book has been applied for at the Library of Congress

Printed by CPI books GmbH, Leck

ISSN 0941-4134
ISBN 978-3-631-66752-1 (Print)
E-ISBN 978-3-653-06384-4 (E-PDF)
E-ISBN 978-3-631-70216-1 (EPUB)
E-ISBN 978-3-631-70217-8 (MOBI)
DOI 10.3726/b10386

Peter Lang Edition is an Imprint of Peter Lang GmbH.

Peter Lang – Frankfurt am Main · Bern · Bruxelles · New York · Oxford · Warszawa · Wien

This publication has been peer reviewed.

www.peterlang.com

Preface

With the advance of communicatively oriented text linguistics in the 1970ies, scholars began to complement the description of text structures with the factors and circumstances behind text production (Gülich & Raible 1975; Ermert 1979). Ermert also coined the term „Kommunikationsform". While researchers soon agreed that *communication form* was an important concept for understanding the emergence of texts and for the recognition of different types of texts, it also became clear that the term was used differently by some authors. At the same time, other terms, such as *medium, affordance, text type* etc. partly covered the same ground or entertained an unresolved status with respect to *communication form*. This state continued for some decades and was possibly even aggravated by the great body of research in media linguistics in the last 20 or so years. After all, this new discipline made the concept *medium*, which is closely related to *communication form*, its main concern. Meanwhile, the under-defined status of the latter term did not stop very valuable research from emerging. However, the different readings of *communication form* have caused some discomfort among researchers, and efforts have been made repeatedly to reach a definitive conceptualisation.

The idea of this volume is to make the concept *communication form* the central point of attention rather than one factor of communication among others. The aim is to highlight its emergence and history as well as its definition and utility in the analysis of empirical data. The inclusion of authors from a range of academic backgrounds ensured the representation of different approaches to the term, and different treatments rather than a unified definition were encouraged. This collection of alternative, yet largely compatible perspectives of *communication form* is hoped to do more justice to its complexity than a unified view. The empirical investigation of communication forms ranges from blogs, print magazines and self-monitoring to computer games and sign systems in cities.

The volume starts with two theoretical texts. **Alexander Brock** and **Peter Schildhauer** give an overview of the emergence and different definitions of the term since the 1970ies, including communication form as (grouping of) genre(s), and communication form as a constellation of communicative potentials. They then suggest a conceptualisation of *communication forms* as clusters of technical and communicative constellations with communicative potentials, which are restricted by conventions.

Matthias Meiler introduces the term *infrastructuring* in order to approach communication form from a praxeological perspective. An infrastructure is a relational term based on organised practice. This concept allows for a more reconstructive analysis of communication forms than lists of (superficial) features.

Christine Domke advocates the extension of features considered in the context of communication forms. By looking at concrete examples of the semiotic landscapes of modern cities, i.e. signage in specific locations, she combines the theoretical discussion of communication forms with examples of how their description should be extended to include aspects of the *locatedness* of communication, of mediality, multimodality, and communication in time. She argues that the concept *communication form* should include all medial and material conditions of communication.

Two texts describe the communication forms of *computer games* and their effects on the language that is used while playing them. **Frederic Zähres** investigates word-formation processes in the lexicon of the English version of the game *League of Legends*. He comes to the conclusion that due to competitiveness and time pressure, shortening processes like clipping and initialisms are the most frequently-used word-formation patterns in the context of this communication form.

Birgit Swoboda analyses the communication in MMORPGs such as *World of Warcraft*®, which offer a multitude of communication forms and genres, such as chat-channels, instant messaging, message-boards, machinimas and *Let's play* videos. In a thorough analysis of the communicative processes involved, she describes MMORPGs as communicative hybrids due to their new combination of communication forms, genres and participants' motivations.

Ina Batzke compares the traditional self-monitoring of personal health and fitness data with modern, digital self-tracking devices as well as the Quantified Self movement as communicative practices and establishes crucial differences between them, which – among other aspects – arise from the different communication forms underlying them.

Peter Schildhauer gives a diachronic account of the development of the blog communication form over approximately fifteen years. He shows that changes in the communication form do not always entail an increase of communicative options and points out some discrepancies between communicative potentials and their actual use, drawing on a diachronic corpus of personal blogs.

Finally, **Jana Pflaeging** compares the material-technical and institutional production conditions of print issues of the *National Geographic* magazine from 1915 and 2015 and points out that in addition to social conventions, other factors also influence the choice of communicative options from the potential available: Production costs, individual decision-making, conscious pattern embedding and coincidence also play a role in making communicative choices.

The editors would like to thank all authors for their contributions, which help to evoke a multi-faceted, complex image of *communications forms* – the aim of this volume. Hopefully, the inspiring discussions that accompanied the work on this volume will continue and fuel media-linguistic work in the future.

Many thanks to John Marcus Sommer for helping us with the technicalities of the manuscript.

Alexander Brock, Peter Schildhauer

Halle/Bielefeld September 2016

References

Ermert, Karl: *Briefsorten. Untersuchung zu Theorie und Empirie der Textklassifikation.* Niemeyer: Tübingen 1979.

Gülich, Elisabeth & Raible, Wolfgang: „Textsorten-Probleme". In: Moser, Hugo (ed.): *Linguistische Probleme der Textanalyse. Jahrbuch 1973.* Pädagogischer Verlag Schwann: Düsseldorf 1975, 144–197.

Table of Contents

Theoretical and Methodological Considerations

Alexander Brock & Peter Schildhauer

Communication Form: A Concept Revisited

Abstract The article starts with a short review of the history and conceptualisation of the terms medium, genre and communication form. For the last of these concepts, two main readings are identified: a) communication form as (grouping of) genre(s), and b) communication form as a constellation of communicative potentials. Mainly based on reading b), we then develop a definition of *communication form* as human-made clusters of technical and communicative constellations with communicative potentials, which are commonly restricted by conventions. This definition is exemplified with the constellations of using pencil and paper for written communication, *Twitter* communication and public speechmaking.

1. Introduction

Digital tools of communication are pervasive in our everyday lives. We use smart phones for writing e-mails and text messages, tweeting, reading newspapers, and, of course, making phone calls. Indeed, today's adolescents will hardly remember a time when phones were primarily used for *calling* people. To them – the digital natives (Prensky 2001) –, it is natural to use digital tools for a wide range of communicative practices.

These developments stirred linguistics as a discipline as well: From the mid-1990ies onwards, research began to focus on language use in various digital environments such as chat, websites, e-mail, and others (see Heyd 2009: 245 for a summary). From researching and comparing language use in various digital environments it was only a small step to asking more generally about how the tools we use for communicating influence communicative practices (and vice versa). This was when linguistics (re)discovered the mediality of language (Holly & Püschel 2007: 148; see also Domke 2013: 102) – and opened a Pandora's Box containing various concepts such as *medium*, *genre*, *communicative practice*, *communication form* and others.

All of these terms divide the academic field in various ways. All of them are also polysemous. Additionally, there are several overlaps among them. Even though a new sub-discipline *media linguistics* has established itself in German Applied Linguistics, some of its main proponents still debate the scope of the central term *medium* in an attempt to clarify the subject-matter of the discipline (see Luginbühl 2015). Besides the term *medium*, the trias *medium – communication form – genre* has become the centre both of debate and media linguistic analysis.

This article attempts to do two things: In a first step, we revisit what has been said about these concepts in order to point out possibly problematic aspects and outline our points of departure for the second step, in which we propose a consistent model that assigns an appropriate place to every element of the trias and sharpens the concepts for media linguistic analysis.[1] Our model rests heavily on previous definitions and discussions, so that our contribution mainly lies in selecting those elements of existing conceptualisations which we consider best suited for an adequate description of technical, medial and situational factors of communication, particularly in the light of recent developments of the New Media.

2. Medium

As long as 30 years ago, Posner (1986) lamented the abundance of different senses of the term *medium*. As a first step, he suggested to keep apart the following readings of the term (Posner 1986: 293–296).[2]

Table 1: Media Concepts Following Posner (1986, translation and examples AB/PS)

Reading	Examples	Definition
biological	voice	body organs contributing to the production, distribution and reception of signs
physical	acoustic media: substances (solid, fluid, gas) that are able to transmit acoustic waves	chemical elements and their forms of existence as needed to establish a connection between organs of production and reception
technological	print media, digital media	tools and material for the transmission of signs
sociological	theatre, opera, publishing houses	social institutions organising biological, physical, and technical means of sign transmission
culture-related	popular music, news, reports, narratives	purposeful messages in re-occurring forms, close to genre
code-related	phoneme systems, various writing systems (syllabic vs. alphabetic, etc.)	sign systems and their inherent rules

1 As we will come to discuss in Sections 4 and 5, *medium*, *communication form*, and *genre* are analytical categories which are mutually dependent and, due to numerous interrelations, hard to separate from one another. We are aware of that difficulty and will still attempt to do so. We will review each concept separately before blending the parts in one model in Section 5.

2 See also Habscheid (2000); Dürscheid (2005: 4).

Traditionally, media linguists have adopted a technological understanding of *medium*. Holly (1997: 69–70), for instance, defines media as specific material tools with which signs can be amplified, produced, stored and / or transmitted.[3] Pen and paper fall under this definition as well as the printing press and the computer. Bittner (2003: 289–290) is an example for a rather widespread view[4] of the relationship between media, understood in a technological way, and communication forms: He states that media are characterised by the sign systems employed as well as the modes of interaction for which they allow. On this basis, then, communication forms establish themselves which use these possibilities in various ways. The computer as a medium, for instance, can process binary code and therefore all kinds of digital data. In terms of interaction modes, it allows for mono-, bi- and multi-directionality, both synchronous and asynchronous. Communication forms established in this medium are, for instance, chat and e-mail (Bittner 2003: 290–291).

Even though the human voice and ears are also tools for communication, Posner's biological media are usually not regarded as media by other authors (Luginbühl 2015: 12). Dürscheid (2005: 14), for instance, argues that media allow for distance communication and, therefore, explicitly states that face-to-face communication does not need a medium. Holly (1997: 65–68) similarly sketches a model of media history whose first stage is the development of tools that amplify signs produced by the body, or ease their reception (such as stages and glasses).

Recently, Luginbühl (2015) has argued against a technological conceptualisation of the medium. He points out that "the concept of the medium has various *interconnected* aspects that are relevant for media linguistics" (Luginbühl 2015: 15). Besides the technical aspect traditionally focused on, Luginbühl stresses

(1) a semiotic aspect of media because the choice of media as tools always influences what sign systems can be used and how they are processed; media leave their traces in the texts which they are applied to produce (Krämer 2008).
(2) a pragmatic aspect dealing with the way media and the potentials they offer are typically used in a certain social group – and how these uses in turn influence the media themselves.

3 „*Medien* sind konkrete, materielle Hilfsmittel, mit denen Zeichen verstärkt, hergestellt, gespeichert und/oder übertragen werden können" (Holly 1997: 69–70, italics in the original). For similar definitions, see Dürscheid (2005: 5); Thaler (2007: 156–157); Marx & Weidacher (2014: 84); Schmitz (2004).

4 See, for instance, Dürscheid (2005: 14) and Holly (1996, 1997, 2011a, 2011b).

Thereby, Luginbühl fuses the technological, culture-related and code-related readings of the term *medium* pointed out in Table 1.

Alongside the conceptualisations mentioned so far, whose main interest is the role of media in the communication process, a sociological reading has long been present, at least implicitly. When we talk about the *mass media* (e.g. Burger & Luginbühl 2014), we often denote a certain social sphere, an *institution*, in which actors follow a common set of social patterns, norms and rules. Thus, Kammer (2013) defines *the media* as

> a diverse and complex constellation of different types of media with various formats, presentational characteristics, audience perceptions, and processes of production and consumption. (Kammer 2013: 142)[5]

Recently, this sociological reading has gained ground in media linguistic studies which investigate processes of *mediatization* as the "proliferation of media communication in all areas of social life" (Androutsopoulos 2014: 10).

As this article attempts to gain the highest possible degree of terminological clarity, we will use the technological reading of the term *medium* in the chapters to follow, and leave the broader conceptualisations aside for the moment.

3. Genre

The term *genre* "has made remarkable ascent in linguistic theories in the past 20 years" (Heyd 2008: 191). To begin with,[6] we would like to consider a reading that has established itself in recent English publications.[7] This reading roughly corresponds to the German term *Textsorte* as "groups of text, which, to a varying extent, share features on a number of heterogeneous dimensions" (Schildhauer 2016: 24).[8] These dimensions have been defined in various ways (see Schildhauer

5 For similar conceptualisations of *the media*, see, e.g., Couldry (2008); Strömbäck (2008); Kunelius & Reunanen (2012), and others. A summary of the field is provided by Lundby (2014) and Androutsopoulos (2014).

6 See the end of this section where we modify this preliminary understanding of *genre*.

7 See, for instance, Giltrow & Stein (2009); Giltrow (2013); Heyd (2008, 2009); Mehler et al. (2011); Lomborg (2014); Schildhauer (2016). A different reading is proposed by Biber & Conrad (2009), who differentiate between *register, genre,* and *style.* In their understanding, *genre* refers to structural characteristics of text exemplars only, including typical formulae (e.g., of greeting and closing a letter).

8 Adamzik (1995) points out that the term *Textsorte* itself gained two distinct readings in German text linguistics. While we follow the *unspecific* reading here (see above), there is also a *specific* reading in which *Textsorte* is a tool for rigid and consistent text classification

2016: 30–38 for a summary); essentially, genres seem to incorporate aspects of multimodal structure (e.g., language and image use), communicative situation (typical participant frameworks, communicative sphere and others), and function.

Since Miller's influential article "Genre as Social Action", genres have been seen as categories of everyday life that also acquire certain labels in a specific community. For instance, members of the academia differentiate genres such as *call for papers*, *conference panel proposal*, and *abstract*, which are rather unfamiliar to members of other social spheres. Therefore, genres have also been defined as "intersubjective mental pattern[s] of knowledge" (Brock 2013: 62) that constitute cognitive devices which ease both text production and reception (see, e.g., Karlgren 2011; Lomborg 2014: 3; Santini et al. 2011: 4).

This aspect, genres as schemata for text production, is usually excluded from the German concept of *Textsorte*, which refers to groupings of texts and their co-occuring features only (e.g., by Heinemann 2000b: 518–519; Sandig 2006: 488; Luginbühl 2014: 31). The schema aspect has been captured by the term *Textmuster*, to which we will henceforth refer as *genre pattern(s)*.[9] While Schildhauer (2014: 21–22) argues that the distinction between *Textsorte* (genre) and *Textmuster* (genre pattern) is not entirely necessary for media linguistic analysis, we would like to keep the distinction here, for reasons to be outlined in Section 5 below.

Most importantly, genres constitute *abstractions* from actual communicative practice that result from grouping existing textual artefacts. For instance, by encountering several *funeral speeches* (actual practice), we acquire knowledge about the features of a typical funeral speech – and that "another one bites the dust" is *not* a typical opener. From that follows that genres are linked tightly to actual communicative practice and, additionally, are prone to change (Brock 2009: 235).

When we abstract away from actual practice (for instance, after encountering several funeral speeches), the genre knowledge we gain tells us something about *conventions*. From the observation that most funeral speeches open with "*We have gathered here today...*" instead of "*Another one bites the dust*", we assume that there is some sort of intersubjective agreement concerning a typical, or rather, *appropriate* opening formula.

This aspect, assumptions and knowledge about conventions, has been subsumed implicitly under *genre*, particularly by authors who understand genre as a device for text production (see above). Here, we rather argue for differentiating

---

with clearly (and often mainly deductively) defined features (e.g., in Heinemann 2000a, 2000b; Heinemann & Heinemann 2002; Heinemann & Viehweger 1991).

9 The term *Textmuster* appears to be polysemous as well. See Schildhauer (2014: 21) for a more detailed account.

between these aspects by splitting up the wide conception of *genre* into three related parts:

- *Genre* as an everyday category, a grouping of existing texts according to similarities on several dimensions, and, therefore, an immediate abstraction from actual communicative practice. Genre knowledge might specifically play a role in text reception, i.e. recognising texts as members of a certain category.
- *Convention* as assumptions and/or knowledge about an intersubjective agreement on what is typical of and *appropriate* for texts of a certain genre.
- *Genre pattern(s)* as schemata, cognitive devices, which guide text production. Genre patterns are formed on the basis of knowledge about genres (actual practice) and conventions (intersubjective agreements).

In the context of the cultural turn in linguistics, genres have also increasingly been viewed under a cultural (and cultural-comparative) perspective (Luginbühl 2014: 40–46). Here, we would like to understand *culture* as a network of norms, assumptions, and beliefs of a community that are instantiated by certain forms of behaviour and their related semiotic products – for instance, forms of greeting, types of food, and textual artefacts (Luginbühl 2014: 55). In our genre framework just outlined, *convention* is the link between genre and culture. The intersubjective agreement on what constitutes (and is appropriate of) a certain genre is part of the network of assumptions and norms of a community's culture as a whole. Actual practice is, then, an expression of these underlying conceptions that might re-affirm but also innovate or challenge them, thus contributing to both cultural stability and change (ibid.).[10]

4. Communication Form

As it is placed between media and genres (see, e.g., Holly 2011b: 155), the concept *communication form* occupies the most difficult position in the trias *medium – communication form – genre*. Where does medium end and communication form start, and where does genre take over? On the one hand and from a conceptual point of view, this is a question of drawing (heuristic) boundaries. Answering it allows for structuring the immense variety of communicative phenomena which we are faced with today (Domke 2013: 121). On the other hand, clarity concerning the scope of these concepts is a precondition for research that aims to grasp the various interrelations that exist among the components of the trias, as, for

10 With *genre profiles*, Luginbühl (2014: 103) proposes an analytic *meso-level* between genres and cultures. For the sake of simplicity, we leave this level aside here.

instance, Domke's (2013, 2014, 2015) work on various kinds of public signage has shown. In what follows, we will review two research strands concerning communication forms in order to outline our points of departure for the model suggested in chapter 5.

4.1. Research Strand Ia: Communication Form as Grouping of Genres

The current discussion of the concept *communication form* can be traced back to Ermert's (1979) study on a classification of *letter* genres. Ermert states that the *letter* itself is not a genre but rather generally a *form of communication*, or, as he puts it, a medium of language-based communicative action,[11] which he defines as *communication form*. This reasoning is grounded in the observation that individual types of letters, such as *love letter* and *business letter*, can be described on all the genre dimensions outlined above; the *letter* itself, however, cannot because it is not specified in terms of communicative functions. Consequently, Ermert states that communication forms such as *letter* are polyfunctional (they are not specified in terms of communicative function yet), while genres are *monofunctional* (Ermert 1979: 59). Communication forms are, according to Ermert, defined by situational characteristics, as, for instance, concerning communicative contact (space and time), semiotic systems, the social relations between communication partners etc.

In Ermert's view, then, communication forms are abstractions of communicative practice just like genres (see above). Consequently, the difference between genres and communication forms is the following: While communication forms are situated on a higher hierarchical level and less specified regarding communicative function, genres are placed on a lower level in the hierarchy as they are richer in features and, thus, have a smaller extension than communication forms. From this perspective, *communication form* denotes what Heinemann & Heinemann (2002: 143) call *Textklasse* (i.e., a group of similar genres such as *texts of the press*) or even *Texttyp* (text type, an even broader group of genres such as *informative texts* or *written texts*).[12]

---

11 In the German original, Ermert writes about „die Rolle des Briefes als Medium sprachlich vermittelten kommunikativen Handelns."

12 This closeness of the communication form concept to genre description does not come as a surprise as soon as Ermert's research context and, thereby, his immediate reference points are taken into account. These lie, according to Meiler (2013: 52–54), in the beginnings of pragmatic text linguistics in Germany (e.g. Sandig 1975; Gülich & Raible 1975). The discipline was characterised by a strong interest in classifying the universe of everyday texts by drawing both on text internal and external criteria. Sandig's (1975: 114–117)

Very soon, Brinker took up Ermert's idea. The latest edition at the time of writing of his popular introduction to text linguistics defines communication forms as entities which are only defined by situational and medial features, but not in terms of communicative function (Brinker et al. 2014: 142). Ziegler, who writes that communication forms are groups of texts (just like genres) which allow for classifying texts, apparently takes the same approach.[13] Ziegler states that communication forms, in contrast to genres, are only defined by external criteria (Ziegler 2002: 24), such as:

Table 2: Criteria for Describing Communication Forms (overview provided by Domke 2010: 266, translation AB/PS)

Criteria for Differentiating Communication Forms	
sign system / potential	language / images / sounds etc., mono- / multicodal
mode of perception	visual / auditory / tactile, mono- / multimodal
direction of communication	unidirectional / bidirectional
communication partners	1:1 / 1:n
social status	private / institutional, public / non-public
Temporality	synchronic / asynchronic
spatial dimension	shared space / distance
medium of communication	computer, pen, paper, telephone etc.
way of transmission	transmitting / storing, electronic / material
media institution, production	institutional / private, provider, postal system etc.

In sum, research strand I defines communication forms as *genre minus functional specification*. To us, this appears an unlucky choice, for the following reasons:

First, the idea of a clear functional specification of genres that this conceptualisation is based on has been challenged convincingly. Several studies highlight the fact that even individual *texts* may serve several functions either for different recipients (Presch 1991: 85), or for the same recipient at different points of time

as well as Gülich & Raible's (1975) external criteria encompass parameters of the communicative situation whereas the internal perspective focuses on genre-specific criteria. Even though Gühlich & Raible (ibid.: 145–146) suggest otherwise, the external criteria theoretically allow for a very abstract classification of texts according to similarities of their communicative situation.

13 „Ebenso wie Textsorten bezeichnen auch Kommunikationsformen Teilmengen von Texten und ermöglichen insofern eine texttypologische Heuristik." (Ziegler 2002: 21).

(Klemm 2002: 155).[14] If this is true for the individual text, then it should be even more so for genres, as, for instance, Askehave & Swales (2001: 200–201) point out. These authors show that the seemingly trivial genre *shopping list* might serve functions as diverse as information (reminder) and prohibition (not to buy anything else). If such a functional heterogeneity is taken into account even for simple genres as the shopping list, then it is hard to think of genres as clearly specified in function, and to use this criterion to distinguish genres from communication forms is impracticable.

Second, we have shown that, with Heinemann & Heinemann's term *Textklasse*, at least German text linguistics already has a term for genres on higher levels of abstraction. This term has the additional advantage that its *signifier* is transparent in that it expresses the gist of this concept: a fairly abstract grouping of texts according to some similarities.

4.2. Research Strand Ib: Communication Form as Genre

The more recent history of the communication form concept is linked tightly to the media linguist Werner Holly. In several publications, he has focused on communication forms from the perspective of semiotics and media sciences (see Meiler 2013: 57–58 for a concise summary). In doing so, however, Holly takes a step that brings his understanding of communication forms close to the genre concept outlined above, in that he defines communication forms as medially conditioned cultural practices (2011b: 155).[15] Thereby, he highlights the fact that cultural processes shape and change communication forms. Holly's definition also tries to capture the intermediate position of communication forms between media and genres mentioned above. In Holly's words, communication forms are not only related to media, nor are they only related to socio-cultural (communicative) needs, which he claims to be the case for genres. Rather, communication forms relate to both – medium and culture (Holly 2011a: 38). By proposing this definition, Holly is the first to highlight explicitly the *practice* aspect of communication forms that was only implicitly present in the earlier accounts discussed

---

14 See also Adamzik (2004: 280) on the interplay of several communicative goals („Zusammenspiel unterschiedlicher kommunikativer Ziele"). Similarly: Eckkrammer (2002: 46). Explicitly focusing on the genre level instead of the individual text, Swales (1990: 47) writes about a "set of communicative purposes".

15 Over the years, Holly's discussion has been much more complex, however. We will outline further aspects of Holly's grasp of the concept below.

above. However, *in what way* communication forms constitute practices remains rather vague in Holly's (2011a/b) accounts.[16]

Meiler (2013) also builds on Holly in developing a practice-based model of communication forms.[17] Additionally, he (2013: 57) credits Holly (1997) for being the first to point out that communication forms are virtual constellations[18] with an ontological status. Starting from that reading of Holly (1997), Meiler (2013: 57) conceptualises communication forms as knowledge structures that influence communicative action and claims that, among others, they can be described by "reconstructing [their] typical use". Similarly, Pentzold et al. (2013: Fn. 2) conceptualise communication forms as typified, socially understandable bundles of activities.[19]

To sum up: According to research strand Ib, communication forms are abstractions from actual practice (Pentzold et al. 2013), practices themselves (Holly 2011a/b), or both (Meiler 2013). With the closeness of this conceptualisation to the widespread understanding of the genre concept outlined above, the conceptualisation of *communication form* according to strand Ib is in need of sharpening to make it a useful tool for media linguistic research.

4.3. Research Strand II: Communication Form as a Constellation of Potentials

The second line of development of the communication form concept also dates back to Ermert's (1979) influential study (see Fn. 12 above): Gühlich & Raible (1975) state that their external criteria of text classification, in fact, do not denote groups of texts but are rather constellations of situational aspects which constitute a

---

16 Meiler (2013: Fn. 19) states that this practice-related conceptualisation of communication forms first appears in Holly & Püschel (2007). Additionally, he claims that the practice aspect is elaborated on in Holly (2011a). We disagree on this last point, however.

17 Meiler (2013: 59) apparently interprets Holly's practice approach as related to the procedures that are necessary to *constitute* a communicative situation. See Schildhauer (2014: 28–30) for an analysis and criticism of Meiler's (2013) approach. In this volume, Meiler distances himself from his earlier understanding and states that communication forms are "not practices. They are, true to their name, 'forms'" (Meiler, this volume: 49).

18 Holly (1997: 69): „Kommunikationsformen sind also virtuelle Konstellationen von einem bestimmten Zeichenspeicherungs- oder Übertragungspotential in eine oder beide Richtungen."

19 „typisierte, routinisierte, raum-zeit-bindende, sozial-verstehbare Bündel von Aktivitäten" (Pentzold et al. 2013: Fn: 2).

frame for text production.[20] The authors term these abstract constellations *types of communication* („Kommunikationsarten", Gülich & Raible 1975: 145). Particularly in some of his earlier articles, Holly also voices this idea (e.g. Holly 1996, 1997).[21]

Other researchers use this aspect in order to draw a clear distinction between communication form and genre. Fritz (2013: 456), for instance, thinks of communication forms as entities that *allow for* specific kinds of use and contrasts them with genres as actual use of these entities with certain functional characteristics.[22] Even though we have pointed out the problematic nature of the functional criterion above, Fritz's definition allows for a distinction between communication forms and genres (as defined above: abstractions from communicative practice) along the lines of *potential* and *use* (i.e. *practice*). Recently, Schildhauer (2016) suggested a conceptualisation in the tradition of research strand II that avoids the aspect of functional specification:

> Here, I conceptualize *communication form* in a simplistic manner as a technical constellation which gives rise to *communicative potentials*. *Potentials* include the semiotic systems available for message production, the possible number of participants and the extent to which distance in space and time can be bridged. The potentials can be used by several genres to a varying extent. (Schildhauer 2016: 30–31, our emphasis, AB / PS)

In the quotation above, we have highlighted formulations that point to the idea of *potentiality*. It becomes apparent that the definition contains aspects such as the number of participants, semiotic systems etc., which were also part of the characterisations of communication forms as outlined in Table 2 above. The essential point is a switch of perspective. Instead of stating, for instance, that an e-mail *is* typically written (see Table 4 below), this definition would describe e-mail as a communication form that *allows* for using written language (and image, too). Questions such as what semiotic systems are most frequently used are from this perspective an issue of genre: Business e-mails usually do not make use of images, whereas Christmas e-mails do.[23]

---

20 See also Meiler (2013: 54).

21 Similarly Dürscheid (2005: 9, 11).

22 Domke (e.g., 2013: 121), similarly to Fritz (2013), stresses that communication forms denote medial and material *conditions*. These conditions are later (Domke 2014: 26) integrated into the concept of the *contingency frame*, according to which communication forms are bundles of conditions that provide potentials (and constraints) for communication.

23 Despite this shift of perspective, we should not forget, of course, that there are indeed typical ways of using the potentials of a communication form (e.g., writing in the case of e-mail). This illustrates the manifold interrelations between *communication form*

To give another example: Dürscheid (2005: 8) characterises the communication form *chat* as *distant* regarding the spatial dimension. Again, this only characterises the *typical* use of chat software. The potentiality reading would define chat as a communication form that allows for communication between partners who are not in the same room – next to other constellations: At LAN-parties, for instance, when players of competing teams possibly share the same room, the players might still use the chat function of their games, possibly for reasons of secrecy. Consequently, they make use of the potentials of the communication form in a different way. Because of these and similar examples, Schildhauer (this volume) argues that the clear distinction between communication form as a frame of potentiality and genre as an abstraction from actual use of this frame allows for interesting insights into what potentials are actually and most frequently used by texts of a certain genre (see also Dürscheid 2005: 12).

Thaler (2007), whose study also follows the potentiality reading, tackles the question of the technological nature of digital communication forms such as chat and e-mail. She suggests that they are, in fact, software-systems, which use the infrastructure of the medium Internet (Thaler 2007: 156–157). Additionally, Thaler argues that different *implementations* of software-systems have to be taken into account to round off the picture of a specific communication form. She supports her argument by referring to several chat implementations, which allow for spatial positioning of chat contributions or attributing specific rights to selected participants.

On the one hand, the conceptualisation developed in strand II provides a clear differentiation between communication forms and genres as defined above. On the other hand, this strand appears to be focused on digital media and still needs to be modified regarding "traditional" communication forms such as Ermert's (1979) letter mentioned above.

---

and *genre*. See, e.g., also Domke (2015: n.p.) on the possible correlations between communication form and textual functions. Domke argues convincingly that "time-bound prohibitions on streets are expressed by means of visible and tactile barriers or moveable signs [i.e., making use of certain types of communication forms, AB/PS], and permanent valid warnings at railway stations are realised by means of fixed and visible signs."

4.4. Combining Research Strand I and II

Even though the typology presented in this chapter so far appears to be clear-cut, both approaches have been combined in several ways. On a conceptual level, some sources define *communication form* both following the practice-reading (strand Ib) and the potentiality reading of strand II.[24] For instance, Holly (2011b: 155, see above) writes about *cultural practices* while earlier (2011b: 150) describing communication forms as *structures* which contribute to establishing sense as conditions of the enablement of communication.[25] Besides the potentiality idea introduced in this passage, the term *structure* is particularly at odds with Holly's *practice*-definition. In the light of the considerations above, which presented the distinct premises of both approaches, combining them appears to be problematic.

However, combining strand I and II takes place not only on the conceptual level but also on a methodological one. In genre research, it is common to use the labels coined by a community and then reconstruct the genre knowledge that they represent. Miller & Shepherd (2004: n.p.) state that "when a type of discourse or communicative action acquires a common name within a given context or community, that's a good sign it's functioning as a genre." The same is done in some studies on communication forms.[26] Holly (2011b: 144) opens his contribution with a listing of what he calls everyday sorting terms that focus on medial aspects: *audio book, leaflet, letter, slide show, telephone call*, and others.

Taking these everyday sorting terms as a starting point for the analysis of communication forms is not problematic at all – if the terms and the polysemy inherent in many of them are handled with care. This polysemy is particularly dangerous from a methodological point of view, as the different senses may denote *both* a communication form and a communicative practice (or an abstraction thereof). This is illustrated in Table 3 using the example of *SMS* and *e-mail*.[27]

---

24 See, e.g., Domke (2013: 119 vs. 121, 2014: 26 vs. 30, 2015); Holly (2011b).

25 „Strukturen, die als Bedingungen der Möglichkeit von Kommunikation an der Genese von Sinn beteiligt sind."

26 A similar approach is taken by Meiler in his study on the blog communication form (Meiler 2013: 71). See Schildhauer (this volume) for a disucssion of this methodology.

27 Dürscheid (2005: 12–13) makes the same point regarding the term *chat*, which also denotes a communication form and a type of communicative practice (*chat-discussions*, *expert chats* etc.). The same is probably true for other sorting terms not related to digital media, e.g. *postcard* and *letter*.

Table 3: Senses of Polysemous Everyday Communication Sorting Terms according to the Oxford English Dictionary (Number in Brackets Indicates Number of Sense in the Dictionary)

	SMS	***E-Mail***
OED-sense related to communication form	(1) Short Message (or Messaging) Service, a system that enables mobile phone users to send and receive text messages	(2) The system of sending messages by electronic means
OED-sense related to communicative practice	(2) A text message that is sent or received using SMS	(1) Messages distributed by electronic means from one computer user to one or more recipients via a network

If these readings are not kept apart from the very beginning for the analyst *and* the recipient, perspectives I and II get confounded easily. Due to the fact that we are so used to these everyday terms that we usually do not notice their polysemy, this is an easy trap to walk into. Consider Table 4 taken from Holly (2011a: 40):[28]

Table 4: Communication Forms E-Mail and Letter (Holly 2011a: 40, translation AB/PS)

	E-Mail	**Letter**
medial and technical basis	PC, Internet	paper, writing tools, postal system
signs / codes	writing (graphics, images)	
channels / modes	visual	
direction of communication	potentially bi-directional	
functionality	storage / transmission	
transmission	electronic	material transport
Temporality	small gap	large gap
communication partners	1:1	
social status	private / institutional (non-public)	

Table 4 sets out by contrasting the tools used in both communication forms (the medium in a narrow sense). Considering *codes*, Holly (2011a: 39) states that primarily writing is used in both forms, but that, of course, also other sign systems are possible (e.g., as attachments), which are apparently bracketed because they are not

28 Holly's chart is presented out of context here for illustrative purposes only and not in order to challenge his sound argument that is clearly aimed at the description of communication forms.

primarily used. Thereby, two perspectives are confounded: a statement on typical use, i.e. actual practice close to genre (strand Ib), and on potentiality (strand II). Under *modes*, Holly apparently makes a statement concerning typical use; earlier on (Holly 2011a: 39), he states that also sound files can be sent via e-mail, which means that, actually, the acoustic channel should be listed as well from a potentiality perspective. Regarding *direction of communication*, Holly explicitly mentions the potentiality aspect. The aspects of *transmission* and *temporality* constitute *absolute parameters* according to Meiler (2013: 84), which could be grouped with the first line of Table 4 as they, in fact, are characteristics of the medial-technical basis itself. The criterion of *communication partners* provides a statement about typical use, as does the final feature *social status*. Both letters and e-mails can *potentially* be 1:n or even n:n, just as letters (e.g., open letters) could be potentially public.

In sum, the apparently clear-cut contrastive analysis of two communication forms shows, at a second glance, traces of two complementary approaches to the concept of communication form. This is possibly supported by the polysemy of the labels *e-mail* and *letter* themselves.

4.5. Interim Summary

We have shown that the term *communication form* has developed two rather distinct senses, which sometimes even exist side by side in one study. We have also shown that research strand I mainly runs parallel to what has been done in genre research and is therefore less suitable to describe phenomena that are thought of as distinct from (even though interrelated with) genres.

After reviewing what has been said on each of the concepts of the *medium-communication form-genre* trias individually, we will move on to suggest a model that integrates the three components. The model is rooted in research strand II and, of course, indebted to many of the contributions reviewed in the chapters 2 to 4 above.

5. Medium – Communication Form – Genre: A Model Based on Potentiality and Convention

In this passage, we develop our understanding of the terms medium, communication form and genre. For this, we use two scenarios: for one thing, using pencil and paper to communicate and tweeting for another. For the sake of our argumentation, we adopt a simplified historical perspective in some passages of this section. We then round off our argumentation by testing our model on the *oral* communication form *public speech*.

Before paper and pencil, there were other writing materials such as clay, parchment and cloth as well as stylus, brush and quill. All these were mostly used for communication across gaps in time and space, even though other uses were always possible, too. For various reasons, new materials became necessary, and paper was invented with roughly the same communicative purpose in mind. For this, wood and similar materials were used. As a natural resource, wood is pre-semiotic. When it is carved into, it becomes semiotic, even though as a sign carrier it still remains in its natural state. It becomes fully semioticised, however, when it undergoes a certain treatment to produce paper, i.e. sheets of a thin material to serve specific semiotic practices such as communication across distance. Similar processes of potential semiotisation can be described for making pencils out of graphite and wood as an alternative to the rather messy ink and quill/pen.[29]

Under the historical perspective outlined above, pencil and paper are the outcome of a communicative *need* seen by their inventors, based on people's experience of previous distance communication. This way, the *convention* of written communication across space and time gaps informed the development of the technical means that made this practice more efficient, and natural resources were transformed into a specific shape to give them the semiotic *potential* to do this. In this process, a technological medium as outlined in Table 1 was created. This technological medium fulfils Schildhauer's definition of *communication form* as "a technical constellation which gives rise to communicative potentials" (Schildhauer 2016: 30; see Section 4.3). Following this broad definition of communication form, we see the technical medium as one of its most basic components.

The next steps towards concrete patterns of communication are obvious and have been described many times:[30] Paper is an efficient carrier for any of the

29 Likewise, it can be argued that the evolutionary development and optimisation of the human speech organs are a similar – though less deliberate – process of a semiotisation, in this case of the human body. In the light of this, excluding face-to-face communication from the discussion of media (Dürscheid 2005: 14) may be unfortunate.

30 The precise causal and temporal order of the emergence of factors is often difficult to determine. While cave walls certainly pre-existed paintings of hunting scenes and the subsequent development of pictograms and ideograms, (alphabetic) writing systems may have been developed along with the materials to carry them or in fact been the reason for the development of new physical media. Fortunately, the exact order of factors has no bearing on the basic conceptualisation of communication forms which we are developing here.

modern human writing systems, which in turn are useful for carrying information across time and space gaps. So, the combination of pencil, paper and writing systems enabled distant 1:1 and also 1:many communication. The postal service completed this constellation by bridging space gaps, and subsequently or simultaneously human societies developed various text genres which made use of the potential for distance communication and permanent data storage which comes with it. Partly, these genres grew out of institutional needs, such as legal documentation. Along with the genres, mental genre *patterns* as defined in Section 3 emerged. They constituted the mental schemata necessary for not only understanding, but also producing texts of a certain genre. Among others, they were explicitly *taught* to apprentices and, in a growing educational system, to pupils. They enabled people to make use of pencil and paper in specific situations to produce concrete texts based on genre patterns which provided procedural plans considering layout and orthography, address forms, content and function of the text.[31]

From the perspective of communicative resources, each of the factors mentioned comes with a specific *potential* of enablement concerning various aspects of communication: pencil and paper enable the usage of alphabetic writing; their combination enables communication across time and space gaps, which enables private letter-writing as well as the storage of court records and the development of newspapers, etc. (see Figure 1). In this potentiality-sequence (Figure 1), we situated *genre patterns* rather than actual genres for the following reason: What *enables* communication via texts of a specific genre are the *schemata* used for text production, i.e. *genre patterns*. These, however, do not strictly *determine* actual use, but only provide *potentials*. Text producers can decide not to follow what their cognitive plan tells them. What is actually *done*, i.e. how the given potentials are

31 Two (mutually compatible) scenarios considering the formation of genre patterns are possible: On the one hand, these schemata might have formed alongside genres, i.e. on the basis of observing an evolving practice. On the other hand, several aspects such as spelling conventions, formulae etc. might have been set by an institution, taught to apprentices and consequently implemented into actual practice. This scenario is possibly true for the institution of the *Chancery* in England, which was responsible for legal documents and, for the sake of efficient communication, chose to use specific spelling variants over others, which were then taught to the apprentices of this institution (see Nevalainen & Tieken-Boon van Ostade 2006 for a more detailed account).

used, is also a question of *genre* as an abstraction from actual use. The genre perspective could tell us that, in fact, 90% of all business letters are produced strictly following the available genre patterns but 10% do not (using less typical closing formulae or greetings, for instance).

Figure 1: Communication Form and Communicative Potentials

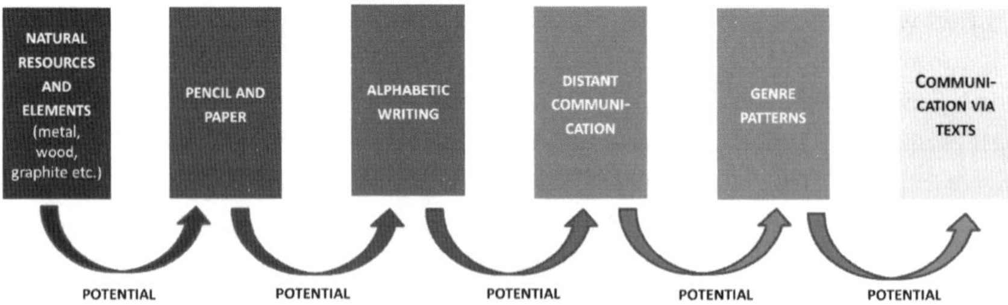

This observation points to a crucial aspect. While pencil and paper, for instance, are mainly used to serve the needs of distant written communication, for which they are typically used, their semiotic potentials are much broader. Paper can be drawn on, it can come in different colours to denote certain moods, it can be folded in meaningful ways, people can write each other notes on it while being co-present in time and space, it can be burned to produce smoke signs, etc. So, each factor enabling communication has a considerably larger potential than is commonly used in standard communication, so that an exhaustive description of communicative potentials for each of the factors is nearly impossible. Also, in order to ascertain the specific communicative options and restrictions behind writing, giving the entirety of communicative potentials is not only impracticable, but also futile.

In order to narrow down the communicative possibilities usefully, *convention* becomes another organising force of communication in addition to potentials. In Section 3, we defined *convention* from a user-centred perspective as assumptions and/or knowledge concerning an intersubjective agreement on what is typical of and *appropriate* for a certain genre. We also stated that convention constitutes the link between *genre* and *culture*, as genre conventions are part of the broader network of a culture's shared assumptions, norms and beliefs that are expressed by semiotic practice.

Figure 2: Restriction of Potentials by Convention

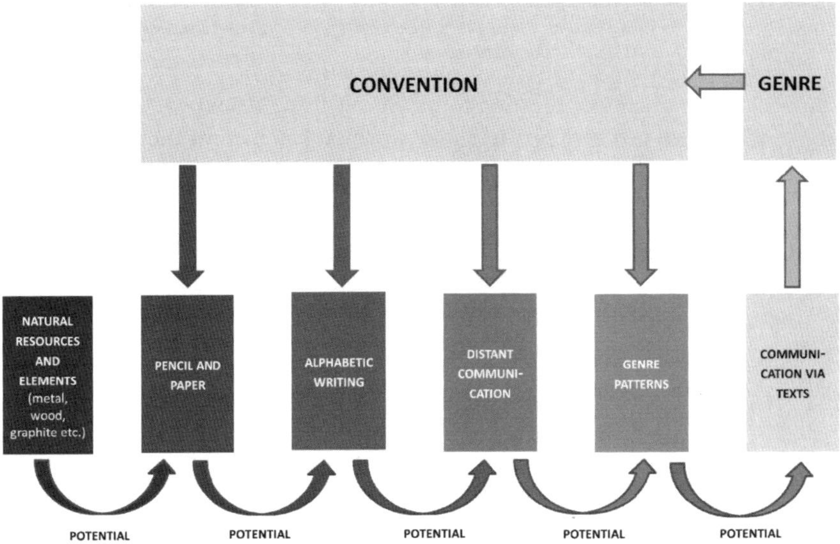

As stated above, the source of convention is mainly communicative and social practice. For instance, before pencil and paper, distance communication by writing on flat surfaces had become a convention, and the potentials of pencil and paper were developed with this convention in mind. Even though the *potentials* exceeded the conventions of distance communication via writing systems by far, the existing *convention* restricted the usage of those potentials, though not completely.

The other factors mentioned are restricted in their potentials along the same lines, as shown in Figure 2. For instance, communication by using pencil and paper can be manifold, but is mainly used for distance communication, etc. Genre patterns for business letters tell producers to end on a polite note; sexual allusions are, however, excluded by convention and the potential frame of topics is, consequently, narrowed down.

The inclusion of convention in addition to potentials is an important step in conceptualising communications forms. We therefore define the term *communication form* as follows:

> Communication forms typically answer communicative needs. They are the factors which influence the *form* of the *communication*, and they arise out of human practice.[32] They are clusters of technical and communicative constellations with certain potentials, which are commonly restricted by conventions.[33]

This definition of communication forms fits anything from pencil and paper to conventionalised text genre patterns – i.e. mental patterns for the production of texts – with specific communicative potentials. Excluded are only

a) the basic natural resources and elements, which go into the production of means of communication, because the raw materials are blind to communication, and
b) the concrete communication, i.e. actual practice and genre as an abstraction from this practice, as shown in Figure 3.

We are aware of the fact that our extension of communication form is wider than usually discussed in the literature – including some authors in this volume. This extension is, however, a logical result of the definition we propose above: Technical and communicative constellations with communicative potentials which shape communication only exclude the communication itself which is shaped by these factors, and its results, i.e. concrete texts. The provision that communication forms arise out of human practice additionally excludes natural resources before their semiotisation by humankind, even though they may also have (latent) communicative potential.

As we shall see in the following, our conceptualisation of communication forms still allows for a detailed analysis of aspects such as medium, situational factors and genre patterns.

---

32 Mostly communicative practice, but also conscious language-political acts, software writing, setting of normative standards for page sizes, etc.

33 As stated above, conventions are part of the broader network of shared assumptions, norms and beliefs of a community's culture. That being said, the role of conventions in the model suggested here relates to Holly's (2011b: 155) use of the attribute *cultural* regarding communication forms. In our suggestion – just as in Holly's – both communication forms and genres are rooted in cultures and are, thereby, genuine cultural phenomena. Our perspective of communication forms as providing potentials restricted by convention is close to Domke's (2014: 26) concept of the *contingency frame*.

Figure 3: The Scope of the Concept Communication Form

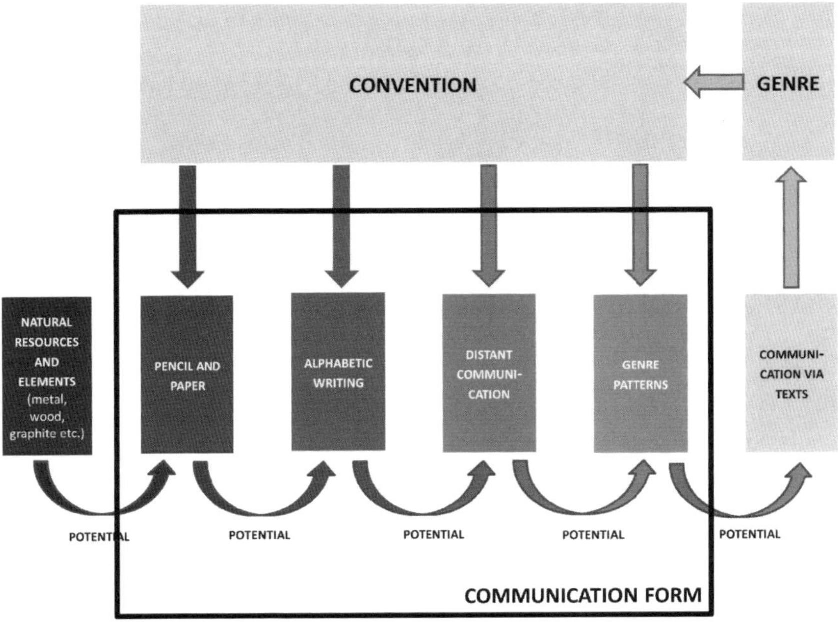

Figure 3 also shows that communication forms have an internal structure, in that they contain technical media, semiotic systems, situational factors and genre patterns.

Now for the relationship between *communication form* and *(technical) medium*: In the case of writing personal letters with pencil and paper, the technical medium is one element of the communication form, which is clearly not identical with, but separate from the other ones (cf. Figure 4):[34]

34 Above, we have treated *medium* and *communication form* as distinct parts of a trias – mainly in order to be able to review contributions to all three concepts first and because the tripartite distinction has been a tradition up to very recent publications such as Marx & Weidacher (2014) and Luginbühl (2015). However, some authors (e.g. Domke 2013; Holly 2011b; Schildhauer 2016) have already opted for integrating the medium into their *communication form* concept, just as we suggest here.

Figure 4: Communication Form and Medium for Pencil and Paper

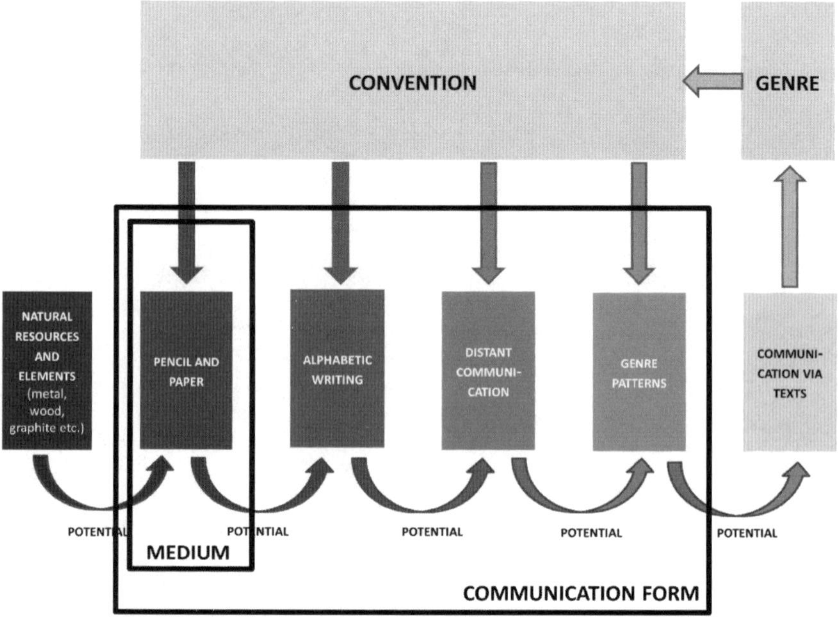

Here, the technical medium enables distance communication, text patterns, etc. without itself containing these other factors.

The case is different for communication via the *Twitter* platform: In this case, the technical medium comprises the computer hardware as well as the Internet connection and the specific programming of the *Twitter* software. The software specifies situational factors (mostly 1:many distance communication,) as well as possible semiotic system(s), layout, text size and coherence (hashtags). So, the technical medium encompasses the majority of factors which make up the communication form, which can be seen in Figure 5:

Figure 5: Communication Form and Medium for Twitter

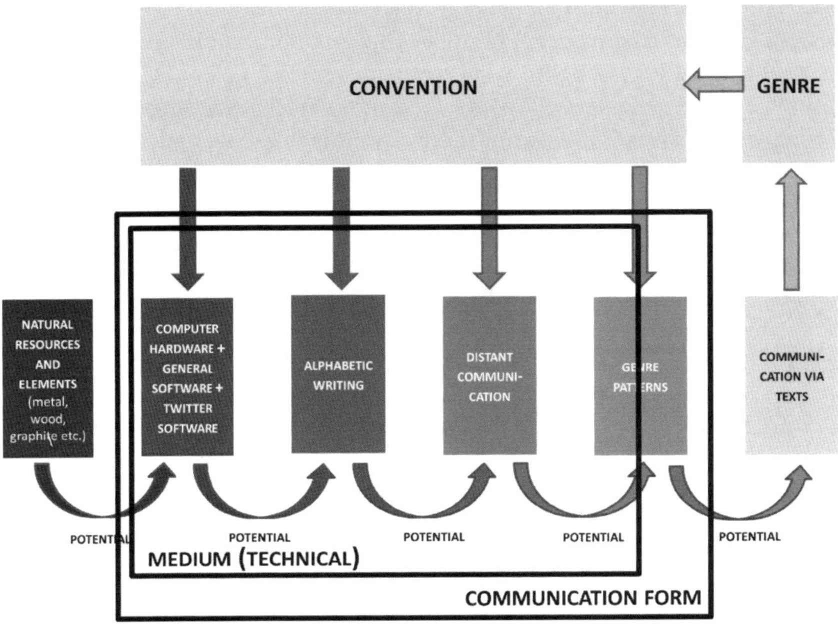

It is obvious that the regulation of many communicative aspects by computer hardware and programming leads to a much narrower set of potentials than in the case of pencil and paper.[35] Thereby, the medium imprints itself on the actual message to a different degree. This shows that the model proposed here is compatible with views such as Krämer's (1998) and McLuhan & Fiore's ([1967]2001), who focus on how the media co-create rather than merely transmit meaning.[36]

So far, we have only considered communication forms that are based on writing. Figure 6 additionally presents a simplified model of the communication form *public speech*. In this case, two media play a key role. On the one hand, the biological medium of the human articulatory apparatus provides the potential of verbal language, which enables space- and time-bound communication. On the other hand, the communication form may potentially be enriched by a sound system

35 Though narrower than for pencil and paper, the potentials of *Twitter* are still wider than its conventional usage suggests.

36 The model also connects to accounts of *mediatization* interested in how media become increasingly important for "the construction of everyday life, society and culture as a whole" (Krotz 2009: 24).

consisting of microphone(s) and speaker(s) as a technical medium, which extends the reach of the human voice and, thereby, enables what we termed "enhanced" space- and time-bound communication. This communication form provides the basis for, e.g., lectures, political speech, and sermons. Of course, other media could be added to the model. For instance, seats, which are arranged in a specific order, provide a means of ensuring that everyone is able to see and hear in the best possible way, which further enhances the time- and space-bound communication enabled by the key media.

Figure 6: Communication Form and Medium for Public Speech (Simplified Model; "convention" and "genre" left out for convenience)

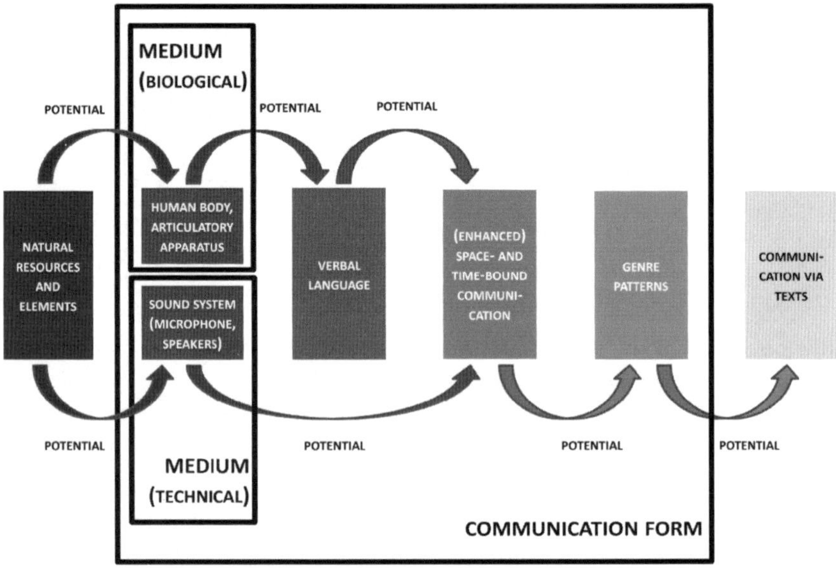

As the examples of pencil/paper, *Twitter*, and public speech show, different communicative practices, and thereby genres, are based on different constellations of communication forms. These communication forms are complex in themselves, and each element of a communication form has certain potentials, which are limited by conventions. *Genre patterns*, for instance, as the element of communication form which consists in the mental patterns necessary for text production, theoretically may have a wider scope than is commonly realised in communication. In these cases, their potential is narrowed down and channelled through actual communicative practice, a fact which is reflected in *genre*, i.e. an abstraction from concrete texts. In other words, genre knowledge (among other things) tells the language user which of the communicative options from a genre pattern not to choose, because they are not conventional.[37]

6. Conclusions and Open Issues

This paper aimed at sharpening the understanding of the terms *medium*, *communication form*, and *genre* as main elements of the media-linguistic tool box. First, we revisited the history of these three terms and pointed out important readings that developed for each of them. Second, we selected and modified specific senses and integrated them into a consistent model that highlights the role of potentiality and convention as factors influencing actual communicative practice. We hope that this model provides a higher degree of conceptual clarity and, therefore, eases future media-linguistic research.

However, we are well aware of the fact that our model is not an all-in-one solution. In particular, we have left aside some aspects for the sake of simplicity here:

(1) We have dealt with communication forms as if they were homogenous entities. In fact, they are abstractions from reality: Talking about *chat*, for instance, entails abstracting away from different software packages offering similar functionalities (Thaler 2007: 156–157). What level of abstraction is chosen will depend on the purposes of a specific study.
(2) We have merely outlined the complex relations between media, communication forms, and genres. Again, these have to be analysed in individual studies in order to show how media and communication forms "co-create and not merely transmit meaning" (Luginbühl 2015: 14).
(3) In the interplay between genre patterns as elements of communication forms with a certain communicative potential and genre as usage, it appears that a

37 For example, it was common for a while (approx. in the mid-to-late 1990s) to tell students that motivational letters and CVs could be submitted in hand-written *or* printed form. Thereby, this facet of the genre pattern *motivational letter* received a relatively wide potential. When these former students of the 1990s have to compose such a document today, a look into actual practice will show them that hand-written documents have become rather uncommon. They will assume that convention has changed and, consequently, decide for the printed version. The potential of their genre patterns has, thus, been restricted by convention. It can also be argued that they, consequently, *update* their genre patterns for CVs and motivational letters, i.e., erase the option *hand-written* in their schemata, which would then no longer be considered for future practice.

prototypical organisation of genre as well as genre change are often the result of language users going beyond genre conventions while staying well within the potentiality of genre patterns. Within the framework of our conceptualisation of medium, communication form and genre, more research is necessary to ascertain the exact mechanisms of pitting potentials against convention.

Acknowledgements

We are indebted to many friends and colleagues for their advice, support, and fruitful discussions that accompanied our work on this article, which began with some first thoughts roughly three years ago. In particular, we would like to thank (in random order): Jana Pflaeging, Martin Luginbühl, Christine Domke, Hartmut Stöckl, Ulrich Busse, and John Marcus Sommer.

References

Adamzik, Kirsten: *Textsorten – Texttypologie. Eine kommentierte Bibliographie.* Nodus-Publikationen: Münster 1995.

Adamzik, Kirsten: *Textlinguistik. Eine einführende Darstellung.* M. Niemeyer: Tübingen 2004.

Androutsopoulos, Jannis: "Mediatization and Sociolinguistic Change". In: Androutsopoulos, Jannis (ed.): *Mediatization and Sociolinguistic Change*. de Gruyter: Berlin, Boston 2014, 3–48.

Askehave, Inger & Swales, John M.: "Genre Identification and Communicative Purpose. A Problem and a Possible Solution". *Applied Linguistics* 22(2), 2001, 195–212.

Biber, Douglas & Conrad, Susan: *Register, Genre, and Style*. CUP: Cambridge 2009.

Bittner, Johannes: *Digitalität, Sprache, Kommunikation. Eine Untersuchung zur Medialität von digitalen Kommunikationsformen und Textsorten und deren varietätenlinguistischer Modellierung*. E. Schmidt: Berlin 2003.

Brinker, Klaus et al.: *Linguistische Textanalyse. Eine Einführung in Grundbegriffe und Methoden*. 8th edition. E. Schmidt: Berlin 2014.

Brock, Alexander: „Zur Variation komischer Textsorten – der Fall britischer Fernsehcomedies". In: Lenz, Friedrich (ed.): *Schlüsselqualifikation Sprache. Anforderungen – Standards – Vermittlung*. Peter Lang: Frankfurt am Main 2009, 235–253.

Brock, Alexander: "On the Corruption of Text Types. The Cases of Comedy and Readers' Commentaries in Online Newspapers". In: Ammermann, Anne et al. (eds.): *Facets of Linguistics*. Peter Lang: Frankfurt am Main 2013, 63–74.

Burger, Harald & Luginbühl, Martin: *Mediensprache. Eine Einführung in Sprache und Kommunikationsformen der Massenmedien.* de Gruyter: Berlin [u.a.] 2014.

Couldry, Nick: "Mediatization or Mediation. Alternative Understandings of the Emergent Space of Digital Storytelling". *New Media & Society* 10(3), 2008, 373–391.

Domke, Christine: „Texte im öffentlichen Raum. Formen medienvermittelter Kommunikation auf Bahnhöfen". In: Bucher, Hans-Jürgen (ed.): *Neue Medien – neue Formate. Ausdifferenzierung und Konvergenz in der Medienkommunikation.* Campus-Verlag: Frankfurt am Main et al. 2010, 257–281.

Domke, Christine: „Ortsgebundenheit als distinktives Merkmal in der Textanalyse". *Zeitschrift für germanistische Linguistik* 41(1) 2013, 102–126, retrieved 22.09.2016, from DOI: 10.1515/zgl-2013-0006.

Domke, Christine: *Die Betextung des öffentlichen Raumes. Eine Studie zur Spezifik von Meso-Kommunikation am Beispiel von Bahnhöfen, Innenstädten und Flughäfen.* Winter: Heidelberg 2014.

Domke, Christine: "Prohibition Signage in Public Spaces. On the Functional Organization of Different Media, Communication Forms, and Text Types". *10plus1. Living Linguistics* 1, 2015, available on 10plus1journal.com.

Dürscheid, Christa: „Medien, Kommunikationsformen, kommunikative Gattungen". *Linguistik online* 22(1), 2005, 1–16.

Eckkrammer, Eva Martha: „Brauchen wir einen neuen Textbegriff?". In: Fix, Ulla et al. (eds.): *Brauchen wir einen neuen Textbegriff? Antworten auf eine Preisfrage.* Peter Lang: Frankfurt am Main 2002, 31–57.

Ermert, Karl: *Briefsorten. Untersuchung zu Theorie und Empirie der Textklassifikation.* Niemeyer: Tübingen 1979.

Fritz, Gerd: *Dynamische Texttheorie.* Gießener Elektronische Bibliothek: Gießen 2013, available on http://geb.uni-giessen.de/geb/volltexte/2013/9243/pdf/Fritz-Gerd_2013.pdf.

Giltrow, Janet: "Genre and Computer-Mediated Communication". In: Herring, Susan et al. (eds.): *Pragmatics of Computer-mediated Communication.* Mouton de Gruyter: Berlin 2013, 717–737.

Giltrow, Janet & Stein, Dieter (eds.): *Genres in the Internet. Issues in the Theory of Genre.* Benjamins: Amsterdam et al. 2009.

Gülich, Elisabeth & Raible, Wolfgang: „Textsorten-Probleme". In: Moser, Hugo (ed.): *Linguistische Probleme der Textanalyse. Jahrbuch 1973.* Pädagogischer Verlag Schwann: Düsseldorf 1975, 144–197.

Habscheid, Stephan: „‚Medium' in der Pragmatik. Eine kritische Bestandsaufnahme". *Deutsche Sprache* 28(1), 2000, 126–143.

Heinemann, Margot & Heinemann, Wolfgang: *Grundlagen der Textlinguistik. Interaktion – Text – Diskurs*. Max Niemeyer Verlag: Tübingen 2002.

Heinemann, Wolfgang: „Aspekte der Textsortendifferenzierung". In: Brinker, Klaus et al. (eds.): *Linguistics of Text and Conversation. An International Handbook of Contemporary Research*. Mouton de Gruyter: Berlin 2000a, 523–546.

Heinemann, Wolfgang: „Textsorte – Textmuster – Texttyp". In: Brinker, Klaus et al. (eds.): *Linguistics of Text and Conversation. An International Handbook of Contemporary Research*. Mouton de Gruyter: Berlin 2000b, 507–523.

Heinemann, Wolfgang & Viehweger, Dieter: *Textlinguistik. Eine Einführung*. Max Niemeyer: Tübingen 1991.

Heyd, Theresa: *Email Hoaxes. Form, Function, Genre Ecology*. Benjamins: Amsterdam et al. 2008.

Heyd, Theresa: "A Model for Describing 'New' and 'Old' Properties of CMC Genres. The Case of Digital Folklore". In: Giltrow, Janet & Stein, Dieter (eds.): *Genres in the Internet. Issues in the Theory of Genre*. Benjamins: Amsterdam et al. 2009, 239–262.

Holly, Werner: „Alte und neue Medien. Zur inneren Logik der Mediengeschichte". In: Rüschoff, Bernd & Schmitz, Ulrich (eds.): *Kommunikation und Lernen mit alten und neuen Medien. Beiträge zum Rahmenthema ‚Schlagwort Kommunikationsgesellschaft' der 26. Jahrestagung der Gesellschaft für Angewandte Linguistik e. V.* Peter Lang: Frankfurt am Main 1996, 9–16.

Holly, Werner: „Zur Rolle der Sprache in Medien. Semiotische und kommunikationsstrukturelle Grundlagen". *Muttersprache* 107(1), 1997, 64–75.

Holly, Werner: „Medialität und Intermedialität in Computerkommunikationsformen". In: Moraldo, Sandro M. (ed.): *Internet-kom. Neue Sprach- und Kommunikationsformen im WorldWideWeb*. ARACNE: Roma 2011a, 27–55.

Holly, Werner: „Medien, Kommunikationsformen, Textsortenfamilien". In: Habscheid, Stephan (ed.): *Textsorten, Handlungsmuster, Oberflächen. Linguistische Typologien der Kommunikation*. de Gruyter: Berlin, New York 2011b, 144–163.

Holly, Werner & Püschel, Ulrich: „Medienlinguistik. Medialität von Sprache und Sprache in Medien". In: Reimann, Sandra & Kessel, Katja (eds.): *Wissenschaften im Kontakt. Kooperationsfelder der Deutschen Sprachwissenschaft*. Narr: Tübingen 2007, 147–162.

Kammer, Aske: "The Mediatization of Journalism". *MedieKultur* 54, 2013, 141–158.

Karlgren, Jussi: "Conventions and Mutual Expectations. Understanding Sources for Web Genres". In: Mehler, Alexander et al. (eds.): *Genres on the Web. Computational Models and Empirical Studies*. Springer: Dordrecht 2011, 33–46.

Klemm, Michael: „Wie hältst Du's mit dem Textbegriff? Pragmatische Antworten auf eine Gretchenfrage der (Text-)Linguistik". In: Fix, Ulla et al. (eds.): *Brauchen wir einen neuen Textbegriff? Antworten auf eine Preisfrage*. Peter Lang: Frankfurt am Main 2002, 143–161.

Krämer, Sybille: „Das Medium als Spur und als Apparat". In: Krämer, Sybille (ed.): *Medien - Computer - Realität. Wirklichkeitsvorstellungen und Neue Medien*. Suhrkamp: Frankfurt am Main 2008, 73–94.

Krotz, Friedrich: "Mediatization. A Concept with which to Grasp Media and Societal Change". In: Lundby, Knut (ed.): *Mediatization. Concept, Changes, Consequences*. de Gruyter: New York 2009, 19–38.

Kunelius, Risto & Reunanen, Esa: "The Medium of the Media Journalism, Politics, and the Theory of 'Mediatization'". *Javnost - the Public* 19(4), 2012, 5–24.

Lomborg, Stine: Social Media, *Social Genres. Making Sense of the Ordinary*. Routledge: New York 2014.

Luginbühl, Martin: *Medienkultur und Medienlinguistik. Komparative Textsortengeschichte(n) der amerikanischen „CBS Evening News" und der Schweizer „Tagesschau"*. Lang: Bern 2014.

Luginbühl, Martin: "Media Linguistics. On Mediality and Culturality". *10plus1. Living Linguistics* 1, 2015, available on 10plus1journal.com.

Lundby, Knut: "Mediatization of Communication". In: Lundby, Knut (ed.): *Mediatization of Communication*. de Gruyter: New York 2014, 3–38.

Marx, Konstanze & Weidacher, Georg: *Internetlinguistik. Ein Lehr- und Arbeitsbuch*. Narr Francke Attempto: Tübingen 2014.

McLuhan, Marshall & Fiore, Quentin: *The Medium is the Massage. An Inventory of Effects*. Gingko Press: Corte Madera Calif. [1967]2001.

Mehler, Alexander et al. (eds.): *Genres on the Web. Computational Models and Empirical Studies*. Springer: Dordrecht 2011.

Meiler, Matthias: „Kommunikationsformenadressen oder: Prozeduren des Situationsvollzugs am Beispiel von Weblogs". *Zeitschrift für Angewandte Linguistik* 59(2), 2013, 51–106.

Meiler, Matthias: "Media Linguistics and Media Studies – Communication Forms and Their Infrastructures". In: Brock, Alexander & Schildhauer, Peter (eds.): *Communication Forms and Communicative Practices. New Perspectives on Communication Forms, Affordances, and What Users Make of Them*. Peter Lang, Berlin, this volume 45–66.

Miller, Carolyn: "Genre as Social Action". *Quarterly Journal of Speech* 70, 1984, 151–167.

Miller, Carolyn & Shepherd, Dawn: "Blogging as Social Action. A Genre Analysis of the Weblog". *Into the Blogosphere. Rhetoric, Community, and Culture of Weblogs* 18(1) 2004, 1–24, retrieved 20.04.2016, from http://tinyurl.com/miller04, 2004.

Nevalainen, Terttu & Tieken-Boon van Ostade, Ingrid: "Standardisation". In: Hogg, Richard M. (ed.): *A History of the English Language*. CUP: Cambridge et al. 2006, 271–311.

Pentzold, Christian et al.: „Online-mediale Texte. Kommunikationsformen, Affordancen, Interfaces". *Zeitschrift für germanistische Linguistik* 41(1), 2013, 81–101.

Posner, Roland: „Zur Systematik der Beschreibung verbaler und nonverbaler Kommunikation. Semiotik als Propädeutik der Medienanalyse". In: Bosshart, Hans-Georg (ed.): *Perspektiven auf Sprache. Interdisziplinäre Beiträge zum Gedenken an Hans Hörmann*. de Gruyter: Berlin / New York 1986, 267–313.

Prensky, Mark: "Digital Natives, Digital Immigrants". *On the Horizon* 9(5), 2001.

Presch, Gunter: „Widersprüche zwischen Textfunktionen als Ausgangspunkt sozialgeschichtlicher Pragmalinguistik". In: Busse, Dietrich (ed.): *Diachrone Semantik und Pragmatik. Untersuchungen zur Erklärung und Beschreibung des Sprachwandels*. M. Niemeyer: Tübingen 1991, 83–100.

Sandig, Barbara: „Zur Differenzierung gebrauchssprachlicher Textsorten im Deutschen". In: Gülich, Elisabeth & Raible, Wolfgang (eds.): *Textsorten. Differenzierungskriterien aus linguistischer Sicht*. Athenaion: Wiesbaden 1975, 113–124.

Sandig, Barbara: *Textstilistik des Deutschen*. de Gruyter: Berlin et al. 2006.

Santini, Marina et al.: "Riding the Rough Waves of Genre on the Web. Concepts and Research Questions". In: Mehler, Alexander et al. (eds.): *Genres on the Web. Computational Models and Empirical Studies*. Springer: Dordrecht 2011, 3–30.

Schildhauer, Peter: *Textsorten im Internet zwischen Wandel und Konstanz. Eine diachrone Untersuchung der Textsorte Personal Weblog*. Dissertation. Martin-Luther-University, Halle-Wittenberg, 2014 retrieved 20.04.2016, from http://tinyurl.com/schild2014.

Schildhauer, Peter: *The Personal Weblog. A Linguistic History*: Peter Lang: Berlin 2016.

Schildhauer, Peter: "Changing Potentials and Their Use: The Case of Blogs". In: Brock, Alexander & Schildhauer, Peter (eds.): *Communication Forms and Communicative Practices. New Perspectives on Communication Forms, Affordances, and What Users Make of Them*. Peter Lang, Berlin, this volume 153–179.

Schmitz, Ulrich: *Sprache in modernen Medien. Einführung in Tatsachen und Theorien, Themen und Thesen*. E. Schmidt: Berlin 2004.

Strömbäck, Jesper: "Four Phases of Mediatization. An Analysis of the Mediatization of Politics". *Press/Politics* 13(3), 2008, 228–246.

Swales, John M.: *Genre Analysis. English in Academic and Research Settings*. CUP: Cambridge 1990.

Thaler, Verena: „Mündlichkeit, Schriftlichkeit, Synchronität. Eine Analyse alter und neuer Konzepte zur Klassifizierung neuer Kommunikationsformen". *Zeitschrift für germanistische Linguistik* 35(1–2), 2007, 146–181.

Ziegler, Arne: „E-Mail – Textsorte oder Kommunikationsform? Eine textlinguistische Annäherung". In: Ziegler, Arne & Dürscheid, Christa (eds.): *Kommunikationsform E-Mail*. Stauffenburg Verlag: Tübingen 2002, 9–32.

Matthias Meiler

Media Linguistics and Media Studies – Communication Forms and Their Infrastructures[1]

Abstract The concept of *communication forms* („Kommunikationsformen“)[2] serves to describe both the evolvement of enabling conditions of communication as well as how different *genres* unfold their communicative purposes within them. In order to inquire these conditions empirically, it seems to be fruitful to address a theoretical concept of recent media studies (Schabacher 2013b; Parks & Starosielski 2015a) taken from science and technology studies: *infrastructures* and *infrastructuring*, respectively. (Bowker 1994; Star & Ruhleder 1996) With this concept, the notoriously vague notion of *media* is graspable in terms of *work*, i.e. as a practical and ongoing accomplishment of the enabling conditions of communication. This will allow to follow the recent tendency to reconsider communication forms in praxeological rather than typological terms, thereby making the analysis of a single communication form more reconstructive, rather than remaining on the surface by merely listing features. Especially in media linguistics, analyses of different domains, like news or science, reconstructions of such kind help to understand what (shifting) organizational conditions or, in other terms, what infrastructural work shapes communicative practices and its domain-specific and social embeddedness. The plea for interdisciplinarity also implies some methodological challenges.

0. Introduction

The aim of this paper is to reconsider one of the key concepts of media linguistics: *communication forms*. For this purpose, I will draw on a concept of recent media studies: *infrastructures* or *infrastructuring*. When brought together, they are useful to shed light on what is meant by calling communication forms 'media-conditioned

1 I will mainly argue from the perspective of the German discussion primarily because 'communication form', the topic of this volume, is a concept that was developed in German text and media linguistics. Besides that, I am convinced that an account along these lines of discussion can also be genuinely interesting in respect of the international exchange of scientific ideas.

2 It is worth noting that the term, in German as well as in English, is somewhat misleading since its conceptual meaning is 'form *for* communication' rather than 'form *of* communication' (which seems to be the more intuitive reading of 'communication forms').

cultural practices' as it has recently been done. That means I will illustrate how the ongoing practical accomplishments that constitute the enabling conditions for communication are empirically accessible and how that set of issues can be conceptualized.

In order to situate my plea for interdisciplinary considerations, I will present a sketch of the outlines of media linguistics as they appear to me (section 1): I will formulate *five main tasks* of media linguistics and the *three assumptions* upon which, in my estimation, they are based. These outlines ought to clarify the conceptual position that communication forms have in media linguistics.

I will then characterize the state of the art of the communication form concept (section 2): In a first step, I will briefly discuss the concept's relation to the notion of *situation*, starting with the notion's linguistic and disciplinary history. That is necessary because communication forms can be understood as typecast forms of speech situations. In the continuum between discourse and text they represent a variety of possible typecast forms of situations that, first of all, enable communication. In a second step, I will summarize the recent developments and tendencies around the communication form concept, and point out the limitations that the concept has within the more praxeological perspective argued for in this article.

This problem will be the point of departure for drawing on the concept of *infrastructure* (section 3): After briefly discussing the relationship between action theory and practice theory, I will give a characterization of the infrastructure concept as it is defined in science and technology studies and how it is taken up in media studies. Finally, I will show how this concept clarifies the challenges that arise with a praxeological perspective for the communication form concept. Such a shift in perspective does, however, bring about new methodological challenges; they will be addressed in the last chapter (section 4).

1. The Outlines of Media Linguistics and a Plea for Interdisciplinarity

If one seeks to consider media linguistics not just as another sub-discipline of linguistics, it has to be understood as a foundational approach investigating the fundamental mediality of language. As such, media linguistics has five main tasks:

i. *Task related to language philosophy*: What role does the materiality of language play in the development of communication, cognition, and sociality as well as culturality (e.g. Jäger 1997; Linz 2010; Schegloff 2006)?

ii. *Task related to language history & typology*: How were the physical and physiological capabilities of humans functionalized for the different development of different languages (e.g. Ehlich 2007)?
iii. *Task related to media history*: How were linguistic means of different complexity functionalized for different communication forms and vice versa: how were communication forms functionalized for different communicative practices by different communities of practice (e.g. Domke 2014: 113–181)?
iv. *Task related to semiology*: How are other types of signs involved in communication by means of language (e.g. Kress & van Leeuwen 1996)?
v. *Task related to discourse analysis*: How do issues and ideas develop through complex inter- and transmedial relations in e.g. political, journalistic, fictional, and also lay discourses (e.g. Rajewsky 2002)?

There may be further, for instance applied, tasks, and of course they are dependent on one another. They, as well, should be and yet already are subjected to empirical concretizations in processes of research.

In order to treat these tasks, media linguistics has to rest on the following three assumptions:

i. *Assumption related to social theory*: Language is inevitably a social phenomenon, i.e. it evolves in social and societal processes through the form/function-dialectics (e.g. Bühler 1990; Redder 2008).
ii. *Assumption related to action theory*: Language is a medium to perform communicative actions (e.g. Austin 1962; important for the German discussion is, e.g., Holly et al. 1984).
iii. *Methodological assumption*: Communication is, under conditions that must not be underestimated, understandable and can hence be reconstructed hermeneutically (e.g. Hermanns & Holly 2007).

As we can see, the third task of media linguistics is concerned with communication forms. That makes communication forms one of its key concepts. For several reasons, and despite their conceptual advantages, communication forms have so far been widely overlooked in the English discussion on media, communication, and language.[3] The central idea of this concept is to make the enabling conditions of communication graspable throughout the spectrum of possibilities (ranging

---

3 However, 'computer-mediated communication' challenges genre-theoretical approaches, as recent works show (cf., e.g., Herring et al. 2005; Herring 2007; Miller & Shepherd 2009; Lomborg 2011). These authors show the complex interrelations between 'genre', 'media', and, e.g., the concept 'affordance'—interrelations that have been implicated

from discourse to text). Lists of features, which make communication forms describable, have therefore been progressively elaborated since the early days of text linguistics (first Ermert 1979).

Unlike the genre-oriented approach, the communication form concept is suited to *equally* consider socio-cultural aspects as well as material and media aspects of communication. This concept provides a link between media technology and processes of conventionalization and standardization through social usage (or domestication) of such technology. Hence, the concept aims to discern and to describe the typecast configurations of media aspects that define a single communication form—aspects such as sign potential, direction of communication, social status, temporality, and spatial dimension. It is only the social usage that configures and stabilizes such media dispositifs, i.e. socio-technical structures that allow for and restrict usages, which thereby gain a specific potential—a potential to enable communication. Communication forms, hence, serve to describe both the evolvement of enabling conditions of communication as well as how different genres unfold their communicative purposes within these conditions.[4]

in the communication forms concept from the very first beginning (see also Brock & Schildhauer, this volume, section 4).

4 Criticism has repeatedly been voiced alleging that the communication form concept addresses an understanding of mediality 'neutral' to the communicative practices which communication forms 'simply transmit' (recently Luginbühl 2015: 13). But the opposite is true (Domke 2014: 25f.; cf. Holly 1996; 2011a; Holly & Püschel 2007: 150): For one part, the concept highlights the *emergent interrelations* of different medialities in the specific configuration that defines a stabilized communication form. For another, the stabilization process itself is not assumed to be technologically deterministic, but rather a *dialectical interplay* between mediality and culturality. The operative point is, then, to differentiate communication forms with their specific 'mediality profiles', enabling us to describe and compare the *co-creative synergy* of different medialities as well as their practical socialization through communicative practices. – To illustrate this briefly with the example of Twitter: With the perspective which the communication form concept provides we are able to address the question of how tweets are going to change if Twitter should abandon the 140-character restriction. It also provides us with a conceptual model to reconstruct the interrelation of the practice of retweeting and the implementation of the retweet button into the Twitter platform. Taking these aspects into consideration, it instructs us to reconstruct the evolvement of Twitter and tweeting as a process in which media technology and social practices influence each other mutually (cf. for a media linguistics point of view e.g. Dang-Anh et al. 2013; for a media studies point of view e.g. Paßmann & Gerlitz 2014). – In summary, the reconstruction of the specific potentials that define different communication forms (and of the way these potentials enable different communicative practices to develop,

Recent works on communication forms called them practices, more precisely, "media-conditioned cultural practices" („medial bedingte kulturelle Praktiken", Holly 2011b: 155; Domke 2014; Meiler 2013a). But such an understanding of communication forms appears to be unserviceable: Communication forms are not practices. They are, true to their name, 'forms'. The concept is, therefore, only suitable to describe a certain kind of structure. To call them practices obscures the relation between communication forms and their performative qualities that are characteristic for practices. However, in order to elaborate that relation, the 'cultural turn' in recent (media) linguistics has to be taken more seriously as it discusses language in the context of social practices (e.g. Deppermann et al. 2016). This terminological problem ('form' vs. 'practice') also raises the question of the ontological status of communication forms and how they take part in *linguistic* and *communicative practices* (cf. Habscheid 2016). An interdisciplinary excursion will help in opening up the black box again, and suggest answers for the question of how communication forms are interrelated with the practices that enable communication.

To inquire communication forms *empirically*, it seems to be fruitful to address a concept of recent media studies taken from science and technology studies: infrastructures and infrastructuring, respectively. It focuses on socio-technical configurations, such as traffic or information systems, their evolvement, and stabilization. With this concept, the notoriously vague notion of media is graspable in terms of *work*, i.e. as a practical and ongoing accomplishment of the enabling conditions of communication. This will follow the recent tendency to reconsider communication forms in less typological but rather in praxeological terms, thereby making the analysis of a single communication form more reconstructive instead of remaining on the surface by merely listing features. Especially in media linguistic analyses of different domains, like news, religion, or science, reconstructions of this kind help to understand what (shifting) organizational conditions or, in other terms, what infrastructural work shapes communicative practices and their domain-specific and societal embeddedness.

---

evolve, and adjust to them) cannot be ascribed to either actors' choices or technological determinism; it is in fact a 'recursive domestication' (cf. Schüttpelz 2006: 93). As a matter of fact, the communication form concept can be perceived as an attempt to follow the 'traces of media' in communicative practices.

2. Communication Forms – State of the Art

The relatively young history of pragmatic linguistics shows that both linguistics of text and linguistics of conversation are eagerly concerned with a notion of 'situations' – but each in a different way. This seems to be because of the medial or merely material characteristics of the two phenomena, text and conversation. Text linguistics, originally interested in the palpable product, used to grasp situations as external features that determine the linguistic activities of texts (cf. Heinemann 2000), whereas linguistics of conversation, interested in the interactive process, focusses on situation as an ongoing accomplishment of the actors itself: How do they define the situation they are a part of right now and how do they constitute it while interacting (cf. Deppermann & Spranz-Fogasy 2001). Just recently these complementary views were mutually adopted (cf., e.g., Hausendorf & Kesselheim 2008; Schmitt 2007). As it turns out, the essence of this bifurcation is a dialectical differentiation of how to comprehend situations as part of the phenomena at hand: a product-view and a process-view.

An etymological analysis, which I cannot outline here, is able to teach us that both views have always been part of the notion of 'situation' (cf. Meiler 2016: 87–96). Throughout the history of the expression, ranging from ancient Latin through Middle French to (e.g.) modern German and English, the process-view and the product-view on situations was alternately stressed. The way the languages mentioned develop different word formations throughout their history, all originating from Latin *situs*, reveals a meandering movement between the two views on situations. If taken seriously, these findings prompt a dialectical synthesis of both views. Hence, situations as such are always both process and product, ongoing accomplishment and determining features, structuration and structure.

What does this have to do with communication forms? The third task of media linguistics, as mentioned above, highlights the empirical reconstruction of how different linguistic means are functionalized for different communication forms. Bühler (1990: 28) put that task in a nutshell by asking: "Must our ultimate slogan be that the old grammar is in need of reform in terms of a decisively *situational theory* of language?" And in objection to Bühler (ibid.), the question has to be answered positively *without restriction*, because even "speech that is largely *removed from the situation*" of face-to-face communication receives its action qualities from the dilation of the speech situation and not its dissolution. Ehlich (1979) (and others) addressed the 'need of reform' from a strictly pragmatic point of view by determining precisely what distinguishes text from discourse (conversation). He justifies his dichotomous definition of text vs. discourse with the differences in the use of linguistic procedures[5] (especially deixeis, see also Ehlich 1989). The main question is therefore whether both interactants, speaker and hearer, are in co-presence or, in any way, not. To enable non-present situations of communication, the linguistic action itself has to become durable to bridge the gap between the production situation of the speaker with the reception situation of the hearer. Deixeis, like other linguistic procedures, too, have to get adjusted to that "dilation of the speech situation" („Zerdehnung der Sprechsituation", Ehlich 1983: 38). But what about more complex linguistic means like, e.g., linguistic action patterns or the turn-taking apparatus (see, also from other theoretical viewpoints, e.g. Beißwenger 2004; Günthner 2012; Mulkay 1986) Is the simple dichotomy of text vs. discourse fit to describe the varieties of linguistic means formed by speech situations beyond these two prototypes? What about the whole, gradually structured spectrum in between?

This is the spectrum that the communication form concept can grasp. Communication forms can be understood as socio-culturally typecast media-material aspects of situations in which speaker and hearer are able to get in communicational contact; they are typecast enabling conditions for communication. As Domke's (2014) work condenses it systematically, the spectrum of enabling conditions can be divided into three major families of communication forms: micro-, meso-, and macro-communication forms.

Since their conceptual launch by Ermert (1979), communication forms were mainly used for purposes of typologizing situational conditions of communication, of mostly several texts (e.g., Brinker [6]2005; Domke 2010; Dürscheid 2005; Schmitz 2004; Ziegler 2002). Communication forms were, thereby, conceptualized as "virtual configurations" („virtuelle Konstellationen"; Holly 1997: 69) with a certain potential to store, process, distribute, and amplify certain types of signs. These configurations assemble several media or medialities in characteristic combinations which, through history, turn out to be useful, and stabilize as communication forms.6 As such configurations, communication forms serve as enabling

---

5 See, e.g., Redder (2008) for the procedures concept in particular and for the Functional Pragmatics approach in general.

6 As far as I know, an *explicit* theory on or at least a theoretical model of the principles of historical change, development, and differentiation of communication forms has not yet been formulated. But what must be avoided (and sometimes linguists' ideas of media change seem to tend in such a direction) is a simplistic, social-deterministic, ex-post rationalization of a complex, indeterministic, socio-technical process (see, e.g., Schröter & Schwering 2014 for an overview on those models).

conditions for a wide variety of possible communicative actions and, on a higher dimension, for communicative genres and practices.

Since Ermert's (1979) early work, the sets of parameters that make describable the properties of communication forms were listed, differentiated, and displayed in different ways.[7] In an earlier paper, I suggested to split up these description parameters in producer's side and recipient's side in order to comprise the various ways in which communicators are involved practically in the media configurations of communication forms (cf. Meiler 2013a).

As mentioned before, another aspect was added recently to the communication form concept: Communication forms were called "media-conditioned cultural practices" (Domke 2014; Holly 2011b: 155; Meiler 2013a). It was an attempt to add the process-view to speech situations that previously were, with the communication form concept, construed from the product-view. But this mere addition of a performative aspect seems to be too simple and neither possible nor fruitful conceptually. Communication forms do not name practices. Instead they name specific forms. Hence, such a conception is, with its elaborated lists of parameters, only suitable to describe structures. A terminological alternation ('practice' *instead of* 'form') or identification ('forms' *are* 'practices') is rhetorically easy but enlightens less than it obscures – it closes the black box upon a concrete communication form rather than opening it up. This raises the question of the ontological status of communication forms.

Because of the virtual quality of communication forms mentioned above, I have argued that they have to be considered a certain kind of social knowledge (cf. Meiler 2013a: 57). There is a rich stock of expressions in our vocabulary which neither name functionally defined genres nor mere technical media but communication forms: e.g. *conversation, meeting, letter, book, paper, journal, radio, TV show, placard, telegram, fax, phone call, videophone call, e-mail, website, chat, video chat, instant messaging, weblog, tweet*, and much else. These more or less common "sorting expressions of everyday language" („alltägliche Sortierausdrücke"; Holly 2011b: 144) give a narrow insight into the structure of the kind of societal knowledge that is of interest here. The knowledge subsumed in these expressions is more or less stereotyped and more or less conscious, and expressible only this way. 'We' have knowledge about how and what is communicable in letters, books, TV shows, or e-mails; 'we' have recently started to gain knowledge about what is communicable in weblogs or tweets, and how; yet 'we' start to forget what a telegram is and how it was used; and 'we' never really established a practice of

7 For an overview, see Brock & Schildhauer (this volume).

videophone calls so that there barely is a structured knowledge of such a practice. It has, of course, to be added that this knowledge is socially distributed in such a way that, e.g., the journalists' notion of periodical communication forms, like newspapers or magazines, differs widely from the readers', and the paperboy has another notion of them yet again. These are first hints on how to tackle the structural bias of the communication form concept: by showing how the actors are involved in the infrastructures of the communicative process they participate in.

As for the attempt to describe communication forms as the practical knowledge communicators themselves gain and have, Gibson's (1979) concept of "affordances" has to be mentioned. It was brought into the discussion of communication forms by Pentzold et al. (2013) to foreground the dialectical process of stabilization of communication forms (with their specific possibilities and constraints) through their usage – i.e. as interplay of materiality and its socialization through practice (more fundamentally Pinkering 1993).

Arguing as a perceptual psychologist, Gibson (cf. 1979: 124–143) tends to highlight mere perceptive qualities of things on the one hand, and on the other marginalizes the role of knowledge in constituting their affordances. He seems to be rather uncertain about the ontology of affordances, as for him they are "both physical and psychical, yet neither" (ibid.: 129). But affordances have to be understood as socio-cultural constructions and as such are clearly mental concepts of generalized social knowledge. It was Norman (1988: 219) who already pointed out that "the mental interpretation of things, based on our past knowledge and experience applied to our perception" is key to the dialectical development of what something affords us to do. For instance, he shows the role of "conceptual models" (ibid.: 12) in the acquisition of a device's operations and functionalities, and how these models shape its actual use and usage problems. So the social knowledge of how and for what a single communication form is used and suitable depends crucially on the continuity of its practical usage. Again, practices play an important role here (see also, e.g., Hutchby 2001; Pentzold 2015). It has therefore to be clarified how communication forms can be conceptually translated in terms of praxeology.

As I have already mentioned, there were certain attempts to comprehend communication forms in terms of praxeology. They propose to recoin the concept by defining communication forms as "media-conditioned cultural practices" (Domke 2014; Holly 2011b: 155; Meiler 2013a). But as I have also already stated, this is too simple and does not unveil any performative qualities of communication forms. It remains a promise that cannot be honored with a structural conception. And indeed, my past attempt to translate the parameters of communication forms into 'medializing and addressing procedures' was misguided because it got trapped in the dark of the unopened black box of practices (cf. Meiler 2013a: 60–67). It is simply not enough to solely say the parameters are, as procedures, part of the practice that constitutes the enabling conditions of communication forms. You have to actually translate them – and that means to understand them from a different perspective. Such a shift in perspective becomes possible with the infrastructure concept.

3. Infrastructures and Infrastructuring

A recent approach in media studies apprehends media as infrastructures (e.g. Parks 2009; Schabacher 2013b). In doing so, media studies took the concept of infrastructure / infrastructuring from science and technology studies, and adopted a practice-theoretical point of view in theory and in empirical research. In order to take advantage of this shift in perspective, media linguistics has to consider how the sociological concept of practice and the linguistic concept of action compare. From the attempts of sociologists to systematize heterogeneous praxeological approaches and to work out a common conceptual core (e.g. Reckwitz 2002; Rouse 2007; Schatzki 2016), we can gather that practice theory is very compatible with linguistic pragmatics and the concepts of practice and action in consequence are, too (cf. Habscheid 2016). Linguistic conceptions of action that were put forward in the past stressed the fact that actions are always complex structured processes depending on collective social knowledge, so that meanings or purposes of actions always depend on the interactional interpretations of their perceptible traces (cf. Holly et al. 1984). But practice theory with its more holistic view reminds us that (linguistic) actions and patterns of actions are fully embedded in ecologies of skilled bodies and minds, and also of socialized things. These three aspects of practices, that also can be rearranged as "people", "material artifacts", and "signs" („Personen", „materielle Artefakte", „Zeichen"; Schüttpelz 2006: 97), shape a certain kind of practice in their interrelatedness determining communicative practices as specific kinds of practices as well. Practice theory thus provides a heuristic device not only to describe communicative practices, but also the manifold practices that constitute the enabling conditions for communication, i.e. the practices of infrastructuring a certain kind of communication form.

But how do we have to understand infrastructures? Star & Ruhleder (1996: 113) state that

> infrastructure is a fundamentally relational concept. [Something] becomes infrastructure in relation to organized practices. Within a given cultural context, the cook considers the water system a piece of working infrastructure integral to making dinner; for the city

planner, it becomes a variable in a complex equation. Thus we ask, *when*—not *what*—is an infrastructure.

The relational quality of infrastructure was initially characterized by Star & Ruhleder (1996: 113) through the following dimensions:

- "*Embeddedness*": Infrastructures are embedded in and therefore depending on other socio-technical structures. Thus infrastructures are (historically) layered.
- "*Transparency*": Infrastructures are invisible during their successful usage; as a result, they are taken for granted.
- "*Reach or scope*": Infrastructures are, by any means, temporally durable beyond merely single events, and they have a wide spatial extent.
- "*Learned as part of membership*": The successful usage of infrastructures requires learning processes in order to acquire a naturalized familiarity.
- "*Links with conventions of practices*": Infrastructures are interdependent with social practices and their conventions to the extent that they shape each other mutually.
- "*Embodiment of standards*": As the scope of infrastructures depends on technical standards that enable the network connections to other infrastructures and between their components, so do standards shape the use of infrastructures, e.g. by device interfaces.
- "*Built on an installed base*": The development of infrastructures is highly dependent on preceding infrastructures that provide a compatible and connectable ground 'to grow'.
- "*Becomes visible upon breakdown*": The transparency of the taken-for-grantedness of working infrastructures loses its invisibility with recalcitrance through failure and breakdown, revealing its wide scope, its different layers of embeddedness, and its socio-technical complexity.
- "*Is fixed in modular increments, not all at once or globally*"[8]: An infrastructure is never developed, installed, or changed from above. Since it holds different meanings depending on where it is in use, it takes situated negotiations, much effort and an amount of time until an infrastructure 'emerges'.

One can understand these (diachronically and synchronically conceivable) dimensions only briefly summarized here as heuristical research tasks. They have to be foregrounded in order to reconstruct an infrastructure. Bowker (1994: 235) called this form of investigation "infrastructural inversion". It means to make visible the 'backstage work' of something that seems to be evidently happening at

8 The last dimension was added to the list in Star (1999: 382).

the 'frontstage'. So the attention shifts away from the practices that make use of a certain infrastructure to the practices of infrastructuring that produce and reproduce it. The fundamental relational quality of infrastructures thereby becomes a clear analytical frame for the investigation of practices that configure and stabilize 'forms' (which themselves enable other practices).

Taking this notion of infrastructuring seriously, the media scholar Gabriele Schabacher (2013b)[9] likewise emphasizes the necessity of not looking at infrastructures as merely stabilized enabling conditions but as *constantly enabled* conditions. She understands infrastructures as "processes of mobilization (infrastructuring) which constituted the basis for mobility" of people, goods, and information – hence, mediation (Schabacher 2013b: 78). By focusing on the dynamic aspects of infrastructures she asks what kind of "allies (people as well as objects)" have to be mobilized to 'take part' in the practices that constitute infrastructures. This concept of "mobilization" is taken from actor-network-theory, a praxeological approach that tries to describe social practices as equally assembling human and non-human actors (see, e.g., Callon 1986; Latour 2005).[10]

While the process of mobilization is quite apparent during the endeavor of establishing an infrastructure, it tends to disappear as it gets stabilized – actor-network-theorists speak of the process of "blackboxing" (Latour 1994: 36). To open up a certain black box means, as Schabacher (cf. 2013b: 85f.) points out referring to Callon (1986), to reconstruct the whole "actor-world" that is concerned with the ongoing accomplishment of stabilizing the relationships between the heterogeneous entities that constitute the infrastructuring practices.

Those reconstructions of actor-worlds behind the mousy labels that seal the black boxes, which we hardly recognize in our everyday practices, cannot be limited to a mere list of all mobilized entities. These entities have instead to be analyzed in their interdependency or mutual co-evolution. Schabacher (2013b: 86–89), therefore, highlights the inevitable co-occurrence of transport and transformation, and it turns out to be a question of perspective whether that co-occurrence

---

9 For slightly different views on 'media infrastructure' see e.g. the works in Parks & Starosielski (2015b). I mainly confine my remarks here to Schabacher's outline because it is decidedly oriented towards praxeology and therefore a coherent approach to mediation as such. In the concept of mediation she follows Schüttpelz's (2006) understanding of mediation as an inextricably and co-constituting entanglement of people, things, and signs through practice.

10 These sociological approaches, science and technology studies in general and actor-network-theory in particular, became recently very important in the German discussion on a praxeological pathway to media research (cf. Thielmann & Schüttpelz 2013).

is analyzed on the level of infrastructural use or / and at the level of infrastructuring. In consequence, the idea of "media" is praxeologically liquefied as "(socio-) technical process of mediation" (Schabacher 2013b: 78; Schüttpelz 2006).[11]

Adopting this perspective for media linguistic research on communication forms means to take a certain kind of labeled black box and therein discover the widespread infrastructure with all its human and non-human actors that are part of the practices that stabilize the enabling conditions defining the features of a certain communication form.[12] Transferring the insight of the inevitable relational quality of infrastructures onto the communication form concept leads to two possible perspectives on communication forms, thereby turning it into a reversible figure.

On the one hand, the *stabilized qualities* of a single communication form can be analyzed. That means to find out either the tacit social knowledge people gain through their communicative practices using different communication forms, or to examine the more or less listable features through a 'system analysis' and to try to relate them to the communicative practices that are observable within a 'media system'. On the other hand, the *dynamic processes* that have a single communication form as their result can be analyzed. That means to liquefy its structural qualities through an infrastructural inversion that sheds light on the manifold practices involved in constituting what is stabilized as a communication form. The effort of organizational work necessary to constitute different types of communication forms as speech situations (see section 2) will become visible, and thus the *Sitz im Leben* of a communication form in a certain "community of practice" (Lave & Wenger 1991) can be reconstructed in more detail. In consequence, the question of what practical realignment is required if a domain adopts, tries to, or is compelled to adopt a new communication form for its purposes becomes

11 That makes the infrastructure concept profoundly useful for media studies especially because thereby a historiography of 'media' is possible beyond asymmetrical emphasis on 'the social' or 'the material' (cf. Schabacher 2013a: 132).

12 Just to point this out briefly, the enablement of the communication form concept to grasp the spectrum between discourse and text (see above) is not reduced by adopting the infrastructuring perspective: "Under some circumstances the human body becomes infrastructure, such as in the study of face-to-face conversations. [There] the targets of study are [e.g.] facial and body muscles, posture and proximity" (Star & Bowker 2006: 151f.). See Schegloff (2006) for an attempt to describe interactions as infrastructures of sociality. Generally both types of infrastructures, 'bodily' and 'technical' infrastructures, are closely interwoven. And in approaching communication forms empirically, it is necessary to take into consideration that the performance of communicative practices depends heavily upon embodied knowledge.

empirical accessible. From such a perspective, it also becomes obvious which communication forms can be reasonably compared with each other. Focusing on domains and their communities of practice provides a perspective that instructs us not just to compare communication forms merely because of their media similarities. What is more, it instructs us to compare how different domain-specific purposes are assessed by actors to get treated in different communication forms (cf., e.g., Meiler forthcoming) – not least because of the infrastructuring processes the actors are, to different degrees, concerned with. Media linguistics would, thereby, not be oriented towards analyses of 'ontologies of single communication forms'[13] but towards analyses of social practices of which communication forms are a part (for a related approach in media studies see, e.g., Bräuchler & Postill 2010; Krajina et al. 2014).

4. Methodological Challenges

If we investigate the everyday and / or the domain-specific changes that emerge with a 'new' communication form from the perspective outlined above, we will not remain mere analysts of communication and its socially guided, hermeneutical interpretation. Investigating such changes means focusing on the practices underlying the communicative processes that are of interest for media linguists traditionally. However, in order to investigate how these processes are socially embedded and thereby enabled through infrastructural work, we have to face certain methodological challenges.

As Star (1999: 383) puts it, one has to apply an "ethnographic sensibility" to the heterogeneous kinds of data that are needed to investigate practices of infrastructuring. As ethnography can be defined roughly as a praxeological approach that investigates small-scale fields holistically through the attempt to acquire an insiders' comprehension of the studied natives' practices,[14] it can make use of many different methods to gain that insight and to tell its story (cf. Wietschorke 2010: 221–223).

---

13 Leschke (2003: 154) speaks of "single-media ontologies" („Einzelmedienontologien") to name the analytical strategy of defining 'an essence' of a single medium by mere ascription of sense. He clearly shows the limits of such an approach that is just capable to sketch out possibilities and disregards concrete practices.

14 That is, in a nutshell, the key condition for hermeneutical analyses of communicative practices: "to recover participants' background assumptions and definitions of reality" (Deppermann 2012: 764).

> The methodological implications of th[e] relational approach to infrastructure are considerable. Sites to examine then include decisions about encoding and standardizing, tinkering and tailoring activities [...], and the observation and deconstruction of decisions carried into infrastructural forms [...]. The fieldwork in this case transmogrifies to a combination of historical and literary analysis, traditional tools like interviews and observations, systems analysis, and usability studies. (Star 1999: 382)

With these methods among others, the main task is to make the invisible work of infrastructuring a communication form analytically visible: What kind of heterogeneous and distributed practices are involved in constituting the enabling conditions that define a single communication form? What interplay of people, things and signs defines these practices? How is their interrelation stabilized so that, in the end, they contribute to the formation of a communication form? These questions mark a direction of questioning that puts us in the position to reconstruct the deep social embeddedness of communication forms instead of merely listing their superficially observable features.

The analysis of the established uses of 'old' and the adoption of 'new' communication forms (and the interplay of both) in and for specific domains, such as science, can be improved with the outlined perspective. It sheds light on the organizational efforts and efforts of organizational changes within the workflows of a single domain, and it can thereby provide answers about how a communication form is embedded in a single domain and why a new communication form might struggle so long to find its suitable place within a domain – may it be ever so useful or highly valued, like, e.g., open access journals. Adopting new communication forms always depends on the difficult task to establish infrastructures within an existing community of practice, which means that infrastructural development is to a great extent an emergent process. Participatory observation is highly useful to investigate that process in depth. However, it might not be necessary in every case for media linguistic research.

Such processes are, as Star (1999) mentioned in the quote above, not just accessible through participatory observation. Archival research, interaction analysis, discourse analysis, and objective hermeneutics also provide insights into infrastructures and infrastructuring, of course each of them from a different angle and with a different epistemological background (cf. Parks & Starosielski 2015a: 16f.; von Grote 1994). Since media studies have a much broader interest in infrastructures, media linguists, interested primarily in how infrastructural aspects effect *communication*, can take a narrower and better-suited perspective. It is possible to look for discourses of 'breakdown' situations in particular. In these situations, the actors themselves have to open the infrastructural black box and give insight into the invisible work of infrastructuring: both into the work of everyday maintaining and the work of repairing a breakdown. So, for instance, the actors' accounts on problems with the infrastructure of his weblog can be analyzed because those accounts give hints on the invisible infrastructuring work beneath the communicative surface (cf. Meiler 2013b). Of course, those analyses are to be combined with related 'system analyses' in order to link the communicative accounts of the actors with the features and properties of the infrastructure and its components. But these 'breakdown' situations give insight in how and to what extent the actors themselves are concerned with infrastructural work, and their accounts hint at the important and influential infrastructural aspects by which they are affected. But by investigating the infrastructures of communication forms, it is impossible to avoid becoming familiar with their constituting practices to a certain degree. And that means going beyond the communicative processes that are analytically focused.

Which research method is appropriate for such an endeavor depends, of course, on the general research interest. If one wants to investigate the historical evolvement of a communication form, or if one wants to accompany the adoption of a communication form in a community of practice, the research endeavor has to be oriented more closely to an individual case, resting on examination of historical documents or on interviews and participatory observation. Which research method is appropriate depends, too, of course, on the communication form that is, or is part of, the research object. Micro-, meso-, and macro-communication forms call for different methods, as they rest on different infrastructural foundations. And finally, which research method is appropriate depends on the question whether the producer's side or the recipient's side is of interest. Each of them is differently involved in what one might call the infrastructural constitution of a speech situation through a communication form. To examine the distributor's side often proves much more difficult, since the field of interest might not be easily accessible and insights in internal processes, like protocols and algorithms, may not be attainable.

More generally speaking, media linguistics is not so much in need of single case studies of infrastructural development as it is in need of systematic determinations of the infrastructural foundations of communication forms – foundations that are important for the communicative practices that we seek to understand in more detail.[15]

15 I extend my sincere gratitude to the editors, Alexander Brock and Peter Schildhauer, who I thank for their helpful and critical commentary and discussion they provided me with. Thanks are also in order to Benjamin Dupke who I'm obliged to for his knowledgeable support throughout the process of writing this article.

References

Austin, John L.: *How to do Things with Words*. Clarendon Press: Oxford 1962.

Beißwenger, Michael: „Sprachhandlungskoordination im Chat". *Zeitschrift für Germanistische Linguistik* 31(2), 2004, 198–231.

Bowker, Geoffrey C.: "Information Mythology. The World of / as Information". In: Bud-Frierman, Lisa (ed.): *Information Acumen*. Routledge: London 1994, 231–247.

Bräuchler, Birgit & Postill, John (eds.): *Theorising Media and Practice*. Berghahn: New York & Oxford 2010.

Brinker, Klaus: *Linguistische Textanalyse*. 6th edition. Schmidt: Berlin 2005.

Brock, Alexander & Schildhauer, Peter: "Communication Form. A Concept Revisited". In: Brock, Alexander & Schildhauer, Peter (eds.): *Communication Forms and Communicative Practices. New Perspectives on Communication Forms, Affordances, and What users Make of Them*. Peter Lang: Berlin, this volume 13–43.

Bühler, Karl: *Theory of Language*. Benjamins: Amsterdam & Philadelphia 1990.

Callon, Michel: "The Sociology of an Actor-Network: The case of the electric vehicle". In: Callon, Michel et al. (eds.): *Mapping the Dynamics of Science and Technology*. Macmillan: Basingstoke 1986, 19–34.

Dang-Anh, Mark et al.: „Kontextualisierung durch Hashtags. Die Mediatisierung des politischen Sprachgebrauchs im Internet." In: Diemannshenke, Hajo & Niehr, Thomas (eds.): *Öffentliche Wörter. Analysen zum öffentlich-medialen Sprachgebrauch*. Ibidem: Stuttgart 2013, 137–159.

Deppermann, Arnulf: "How does 'Cognition' Matter to the Analysis of Talk-in-Interaction?". *Language Sciences* 34(6), 2012, 746–767.

Deppermann, Arnulf et al. (eds.): *Sprachliche und kommunikative Praktiken*. de Gruyter: Boston & Berlin 2016.

Deppermann, Arnulf & Spranz-Fogasy, Thomas: „Aspekte und Merkmale der Gesprächssituation". In: Brinker, Klaus et al. (eds.): *Text- und Gesprächslinguistik. Linguistics of Text and Conversation*. de Gruyter: Berlin & New York 2001, 1148–1161.

Domke, Christine: „Texte im öffentlichen Raum: Formen medienvermittelter Kommunikation auf Bahnhöfen". In: Bucher, Hans-Jürgen et al. (eds.): *Neue Medien – neue Formate*. Campus: Frankfurt & New York 2010, 257–281.

Domke, Christine: *Die Betextung des öffentlichen Raumes. Eine Studie zur Spezifik von Meso-Kommunikation am Beispiel von Bahnhöfen, Innenstädten und Flughäfen*. Winter: Heidelberg 2014.

Dürscheid, Christa: „Medien, Kommunikationsformen, kommunikative Gattungen". *Linguistik online* 22(1), 2005, 3–16.

Ehlich, Konrad: *Verwendungen der Deixis beim sprachlichen Handeln.* 2 Vols. Lang: Frankfurt a.M. et al. 1979.

Ehlich, Konrad: „Text und sprachliches Handeln. Die Entstehung von Texten aus dem Bedürfnis nach Überlieferung“. In: Assmann, Aleida et al. (eds.): *Schrift und Gedächtnis.* Fink: München 1983, 24–43.

Ehlich, Konrad: “Deictic Expressions and the Connexity of Text”. In: Conte, Maria-Elisabeth et al. (eds.): *Text and Discourse Connectedness.* Benjamins: Amsterdam 1989, 33–52.

Ehlich, Konrad: „Sprachmittel und Sprachzwecke“. In: Ehlich, Konrad (ed.): *Sprache und sprachliches Handeln.* Vol. 1. de Gruyter: Berlin & New York 2007, 55–80.

Ermert, Karl: *Briefsorten.* Niemeyer: Tübingen 1979.

Gibson, James J.: *The Ecological Approach to Visual Perception.* Mifflin: Boston 1979.

Günthner, Susanne: „‚Lupf meinen Slumpf‘: Die interaktive Organisation von SMS-Dialogen“. In: Ayaß, Ruth & Meyer, Christian (eds.): *Sozialität in Slow Motion.* VS: Wiesbaden 2012, 353–372.

Habscheid, Stephan: „Handeln in Praxis. Hinter- und Untergründe situierter sprachlicher Bedeutungskonstitution“. In: Deppermann, Arnulf et al. (eds.): *Sprachliche und kommunikative Praktiken.* de Gruyter: Berlin & Boston 2016, 127–151.

Hausendorf, Heiko & Kesselheim, Wolfgang: *Textlinguistik fürs Examen.* Vandenhoeck & Ruprecht: Göttingen 2008.

Heinemann, Wolfgang: „Aspekte der Textsortendifferenzierung“. In: Brinker, Klaus et al. (eds.): *Text- und Gesprächslinguistik. Linguistics of Text and Conversation.* de Gruyter: Berlin & New York 2000, 523–546.

Hermanns, Fritz & Holly, Werner (eds.): *Linguistische Hermeneutik.* Niemeyer: Tübingen 2007.

Herring, Susan C.: “A Faceted Classification Scheme for Computer-Mediated Discourse”. *Language@Internet* 4(1), 2007, 1–37, retrieved 22.09.2016, from http://www.languageatinternet.org/articles/2007/761.

Herring, Susan C. et al.: “Weblogs as a Bridging Genre”. *Information Technology & People* 18(2), 2005, 142–171.

Holly, Werner: „Alte und neue Medien. Zur inneren Logik der Mediengeschichte“. In: Rüschoff, Bernd & Schmitz, Ulrich (eds.): *Kommunikation und Lernen mit alten und neuen Medien.* Lang: Frankfurt a.M. et al. 1996, 9–16.

Holly, Werner: „Zur Rolle von Sprache in Medien. Semiotische und kommunikationsstrukturelle Grundlagen“. *Muttersprache* 107(1), 1997, 64–75.

Holly, Werner: „Medialität und Intermedialität in Computerkommunikationsformen". In: Moraldo, Sandro M. (ed.): *Internet.kom.* Vol. 2: *Medialität, Hypertext, digitale Literatur.* Aracne: Roma 2011a, 27–55.

Holly, Werner: „Medien, Kommunikationsformen, Textsortenfamilien". In: Habscheid, Stephan (ed.): *Textsorten, Handlungsmuster, Oberflächen.* de Gruyter: Berlin & Boston 2011b, 144–163.

Holly, Werner et al. (1984): „Für einen ‚sinnvollen' Handlungsbegriff in der linguistischen Pragmatik". *Zeitschrift für Germanistische Linguistik* 12(3), 275–312.

Holly, Werner & Püschel, Ulrich: „Medienlinguistik. Medialität von Sprache und Sprache in Medien". In: Reimann, Sandra & Kessel, Katja (eds.): *Wissenschaften im Kontakt.* Narr: Tübingen 2007, 147–162.

Hutchby, Ian: "Technologies, Texts and Affordances". *Sociology* 35(2), 2001, 441–456.

Jäger, Ludwig: „Die Medialität der Sprachzeichen. Zur Kritik des Repräsentationsbegriffs aus Sicht des semiologischen Konstruktivismus". In: Baum, Richard et al. (eds.): *Kunst und Kommunikation.* Stauffenburg: Tübingen 1997, 199–220.

Krajina, Zlatan et al.: "Non-Media-Centric Media Studies. A Cross-Generational Conversation". *European Journal of Cultural Studies* 17 (6), 2014, 682–700.

Kress, Gunther R. & van Leeuwen, Theo: *Reading images.* Routledge: London 1996.

Latour, Bruno: "On Technical Mediation – Philosophy, Sociology, Genealogy". In: *Common Knowledge* 3(2), 1994, 29–64.

Latour, Bruno: *Reassembling the Social.* Oxford University Press: Oxford & New York 2005.

Lave, Jean & Wenger, Etienne: *Situated Learning.* Cambridge University Press: Cambridge 1991.

Leschke, Rainer: *Einführung in die Medientheorie.* Fink: München 2003.

Linz, Erika: "The Reflexivity of Voice". In: Jäger, Ludwig et al. (eds.): *Media, Culture, and Mediality.* Transcript: Bielefeld 2010, 333–347.

Lomborg, Stine: "Social Media as Communicative Genres". *MedieKultur. Journal of Media and Communication Research* 51, 2011, 55–71.

Luginbühl, Martin: "Media Linguistics: On Mediality and Culturality". *10plus1. Living Linguistics* 1(1), 2015, 9–26.

Meiler, Matthias: „Einige Spezifika soziologischen Bloggens". In: Zhu, Jianhua et al. (eds): *Germanistik zwischen Tradition und Innovation. Akten des XIII. Kongresses der Internationalen Vereinigung für Germanistik (IVG), Shanghai, 23.-30.08.2015.* Band 2. Lang: Frankfurt a.M. et al.: Lang forthcoming, 61–65.

Meiler, Matthias: *Eristisches Handeln in wissenschaftlichen Weblogs. Medienlinguistische Grundlagen und Analysen.* 3 Vols. Dissertation: University of Siegen 2016.

Meiler, Matthias: „Kommunikationsformenadressen oder: Prozeduren des Situationsvollzugs am Beispiel von Weblogs". *Zeitschrift für angewandte Linguistik* 59(1), 2013a, 51–106.

Meiler, Matthias: „Geoberg.de – ein wissenschaftlicher Weblog. Kommunikationsform und institutionelle Position". In: *Navigationen. Zeitschrift für Medien- und Kulturwissenschaften* 13(2), 2013b, 57–99.

Miller, Carolyn R. & Shepherd, Dawn: "Questions for Genre Theory from the Blogosphere". In: Giltrow, J. & Stein, D. (eds.): *Genre in the Internet*. Benjamins: Amsterdam 2009, 263–290.

Mulkay, Michael: "Conversation and Texts". *Human Studies* 9(2–3), 1986, 303–321.

Norman, Donald A.: *The Psychology of Everyday Things*. Basic Books: New York 1988.

Parks, Lisa: "Signals and Oil. Satellite Footprints and Post-Communist Territories in Central Asia". *European Journal of Cultural Studies* 12(2), 2009, 137–156.

Parks, Lisa & Starosielski, Nicole: "Introduction". In: Parks, Lisa & Starosielski, Nicole (eds.): *Signal Traffic*. University of Illinois Press: Urbana 2015a, 1–27.

Parks, Lisa & Starosielski, Nicole (eds.): *Signal Traffic. Critical Studies of Media Infrastructures*. University of Illinois Press: Urbana 2015b.

Paßmann, Johannes & Gerlitz, Caroline: „'Good' Platform-Political Reasons for 'Bad' Platform-Data. Zur sozio-technischen Geschichte der Plattformaktivitäten Fav, Retweet und Like." In: *Mediale Kontrolle unter Beobachtung* 3(1), 2014, 1–40.

Pentzold, Christian: „Praxistheoretische Prinzipien, Traditionen und Perspektiven kulturalistischer Kommunikations- und Medienforschung". *Medien und Kommunikationswissenschaft* 63(2), 2015, 229–245.

Pentzold, Christian et al.: „Online-mediale Texte: Kommunikationsformen, Affordanzen, Interfaces". *Zeitschrift für Germanistische Linguistik* 41(1), 2013, 81–101.

Pinkering, Andrew: "The Mangle of Practice: Agency and Emergence in the Sociology of Science". *American Journal of Sociology* 99(3), 1993, 559–589.

Rajewsky, Irina O.: *Intermedialität*. Francke: Tübingen 2002.

Reckwitz, Andreas: "Toward a Theory of Social Practices. A Development in Culturalist Theorizing". *European Journal of Social Theory* 5(2), 2002, 243–263.

Redder, Angelika: "Functional Pragmatics". In: Antos, Gerd & Ventola, Eija (eds.): *Handbook of Interpersonal Communication*. de Gruyter: Berlin & Boston 2008, 133–178.

Rouse, Joseph: "Practice Theory". In: Turner, Stephen P. & Risjord, Mark W. (eds.): *Philosophy of Anthropology and Sociology*. Elsevier: Amsterdam et al. 2007, 639–682.

Schabacher, Gabriele: „Medium Infrastruktur. Trajektorien soziotechnischer Netzwerke in der ANT". *Zeitschrift für Medien- und Kulturforschung* (3), 2013a, 129–148.

Schabacher, Gabriele: "Mobilizing Transport: Media, Actor-Worlds, and Infrastructure". *Transfers* 3(1), 2013b, 75–95.

Schatzki, Theordor: „Praxistheorie als flache Ontologie". In: Schäfer, Hilmar (ed.): *Praxistheorie. Ein soziologisches Forschungsprogramm*. Transcript: Bielefeld 2016, 29–44.

Schegloff, Emanuel A.: "Interaction: The Infrastructure for Social Institutions, the Natural Ecological Niche for Language, and the Arena in which Culture is Enacted". In: Enfield, N. J. & Levinson, S. C. (eds.): *Roots of Human Sociality*. Berg: New York 2006, 70–96.

Schmitt, Reinhold (ed.): *Koordinationen. Analysen zur multimodalen Interaktion*. Narr: Tübingen 2007.

Schmitz, Ulrich: *Sprache in modernen Medien*. Schmidt: Berlin 2004.

Schröter, Jens & Schwering, Gregor: „Modelle des Medienwandels und der Mediengeschichtsschreibung". In: Schröter, Jens (ed.): *Handbuch Medienwissenschaft*, Metzler: Stuttgart, Weimar 2014, 179–190.

Schüttpelz, Erhard: „Die medienanthropologische Kehre der Kulturtechniken". *Archiv für Mediengeschichte* 6, 2006, 87–110.

Star, Susan Leigh: "The Ethnography of Infrastructure". *American Behavioral Scientist* 43(7), 1999, 377–391.

Star, Susan Leigh & Bowker, Geoffrey C.: "How to Infrastructure". In: Lievrouw, Leah A. & Livingstone, Sonia M. (eds.): *Handbook of New Media*. Updated student edition. Sage: London & Thousand Oaks, CA 2006, 151–162.

Star, Susan Leigh & Ruhleder, Karen: "Steps Toward an Ecology of Infrastructure: Design and access for large information spaces". *Information Systems Research* 7(1) 1996, 111–134.

Thielmann, Tristan & Schüttpelz, Erhard (eds.): *Akteur-Medien-Theorie*. Transcript: Bielefeld 2013.

von Grote, Claudia: „Anschlüsse an den Alltag. Versuche zu einer Hermeneutik technischer Infrastrukturen“. In: Braun, Ingo & Joerges, Bernward (eds.): *Technik ohne Grenzen*. Suhrkamp: Frankfurt a.M. 1994, 251–304.

Wietschorke, Jens: „Historische Ethnografie. Möglichkeiten und Grenzen eines Konzeptes“. *Zeitschrift für Volkskunde* 106, 2010, 197–224.

Ziegler, Arne: „E-Mail – Textsorte oder Kommunikationsform“. In: Ziegler, Arne & Dürscheid, Christa. (eds.): *Kommunikationsform E-Mail*. Stauffenburg: Tübingen 2002, 8–32.

Christine Domke

From the Space/Place-issue to Mediatization: On the Potential of the Concept of Communication Forms

Abstract My contribution argues for the inclusion of all medial and material features of any communication in text analysis in general and in particular. It points out the significance of the locatedness of communication for a text's semiotic and medial structure as well as its function. It is highlighted that the current focus on mediality of communication in linguistic studies needs additional thought on the impact of where the communication takes place, is to be read, heard or felt. Related to that is the focus on the semiotic resources used for both specific communication forms *and* specific places in the public sphere. With regard to the studies on linguistic and semiotic landscapes (cf. Jaworski & Thurlow 2010), it is pointed out on the one hand that current text analysis of communication in the public sphere (cf. Papen 2012) has to expand the subject-matter by mediality – and therefore modes of perception – and on the other hand that the concept of communication forms elaborated so far (cf. Domke 2014; Holly 2011) needs distinctive categories concerning a text's place and locatedness as well as the time-bound possibilities to perceive a text. The paper argues in general that analyzing communication basically means to include – theoretically and methodologically – all medial and therefore material conditions shaping the way one can communicate to another for different pragmatic purposes.

0. Introduction

With reference to recent linguistic work in the field of multimodality (cf. Jewitt 2011; Klug & Stöckl in print), mediatization, mediality and materiality (cf. Androutsopoulos 2014a; Domke 2014, 2015; Scollon & Scollon 2003), a critical observer could be relieved: The former lack of contextuality and basic mediality (cf. discussed in Habscheid 2011; Holly 2011; Jäger 2002) of every communication taking place has been overcome. In any field of applied linguistics, analyzing texts including oral as well as written communication currently entails the media used, as well as the local setting or the semiotic resources beyond language. For very different fields, this expanded perspective demonstrates the immense scope of linguistic work with reference to, for example, language-image relations gaining more and more importance, gestures as a crucial part in the process of meaning-making or typography as a constitutive part of texts. Regarding these more recent developments in linguistics, it also becomes quite clear at which point linguistic analysis benefits from broader perspectives (e.g. on mediatization, cf. Androutsopoulos 2014b; Domke 2014 and forthcoming) from sociology or media studies – and on the other hand where more specific, i.e. linguistic research on language or other semiotic resources can make a crucial contribution to the understanding of the communicative and mediatized world we are living in.

However, besides new linguistic findings on mediality and materiality of communication and new analytic and disciplinary interplay, some remarks on the relation language/mediality/theorization are to be made: The more recent work on multimodality and mediality is often still linked to the classic dichotomies of linguistic research; this means that either written or oral communication are prioritized, either texts or speech (interactions) are brought into focus. Thus, it can be noticed that, for example, multimodality is often (still) examined using the preferred example of written and/or digital communication (cf. Klug & Stöckl 2014; Machin 2007). On the other hand, the much-discussed space/place[1] issue is either investigated for "interaction space" (cf. Hausendorf et al. 2012) or "place making" by means of semiotic (and almost always visual) landscapes (cf. Warnke & Busse 2014): Broader perspectives which focus on communication *in general* instead of written or oral (or analog or digital) communication and which discuss the relevance of place/space for every kind of language perception have to be considered rare (cf. Domke 2014).

This is where the present contribution takes up. The aim is to suggest the scope of the concept of *communication form,* which is this volume's key issue as a useful foundation for the analysis and characterization of communication *in general.* Therefore, the next chapter's aim is to point out how focusing on communication forms enables discussing any communication's mediality, materiality and participants as a distinctive basis for further analysis. Using the example of public texts, the paper will outline what kind of insights *communication forms* allow. This leads to the question to what extent the concept used in media linguistics so far needs additional thoughts or rather more categories concerning new findings on place, space and perception. Therefore, the general importance of the distinctive feature place-bound/non-place-bound is to be elaborated.

First of all (see chapter 1), the contribution briefly discusses the relation between public places and current forms of "mediatization" (Krotz 2007) and therefore gives a 'typical' example for more recent 'textscapes'. Secondly, the analytic use

1 Space/Place are well established categories in social sciences but far from homogeneously defined. See, for example, Auer et al. (2013), Döring & Thielmann (2008), Hubbard & Kitchin (2010), and Warnke & Busse (2014).

of the concept will be focused on and the concept is to be expanded by including the category "place-bound". Thirdly, the methodological consequences (like using photographs, records) of a pronounced focus on communications forms will be traced. With reference to texts in public places, empirical examples will be given and discussed as a crucial part of everyday life's mediatization, which is shaped by using different (place-bound) communication forms with very different modes and codes.

1. 'Textscapes' in the City as a Part of Mediatized Everyday Life

Walking through a city means – besides obvious purposes like getting somewhere – seeing signs, billboards and stickers, hearing announcements of trains and busses and perceiving tactile guidance systems on the pavement. It is almost impossible to take a train at the station or to view a city's places of interest without perceiving any of the many public signs, graffiti, announcements, stickers, display panels, notices, QR-codes, semiotic and physical barriers and commercial signs (see Pictures 1 and 2).

Picture 1: Vienna, Mariahilfer Street

Picture 2: Frankfurt, Main Station

The perception of some of these texts is time-bound, written on paper or boards which are not weatherproof; some of the texts are visible permanently, printed on fixed materials; they differ with reference to their material, local placement (on walls, the ground, boards) and the semiotic resources used (such as oral or written languages, sounds, pictograms, color, tactile stripes and dots, see Pictures 3 and 4). Outlining a city's publicly perceivable communication[2] as just demonstrated makes quite clear that the texts shape an extensive semiotic landscape differentiated in both the media and materials used and the pragmatic purpose they are produced for. In view of the linguistic and functional diversity, one could actually highlight this textual presence and consider it a 'textscape' of its own.

Picture 3: Leipzig, Main Station/Tram

Picture 4: Erfurt, Main Station

This public textscape 'accompanies' us and determines our perception of a place; it is an important part of the "social construction" of public space (cf. Domke 2014; Döring & Thielmann 2008). In Jäger's terms, the global function of all these different texts, which are bound to a specific corner or wall or shop, may be defined as making a place "readable" (cf. Jäger 2010) as a specific social space: The texts ascribe specific characteristics to 'their' place, like being public vs. private,

2 It is important to mention that this paper deals with publicly perceivable texts such as signs, announcements or demonstrations. This includes every communication perceivable by different local attendees but excludes private conversation which may just be overheard by chance. To investigate publicly perceivable communication means to ascertain by means of which media and resources the local attendees are addressed, and for what purpose.

or walkable or drivable, or being historically relevant. The broad pragmatic use of texts is perceivable only in 'their' specific place: They belong to very different discourses such as the commercial, political, regulatory and transgressive discourse (cf. Scollon & Scollon 2003; also Domke 2014, 2015, and forthcoming; Kallen 2010; Warnke 2011). Especially the signs from the regulatory discourse can be linked to the work of the anthropologist Augé (1994) who defines these texts as public "instruction manuals" for unfamiliar places or, to speak in Augé's terms: non-places. But even when we are not traveling but walking through our very own hometown trying to overlook the many direction signs, we may be 'caught' by a commercial waiting at a bus stop: The public textscape obviously serves very different communicative purposes.

Regarding the given diversity, one further observation seems to be quite evident: The differentiation of the public texts correlates with what is usually claimed for online or digital texts: They are semiotically differentiated, convergent, produced for different addressees, and they shape social practices (cf. Androutsopoulos 2014; Jewitt 2011). Likewise, the public textscape uses very different media options, semiotic resources, addresses different groups (such as tourists, drivers, visually impaired pedestrians), allows individual and more conventional text layout and intertextual relations and offers new communicative, and therefore social, activities (finding places of interest, knowing local rules, getting access to current travel information etc.). Some texts can be related to each other due to their specific design like regulatory signs; some refer to other texts by means of shape (such as prohibition signs) and some – like QR-codes – connect the public place with virtual places: Using a smartphone enables us to perceive certain online texts that are linked to place-bound posters, for example – thus participating in what in terms of Jenkins is called "convergence culture" (Jenkins 2006). Public communication as well as online-communication is genuinely multimodal – considering modes at this point from a social semiotic point of view (cf. Kress 2009; van Leeuwen 2005): Different semiotic resources are merged to multimodal texts and thus connect analog (such as posters with QR-codes) and digital communication forms (such as websites).

Thus, with reference to the increasing number of text types for different public discourses (see above), the public textscape can be considered an important but at the same time overlooked part of everyday life's "mediatization" (Krotz 2007; Krotz & Hepp 2012). Mediatization refers to the increasing existence and use of different media in our everyday life *and* the cultural impact following these changes (Androutsopoulos 2014b). Accordingly, mediatization is not only to be linked to the present but also to every media development (such as the printing press in the 15th century). What has to be considered special today is the number of developments at the same time, the speed at which the developments are challenging social practices and ourselves and the increasing interplay between media and new communication forms.

Accordingly, being interested in public texts means to elaborate on their linguistic and functional diversity and their interplay for different communicative and social activities as well. Thus, the linguistic contribution to exploring the *public textscape* as a part of our mediatized everyday day life includes first of all identifying the forms used for different pragmatic purposes to be able to discuss their communicative usefulness. Here, the concept of communication forms serves as a crucial possibility to find order in a city's texts' variety. Therefore, it is discussed in the next section.

2. The Potential of the Concept of Communication Forms

Walking through a city reveals – as mentioned above – a communicative diversity which is still often overlooked in the research of semiotic and media differentiation. To analyze and classify the textual tokens such as commercials and prohibition signage which have framed our walk, we need considerations on types and, therefore, distinctive features. At this point, the concept of *communication forms* turns out to be useful. The concept was established by Ermert's study on "letter communication" and his sustainable finding that a letter is not yet a text type but rather a more abstract class (cf. Ermert 1979; cf. also Meiler and Schildhauer & Brock in this volume). It has been utilized since by many media-orientated linguistic works. Accordingly, it implies and contains the basic *analytic* differentiation (cf. Domke 2013, 2014, and forthcoming; Holly 2011) between structural and media-based frames of any text (the very communication form such as a sign, see below) and the specific pragmatic use for which a specific communication form may be used (realized by means of the *text type* such as prohibition or direction signs).[3]

3 It is of consequence to distinguish the media features of communication (e.g. is a text visible or audible, is it printed or broadcast, how many recipients are possible at a time?) from its purpose (is a text produced to inform, prohibit, to promote something, to look for something…). In that we find the concept's range: to be able to distinguish a text's aim from what allows to produce or realize it. The achievement and usefulness of medialinguistic research lies at this point in finding order in the variety of communicative possibilities. Based on the concept, we are able to discuss the interplay between communication forms and the pragmatic use they are applied for.

In this understanding, a medium is a constructed device usable for different communicative intentions: In the concept of communication forms influenced by the work of Holly (cf. 1997, 2011), the cultural features of media are considered to be reflected in the development of communication forms for different communicative purposes. *Communication forms emerge from media use and reflect the medium's specific mediality*. The medium *paper*, for example, may be used for the communication form "letter" and text types as "letter of application", "love letter" or "letter of complaint". Paper is also used for the communication form "notice" or "tear-off", which is often used for flat hunting or searching for lost belongings. A love letter may include a handwritten text, private pictures and drawings whereas a letter of application may be printed and may make use of conventionalized typography. Apparently, what semiotic and structural resources are used differs from the concrete realization of a communication form in different text types. *Thus, the cultural dimension of media reveals itself in the differentiated use of specific structural frames for specific communicative intentions.*[4] Therefore, the trias medium, communication form and text type consists of an ongoing interplay and makes it possible to analyze concrete texts as parts of cultural practices which are based on manifest communicative possibilities: communication forms.[5] In their development we may discover the particular mediality. To identify communication forms, one may define for example

4 It has to be emphasized (again) that the cultural aspect of all media as a basic and crucial feature (cf. the work of Krämer 1998; McLuhan 1995) does not get lost in this concept. In fact, the cultural shape is reflected in the communication forms which are developed gradually by using the existing media. Their mediality allows to generate communication forms which serve different pragmatic purposes.

5 The understanding that communication forms are to be considered as possibilities/po-tentialities is well established by the work of Holly (e.g. 1997). It is important to mention that he has highlighted the interplay between mediality and culturality especially in his more recent work (e.g. 2011) but not distinguished the communication form from its realization. To emphasize the status of communication forms as frames which offer established communicative possibilities I prefer to speak of frames of contingency, a term I have elaborated before. (Domke 2014: 26 i.a.) Thereby it gets into focus that only the concrete realization (the text) reflects which possibilities shaped by a communication form are being used. Schildhauer & Brock (in this volume) also highlight the relevance of this basic differentiation but do not elaborate its impact on concrete analysis.

- the possible number of the *participants* (such as one-to-one communication, one-to-many and so on),
- the *mediality/materiality* (such as analog or digital, printed, broadcast, fixed, moveable, embodied, technical, and so on),
- the *semiotic resources* available (such as oral or written language, pictograms, images, sounds, typography)
- the mode of perception (such as visible, audible or tactile)
- the material locatedness (place-bound, non-place-bound, see below)
- the time-boundness (such as temporary, permanently perceivable).

However, with reference to research on communication forms in different discourses, it has to be mentioned that the differentiation of the communication form's *perception possibilities* (are they visible, audible, tactile or multimodal perceivable) as well as the communication form's *placements* have not been a major issue yet (see below). But in particular these categories allow combining the analysis of recent communication forms with the broader discussion on multimodality, mediatization and social construction of space: The recent and often emphasized differentiation of the communicative options (cf. Androutsopoulos 2014b; Krotz & Hepp 2012; Jenkins 2006) from which we may choose to realize our pragmatic intentions only gets into focus by elaborating which medium is used in what constellation for what communicative purpose. Prohibiting smoking in public places for example may include stickers, announcements and signs, amongst others. And in this case all these communication forms rely on different media and realize the same textual function: to prohibit something (as non-smoking sticker, non-smoking sign and so on). At the same time, we may notice other stickers (and thereby the same medium) which realize different functions (see Picture 4) such as promoting something or informing about handicapped accessible services. Obviously, differentiation exists on different levels.

→ Considering all these distinctive features, **communication forms** can be considered at this point to be the structural basis and a frame of communicative potentialities by which communicative and therefore cultural practices may be realized. *They emerge from the differentiated use of media and become established options.* In this sense communication forms are to be considered *frames of contingency* (cf. Domke 2014, see above) from which the person who wants to communicate has to choose for their communicative purpose. Communication forms are the foundation for communicative practices and therefore for concrete text types, and they are culturally shaped by the media which may be used for their realization. In their development, we may discover the particular mediality of the media resources used. Accordingly, media and mediality may be examined and understood entirely only by analyzing how they are utilized in a society's everyday communication.

It is important to mention – and often overlooked – that different communication forms make it possible to realize the same text type such as prohibitions (see above) by means of fixed signs or stickers or temporary notices or barriers, which differ obviously with reference to their permanence or, rather, their validity and visibility. This means that the media that are characteristic for a communication form (such as paper for a notice or fixed and big screens for display panels) are an important part of the meaning of the text realized by them. A notice as well as a sign may prohibit entering a building and may thus realize the text type "prohibition", but they differ obviously with reference to their scope: The notice seems to be only of temporary validity and may be individually produced, while the sign fixed on the door indicates permanence.

Evidently, the concept of communication form does neither determine nor neglect the cultural relevance of media as criticized at times (cf. Luginbühl 2015; Schneider 2006, 2008); as discussed above, the concept's aim is to reflect a medium's specific mediality in the culturally shaped communication form. *The cultural shape of a medium shows itself just where we can observe what communicative possibilities have emerged.*

Therefore, it helps to elaborate the difference between, for example, prohibitions by means of paper, fixed signs or announcements (see and hear Domke 2015), and the difference between different communication forms by means of the same medium (see above). The differentiation between communication forms on the one hand and text types on the other also includes the finding that using one specific communication form makes it possible to realize very different pragmatic purposes. Signs demonstrate the scope of activities realized by means of this communication form: Signs in public places serve, for example, as prohibitions, direction instructions, namings, cultural references.

Furthermore, it seems to be quite evident that regarding and analyzing the many different communication forms just given in public places offers deep insights into the meaning-making of both the media and the semiotic resources used. Communication forms allow for differentiation concerning the media used (like analog or digital), the mode of perception – as mentioned, visible, audible or tactile, semiotic resources – like language, color, pictures. Accordingly, we can elaborate many different communication forms in public places (such as billboards, stickers, announcements, display panels, guidance systems, conventionalized public signs, handwritten notices, posters, QR-codes, semiotic and physical barriers, see Picture 6). These communicative possibilities may be related to concrete text types such as time tables, prohibitions like stopping restrictions, direction signs, tear-offs for sale, advertisements. Thus, it is possible to differentiate the media and materiality and, therefore, the communication form from the specific pragmatic use it has been put to. The interplay between form and function gets into focus – and the question arises: Can we find order among communication forms, pragmatic use and addressees (see chapter 3)?

The understanding of communication forms outlined so far enables us to elaborate, for example, many different forms in public places. This indicates diversity and differentiation. But it also evokes the question of what all public texts have in common. This leads to one basic feature which has been overlooked in analyzing communication forms and communication in general: The texts discussed so far are all based on place-bound communication forms. For example stickers, direction signs, display panels, announcements are – permanently or temporarily – visible, audible and tactually perceivable in 'their' places. This also applies to public communication forms based on attendees such as demonstrations or outdoor or public screenings of sport events. Apparently, the latter gains its popularity just in comparison to its non-place-bound equivalent at home, with a smaller screen. The functionality of place-bound communication is obviously based on the presence of its addressees at their location and provides for the discourses mentioned above (such as regulatory, commercial, private) the possibility to address for example tourists, passers-by, and costumers locally.

To categorize communication into place-bound (such as stickers, signs) and non-place-bound (such as books, websites) obviously allows discussing the question of where a certain type of communication is readable or audible or rather where the potential recipient has to be. In addition to that, the distinction between place-bound and non-place-bound communication forms refers to the broader perspective of pragmatic use. With reference to the recent amount of digital and non-place-bound communication, the question comes into view for what purpose communication forms are used which require the recipients' presence in certain places. As mentioned above, place-bound texts make their places "readable" as specific places such as being public, reserved for pedestrians, and historically of relevance, amongst others. Accordingly, public communication contributes to the social construction of space (cf. Döring & Thielmann 2008; Jaworski & Thurlow 2010; Rau 2014). Based on de Certeau's (1988) famous distinction between place/space (cf. Hubbard & Kitchin 2010), these place-bound communication forms generate specific "social spaces with specific features" (cf. Domke 2014).

With reference to the amount of recent communicative possibilities, it seems quite clear that place-bound communication fulfills special tasks for the construction of public space. This will be discussed in the following chapter on the basis of some examples from mostly German large cities. They are part of a corpus of about 2900 pictures and 50 recordings collected for a larger study on public communication (cf. Domke 2014) and for more recent questions on the interplay between place-bound and non-place-bound communication.

3. The Pragmatic Use of Place-Bound Texts: Empirical Examples

The focus on the variety of communication forms realized in public places goes along with the need to collect them. At this point, pictures become an important device of documentation as they allow for reconstructing the communicative structure of a place. They expand the well-established linguistic methods of audio recording. Because of the unquestionable subjectivity of every picture, its perspective, or rather its "making-of" has to be reflected (cf. Domke 2014; Meier 2012). I took all those pictures while walking through mostly German large cities. As a pedestrian or tourist or visitor, I was on my way to places of interest or appointments or stations. And while being on my way to my destination, I photographed or recorded the texts visible at the time. The texts captured in the pictures are part of the publicly perceivable communication. With reference to de Certeau's distinction of place/space and his considerations of how "users re-appropriate the space" (de Certeau 1988: xiv), two things have to be considered relevant: First, the texts ascribe specific features to their places, such as being public, regulated or touristy. Second, due to a walker's individual route through a city and individual perception of the texts, two different walkers may generate two uneven readings of a city. That causes the need of very many pictures and recordings of similar routes to be able to elaborate patterns and frequencies. Some of them are presented here:

Steady Order

Walking through a city reveals – as mentioned above – a variety of different text functions and different communication forms. One of them seems to be quite typical of a city's textscape – signs. A closer look at only some examples (see Pictures 1, 2 and 5) already brings their broad functionality into focus. Signs as a communication form are realized by means of fixed media material. They are used for text types such as direction advice, prohibition and naming. Because of their materials and fixed placement they are permanently perceivable and therefore utilizable for information of non-time-bound validity (cf. Domke 2015) such as information on directions (see Picture 5), infrastructure (see Picture 2), a place's history or access to it.

One could say that these texts' function lies in arranging a place's basic (and obviously permanent) character as public or drivable or historic (see Picture 5, baroque quarter). Signs as well as fixed positioners and boards provide everyday order in public places. The relevance of signs as possibilities to address the local attendees seems to be even quite evident in exceptional circumstances. When they get obsolete during redirections or reconstructions, their steady functionality is reflected through the need of temporary notices or barriers. Signs are frequently used for infrastructural information, which underlines their "empractical" (Bühler 1982) use: They make the place readable as a space which we may (or may not) use in a certain way.

Picture 5: Fulda, in front of the Main Station

Picture 6: Kassel, Tram Station Friedrichsplatz

It is important and often overlooked by the linguistic and semiotic research on public 'textscapes' so far (cf. Jaworski & Thurlow 2010) that permanently perceivable texts are not only realized by means of *visible* communication forms like signs. This leads to the group of tactilely perceivable texts (cf. Domke 2014, 2015). Communication forms such as guidance systems on pavements (see Picture 3) are used for direction information; these communication forms are permanently perceivable by sense of touch and make it possible for visually impaired people to follow the coded paving consisting of stripes and dots with their white cane. In addition to that, tactile tablets in front of famous buildings or inside railway stations are fixed by robust media materials and serve different pragmatic uses: They contain tactilely perceivable floor plans as well as cultural information in braille concerning a place's history. With reference to the material used, it seems quite clear that guidance systems, and tactile communication forms in general, are only used for permanently valid information. It is also obvious that these texts may be received only by one person at a time.

Temporary Advice and Temporary Requests

Place-bound communication forms as discussed above make their place permanently readable in the same way. The fixed and robust media-material of the different communication forms indicates steady validation of the perceivable content. But in addition there are others forms to generate public space by means of communication. At this point, it comes into focus what may be seen or heard only temporarily. Besides the signs and guidance systems, we may discover a group of communication forms which is used for time-bound information such as arrivals and departures, cancellations, changes of locations, and search for lost belongings, among others. Time-bound contents are realized by using communication forms such as announcements, notices (see Picture 7), display panels (see Picture 6), mobile positioners and physical barriers. They are based on more flexible media-material like paper or digital displays. This group of communication forms is used, for example, for infrastructural (like digital arrival boards), commercial (like mobile positioners in front of restaurants or bars, see Picture 5) or private (like tear-offs for lost belongings) matters and reflect the variety of media and functions of the public textscape. With reference to their time-limited validation and their media-material, their broad usefulness becomes clear. Accordingly, they ascribe more differentiation to their places: With reference to, for example, the many different notices in public, we are able to differentiate job offers, requests for lost belongings (see Pictures 7 and 8) or new apartments, event promotions, invitations to religious or band meetings.

Picture 7: Tram Station Leipzig/Plagwitz

Picture 8: Park-Entrance, Leipzig

Obviously, they make their location "readable" as a social space useable by individuals. They are often less conventionalized than the permanently visible empractical texts, which is reflected in individual layouts and handwritings. Example 7 (see Picture 7) may illustrate the range of possibilities that the use of the communication form notice offers. The notice addresses "Dear adults and children. Have you seen a shoebox with my Schleich toys. (This is for a school project) I'm missing it very much. Please call. Cell phone number. Thanks. There will be reward for return!" It is most likely written by a child and contains spelling mistakes and a smaller written differentiation between the lines (This is for a school project) by another writer, probably a parent. The creative use of typographic design correlates with the medium paper and is to be regarded as individualizing the public space (cf. Domke forthcoming). It also helps to attract the attention of the people waiting at the station or walking by. With reference to the less expressive search for a lost cell phone in example 8 (see Picture 8), the difference between medium (paper, adhesive tape), established communication form (notice), pragmatic use (request for help) and text design comes into focus (again). Both notices make use of supporting media at transition places (a bus and tram shelter and a barrier in front of a park) where possible recipients have to pause for at least a moment and may perceive the place-bound texts.

In relation to all the examples discussed so far, the place-shaping character of public texts seems to be evident. Both permanent and temporary texts are important parts of the social construction of social space: They use different communication forms and serve different pragmatic purposes. And they ascribe different features to their place, such as being public and regulated or individually usable.

The feature "only temporarily perceivable" also applies to audible communication in public places. Besides more recent studies on more private conversation in cities (cf. Scarvagleri et al. 2013), these forms of linguistic soundscaping (cf. Pappenhagen et al. 2013) have been mostly overlooked (overheard) in semiotic landscapes research (cf. Domke 2015). Audible communication in public places includes mainly announcements and is used for both verbal information (human or computer-generated) about, for example, arrivals, departures and cancellations of trains or busses and non-verbal information by means of coded acoustic signals. By contrast with non-time-bound and visible texts in public places, announcements may be described as "omnipresent" (Raffaseder 2010) due to the fact that we are not able to 'unfocus' or ignore what is publicly announced via PA systems: Audible communication such as standard warnings at platforms like "Please take care while the train is approaching" can be heard by every person in the location. Due to this basic relevance of public announcements, they are mostly restricted to time-bound information, such as deviations from a time-schedule. For issues not relevant for every attendee at a place, visible texts are used in general. And the walker or traveler is able to create his own "reading" by focusing on some of them. However, audible communication shapes public spaces more directly, sustainably and inescapably, which explains their restricted use mainly for infrastructural matters or political events only on occasion.

Finally, this (short) discussion of different groups of communication has to include the increasing number of digital display panels in, for example, railway or tram stations (see Picture 6), in front of cinemas or museums. This more recent realization of the communication form *display panel* allows information which is updated frequently and visible just for a short time. In contrast to permanently visible texts on analog media (such as printed time-schedules), their main function can be considered to be offering news (cf. Domke 2014). Digital displays are permanently fixed by means of their media-material such as screens or big boards and perceivable either overhead or vis-à-vis. Digital information in cities underlines the media and pragmatic differentiation discussed above. As place-bound perceivable texts, they are an increasing part of the variety of the public *textscape* – and of the mediatization of our everyday life.

4. Conclusion

Elaborating media structure and perceptive possibilities of recent communication as demonstrated before allows insights into the relation between form and function. With reference to the examples this paper deals with, two considerations are clear: First, to communicate we are able to choose from a broad range of possibilities which have emerged through media developments. These established communication forms coexist, which sometimes leads to interplays. Second, the many communicative possibilities that exist go along with a differentiation concerning both the structural framework of communication and its pragmatic use. The contribution's issue – a city's textscape – highlights that differentiation is to be considered for communication in general and not only for digital communication in the "new media".

Analyzing publicly perceivable texts includes findings on the broad use of different media, resources and places for different pragmatic purposes. In this study on variety and differentiation, the concept of communication form proves to be of relevance: It is based on the analytic difference between communication structure and the concrete realization of this frame of contingency (see above, cf. Domke 2014). It allows, for example, to distinguish between the communication form "sign" based on robust media material and the pragmatic function it is used for, such as pointing out directions or prohibiting something. Due to the concept's focus on mediality and materiality, it also allows to elaborate on correlations on different levels:

- between pragmatic functions such as prohibitions and the communication forms by which they may be realized such as visible signs or tactilely perceivable guiding systems or audible announcements,
- or between communication forms such as digital display panels and the established practice to use them for time-bound contents such as arrivals or departures of trains in stations, tickets for events in front of museums or news in trams,
- or between modes of perception and their relevance for different discourses, purposes and addressees such as the amount of permanently visually perceivable texts for the regulatory and commercial discourse because of the more exclusive use of audible texts for time-bound information.

It seems to be evident that the concept of communication forms offers differentiation for any analysis of communication. This is useful for understanding the consequences of media development and mediatization (cf. Krotz 2007). This applies also to the mostly overlooked distinction between place-bound and non-place-bound communication forms (see above, Domke 2014, forthcoming). With reference to the increasing amount of communication forms that are realizable only digitally and in virtual space (like websites), this distinction makes it possible to investigate the purposes of place-bound communication forms (like posters, signs, notices, guided tours) and their contribution to the communicative construction of social space (cf. Domke 2014; Warnke & Busse 2014). Besides the reason to serve as "instruction manuals" (cf. Auge 1994, see above), public communication uses the presence of the attendees in specific places for their own purposes. Commercials at bus stations may be seen while someone is waiting and political demonstrations are taking place where they can be seen and heard by many. This functionality of place-bound communication also comes into focus when it is linked to non-place-bound communication. With QR-codes printed on posters, for example, their producers try to grab the attention of the attendees on location; scanning the QR-codes implies the possibility to perceive a website with articles or audio-files promoting restaurants, events or books. This relatively new form of intertextuality combines place-bound posters with non-place-bound websites – and reflects the media in existence and the range of recently-emerged communication forms from which we may choose at a given moment and which are the basis for the concrete textscape/soundscape shaping the social space of our everyday life.

References

Androutsopoulos, Jannis (ed.): *Mediatization and Sociolinguistic Change*. de Gruyter: Berlin & Boston 2014a.

Androutsopoulos, Jannis: "Mediatization and Sociolinguistic Change. Key Concepts, Research Traditions, Open Issues". In: Androutsopoulos, Jannis (ed.): *Mediatization and Sociolinguistic Change*. De Gruyter: Berlin & Boston 2014b, 3–48.

Auer, Peter et al. (eds.): *Space in Language and Linguistics: Geographical, Interactional and Cognitive Perspectives*. (Linguae & Litterae, 24). De Gruyter: Berlin & Boston 2013.

Augé, Marc transl. by Bischoff, Michael: *Orte und Nicht-Orte. Vorüberlegungen zu einer Ethnologie der Einsamkeit*. Fischer: Frankfurt a. M. 1994.

Brock, Alexander & Schildhauer, Peter: "Communication Form. A Concept Revisited". In: Brock, Alexander & Schildhauer, Peter (eds.): *Communication Forms and Communicative Practices. New Perspectives on Communication Forms, Affordances, and What Users Make of Them*. Peter Lang: Berlin, this volume 13–43.

Bühler, Karl: *Sprachtheorie*. Lucius & Lucius: Stuttgart 1982.

Certeau, Michel de transl. by Rendall, Steven: *The Practice of Everyday Life*. University of California Press. Berkeley et al. 1988.

Döring, Jörg & Thielmann, Tristan (eds.): *Spatial Turn. Das Raumparadigma in den Kultur- und Sozialwissenschaften.* transcript: Bielefeld 2008.

Domke, Christine: „Mediatisierter Alltag: Zum Verhältnis von Alltagsorten, Texten und Medien". In: Coelsch-Foisner, Sabine (ed.): *Transmedialisierung.* Winter: Heidelberg forthcoming.

Domke, Christine: "Prohibition Signage in Public Places: On the Functional Organization of Different Media, Communication Forms, and Text Types". *10plus1. Living Linguistics. Media Linguistics (Issue 1)*, 2015, retrieved 20.09.2016, from http://www.10plus1journal.com.

Domke, Christine: *Die Betextung des öffentlichen Raumes. Eine Studie zur Spezifik von Meso-Kommunikation am Beispiel von Bahnhöfen, Innenstädten und Flughäfen.* Winter: Heidelberg 2014.

Domke, Christine: „Ortsgebundenheit als distinktives Merkmal in der Textanalyse". *Zeitschrift für Germanistische Linguistik (ZGL)*, Themenheft Textualität und Sichtbarkeit 2013, 102–126.

Domke, Christine: „Der Ort des Textes – Überlegungen zur Relevanz der Platzierung von Kommunikaten am Beispiel von Flughäfen". In: Stöckl, Hartmut (ed.): *Mediale Transkodierungen. Metamorphosen zwischen Sprache, Bild und Ton.* (Wissenschaft und Kunst 17). Winter: Heidelberg 2010, 85–104.

Habscheid, Stephan: „Das halbe Leben. Ordnungsprinzipien einer Linguistik der Kommunikation – Zur Einleitung in den Band". In: Habscheid, Stephan (ed.): *Textsorten, Handlungsmuster, Oberflächen. Linguistische Typologien der Kommunikation.* De Gruyter: Berlin & New York 2011, 3–29.

Hausendorf, Heiko et al. (eds.): *Raum als interaktive Ressource.* (Studien zur Deutschen Sprache 62). Narr: Tübingen 2012.

Hubbard, Phil & Kitchin, Rob (eds.): *Key Thinkers on Space und Place.* Sage: London 2010.

Holly, Werner: „Medien, Kommunikationsformen, Textsortenfamilien". In: Habscheid, Stephan (ed.): *Textsorten, Handlungsmuster, Oberflächen. Linguistische Typologien der Kommunikation.* De Gruyter: Berlin & New York 2011, 144–163.

Holly, Werner: „Was sind ‚Neue Medien'? – Was sollen ‚Neue Medien' sein?". In: Voß, G. Günter et al. (eds.): *Neue Medien im Alltag.* Leske + Budrich: Opladen 2000, 79–106.

Holly, Werner: „Zur Einführung: Was sind Medien und wie gehen wir mit Medien um?". *Der Deutschunterricht* 49(3), 1997, 3–9.

Jäger, Ludwig: „Intermedialität – Intramedialität – Transkriptivität. Überlegungen zu einigen Prinzipien der kulturellen Semiosis". In: Deppermann, Arnulf &

Linke, Angelika (eds.): *Sprache intermedial. Stimme und Schrift, Bild und Ton*, Tübringen 2010, 301–323.

Jäger, Ludwig: „Transkriptivität. Zur medialen Logik der kulturellen Semantik". In: Ludwig, Jäger & Stanitzek, Georg (eds.): *Transkribieren – Medien/Lektüre*. Fink: München 2002, 19–41.

Jaworski, Adam & Thurlow, Crispin (eds.): *Semiotic Landscapes. Language, Image, Space*. Continuum: London & New York 2010.

Jenkins, Henry: *Convergence Culture. Where Old and New Media Collide*. New York University Press: New York 2006.

Jewitt, Carey (ed.): The *Routledge Handbook of Multimodal Analysis*. Routledge: London 2009.

Kallen, Jeffrey L.: "Changing Landscapes. Language, Space and Policy in the Dublin Linguistic Landscape". In: Jaworski, Adam & Thurlow, Crispin (eds.): *Semiotic Landscapes. Language, Image, Space*. Continuum: London & New York 2010, 41–58.

Klug, Nina-Maria & Stöckl, Hartmut (ed.): *Handbuch Sprache im multimodalen Kontext*. (Band 7). De Gruyter: Berlin 2017 (in print).

Klug, Nina-Maria & Stöckl, Hartmut: „Sprache im Multimodalen Kontext". In: v. Felder, Ekkehard & Gardt, Andreas (eds.): *Handbuch Sprache und Wissen*. De Gruyter Mouton: Berlin 2014, 242–264.

Krämer, Sybille: „Das Medium als Spur und als Apparat". In: Krämer, Sybille (ed.): *Medien, Computer, Realität: Wirklichkeitsvorstellungen und neue Medien*. Suhrkamp: Frankfurt a. M. 1998, 73–94.

Kress, Gunther: "What is Mode?" In: Jewitt, Carey (ed.): *The Routledge Handbook of Multimodal Analysis*. Routledge: London 2009, 54–67.

Krotz, Friedrich: *Mediatisierung: Fallstudien zum Wandel von Kommunikation*. VS Verlag: Wiesbaden 2007.

Krotz, Friedrich & Hepp, Andreas (eds.): *Mediatisierte Welten. Forschungsfelder und Beschreibungsansätze*. VS Verlag: Wiesbaden 2012, 7–23.

Landry, Rodrigue & Bourhis, Richard Y.: "Linguistic Landscape and Ethnolinguistic Vitality. an Empirical Study". *Journal of Language and Social Psychology* 16(1), 1997, 23–49.

Leeuwen van, Theo: *Introducing Social Semiotics*. Routledge: New York 2005.

Luginbühl, Martin: "Media Linguistics. On Mediality and Culturality". *10plus1. Living Linguistics* (Issue 1), 2015, 9–26, retrieved 20.09.2016, available on http://10plus1journal.com.

Machin, David: *Introduction to Multimodal Analysis*. Bloomsbury: London 2007.

McLuhan, Marshall transl. by Nänny, Max: *Die Gutenberg-Galaxis. Das Ende des Buchzeitalters.* Addison-Wesley: Bonn 1995.

Meier, Stefan: „Die Simulation von Fotografie. Konzeptuelle Überlegungen zum Zusammenhang von Materialität und digitaler Bildlichkeit“. In: Finke, Marcel & Halawa, Mark A. (eds.): *Materialität und Bildlichkeit. Visuelle Artefakte zwischen Aisthesis und Semiosis.* Berlin: Kadmos 2012, 126–142.

Meiler, Matthias: “Media Linguistics and Media Studies – Communication Forms and Their Infrastructures”. In: Brock, Alexander & Schildhauer, Peter (eds.): *Communication Forms and Communicative Practices. New Perspectives on Communication Forms, Affordances, and What Users Make of Them.* Peter Lang: Berlin, this volume 45–66.

Papen, Uta: “Commercial Discourses, Gentrification and Citizens' Protest: The Linguistic Landscape of Prenzlauer Berg, Berlin”. *Journal of Sociolinguistics* 16(1), 2012, 56–81.

Pappenhagen, Ruth et al.: „Hamburgs mehrsprachige Praxis im öffentlichen Raum – sichtbar und hörbar“. In: Redder, Angelika et al. (eds.): *Mehrsprachige Kommunikation in der Stadt. Das Beispiel Hamburg.* Waxmann: Münster 2013, 127–160.

Raffaseder, Hannes: *Audiodesign. Akustische Kommunikation, akustische Signale und Systeme, psychoakustische Grundlagen, Klangsynthese, Audioediting und Effektbearbeitung, Sounddesign, Bild-Ton-Beziehungen.* (2nd edition). Hanser: München 2010.

Rau, Susanne: *Räume. Konzepte, Wahrnehmungen, Nutzungen.* Campus: Frankfurt & New York 2013.

Scarvaglieri, Claudio et al: “Capturing Diversity. Linguistic Land- and Soundscaping”. In: Duarte, Joana & Gogolin, Ingrid (eds.): *Linguistic Superdiversity in Urban Areas.* Benjamins: Amsterdam 2013, 45–74.

Schneider, Jan G.: *Spielräume der Medialität. Linguistische Gegenstandskonstitution aus medientheoretischer und pragmatischer Perspektive.* (Linguistik – Impulse & Tendenzen 29). De Gruyter: Berlin & New York, 2008.

Schneider, Jan G.: „Gibt es nichtmediale Kommunikation?“. *Zeitschrift für Angewandte Linguistik* 44(1), 2006, 71–90.

Scollon, Ronald & Scollon, Suzie: *Discourses in Place. Language in the Material World.* Routledge: London 2003.

Warnke, Ingo H.: „Die Stadt als Kommunikationsraum und linguistische Landschaft“. In: Hofmann, Wilhelm (ed.): *Die Stadt als Erfahrungsraum der Politik. Beiträge zur kulturellen Konstruktion urbaner Politik.* LIT: Münster 2011, 343–363.

Warnke, Ingo H. & Busse, Beatrix (eds.) 2014: *Place-Making in urbanen Diskursen.* De Gruyter: Berlin et al. 2014.

Communication Forms and Communicative Practices

Frederic Zähres

"*pentakill inc*" – A Case Study of Shortening Processes in Ludolects

Abstract While video games have become an omnipresent medium over the last decades, linguistic research has only scratched the surface of the language of gamers and gaming. Ludolects – a term coined by Astrid Ensslin for the language variety used in metaludic discourse by gamers – offer particularly interesting angles for linguistic research, as language and communication are shaped by the rules and constraints of the respective games. This case study serves as an attempt to describe the word-formation processes at work in the lexicon of the English *League of Legends* ludolect, which is one of the most popular video games of recent times. Due to high competitiveness of the community and fast-paced gameplay, the players rely on brevity and make extensive use of shortening processes, most notably clippings and initialisms, but also different, more creative strategies.

1. Introduction

Over the last 40 years, video games have changed substantially: There was Atari's rather abstract digital representation of table tennis called *Pong*, which was one of the first commercially successful video games (cf. Beil 2013: 7 f.) and brought video games to the living rooms. More recently, games like Blizzard's *World of Warcraft*, which captivates and digitally connects millions of players in an online world, and the high competitiveness of Riot's *League of Legends,* that evokes all kinds of emotional outbursts in millions of players and their audiences from all over the world on a daily basis, have found their way into the players' homes (cf. Evans 2014; Sherr 2014). Once a niche product, video games have become a ubiquitous mainstream medium with a serious economic market (cf. BIU 2015; McDonald 2014). Not only do four out of five households in the US own a device to play video games (cf. ESA 2015: 2), but video games can also be found in cinemas,[1] in concert halls,[2] in the news, in kindergartens, schools and universities (cf. Beil 2013: 1, 21ff.; Mueller 2015), and all over the Internet.

1 Big electronic sports tournaments and video game documentaries are shown in cinemas. Cf. *http://www.esportsincinema.com/*.

2 Just like film soundtracks and scores, video game music is regularly performed live. Cf. *http://www.spielemusikkonzerte.de/* or *http://www.videogameslive.com/*.

Considering its culture, its industry, its impact and status as a medium, the video game has truly become a global player, which has also been recognized by scholars. Over the last decades, numerous studies in various fields have been conducted to discover the impact and effects of this dynamic medium. At first, the main academic fields in this regard were the cognitive and educational sciences. But soon, interdisciplinary connections became apparent and the discipline of (digital) *game studies*, or *ludology*, was formed, which unites the social-scientific, computer-scientific and humanistic approaches to video game research (cf. Beil 2013: 1ff.; Ensslin 2012: 1ff.; Wolf & Perron 2003).

While several disciplines are actively involved in studying video games, the field of linguistics is nearly absent in this matter. Video games, by now, have moved from the offline single player experience to an interconnected space of cooperative and competitive, massively multiplayer experience. It is exactly this space that can present ideas and opportunities for linguists. For one thing, new communication strategies among players are deployed in the absence of face-to-face communication on the Internet, and, additionally, quite large communities form around certain topics of video gaming, certain genres and, of course, individual games, which mostly exist in an exclusively online environment. This creates an attractive point of departure for research on identity-formation and expression, in-group communication strategies and dynamics, pragmatics / politeness strategies during online games, and language change in general, just to name a few examples. A number of these topics are addressed in Ensslin's *The Language of Gaming* (2012), which, to my knowledge, was the first monograph presenting a comprehensive linguistic perspective on video games and gamers.

In her book, Ensslin coins the term *ludolect* (cf. 2012: 66), which refers to the language variety that gamers use either while actually playing a video game or when using channels like chats, message boards, or face-to-face communication for discussions. As Ensslin presents rather general linguistic descriptions and observations concerning ludolects, further investigation to assess Ensslin's observations is needed. My personal point of departure in this regard will be the examination of word-formation processes, especially shortening processes, of a ludolect – a topic that Ensslin only covers in a cursory way. Due to the lack of an available corpus, new data had to be collected and while there is generally a lot of data available on the Internet, the collection for this case study focused on one particular community. To guarantee easy access and availability of data, a fairly popular game had to be chosen. Today, one of the globally most successful online games is Riot Game's *League of Legends*, in short *LoL*, whose community's lexicon will be under scrutiny in this paper.

Considering that, section 2 will present my working hypotheses after discussing the relevant background for this study – the previous linguistic research regarding video gaming and online communities, and information on the object of research, the game League of Legends. Section 3 explains the method of data collection and analysis while section 4 presents the respective results which will then be discussed in section 5. This is followed by a conclusion including a short outlook in section 6.

2. Background

The discipline of game studies, a recent development in the academic world, is still a rather small field. As previously stated, especially linguistic research in this interdisciplinary area is scarce. However, a substantial amount of linguistic research in the area of *computer-mediated communication* (*CMC*) and online communities exists, which is highly relevant for the gaming community context as communication in and about online gaming is by its nature mostly computer-mediated. There are monographs, collected volumes and various papers with socio-psychological and sociolinguistic perspectives, focusing on language use on the Internet and in respective online communities.

2.1. Previous Research

Ensslin divides the language of video gaming and gamers into five different categories:

(a) *language about games and gaming used by gamers across different media and communication platforms,*
(b) language about games and gameplay used by industry professionals, such as game designers and developers,
(c) language about games and gaming used by journalists, politicians, parents, activists and other media stakeholders
(d) language used within games as part of their user interfaces, scripted dialogues, instructions and backstories, and
(e) language used in instruction manuals, blurbs, advertising and other 'peri-texts'. (cf. 2012: 6; my emphasis, F.Z.)

Language of type (a) is what Ensslin describes as ludolect (cf. 2012: 66f.). Ludolects are positioned between – at one end of the spectrum – technical and academic ludological jargons (type (b)) and, at the other end, popular discourse (type (c)). Ensslin characterizes ludolects as being highly encoded (ibid.: 16), highly specific and technical in-group codices (ibid.: 64f.) that are very adaptive to change within the game, genre or medium (ibid.). The degree of specificity and, thus, the degree of transparency of the ludolect can vary depending on the amount of expertise that is required to understand or master the respective game, or the focus of the actual metaludic discourse. The more general concepts of gaming a conversation between gamers addresses, which tend to be less specific and do not require much expertise, the more transparent it becomes for outsiders, and vice versa (ibid.: 68f.). Hence, proficient use of a ludolect among a group of speakers identifies them as experienced gamers and signals in-group status, whereas a lack of proficiency labels a speaker as an outsider or possible intruder to the group, which can also be a deliberately-employed instrument for social exclusion (cf. Consalvo 2009: 308; Ensslin 2012: 68; see also Swoboda, this volume). While the correct usage of ludolects is usually connected to positive social prestige within the community, its members do not rely solely on language to determine their own and others' position within the group's hierarchy: Successful gaming is, of course, much more valuable in this regard. More so, as language does not constitute the only social component of gaming communities, Ensslin argues that gamers form "not only [...] discourse communities but communities of practice [...], because they share and creatively operate upon a shared set of social practices, of which language is only one – albeit important – element" (cf. 2012: 22).[3] Due to the facelessness of the online world, language, however, is often the very first piece of the puzzle of someone's identity that others will receive in the form of chat messages or online message board postings, which would consequently place language among the most important factors of impression formation, even in gaming communities.

Ensslin makes the important remark that there is not one monolithic ludolect (2012: 42). Due to the diversity in genres and games,[4] a vast amount of variety in game mechanics and dynamics can be found that requires the players to employ different ways of thinking, acting and, sometimes, communicating. An educational farming simulation, for example, works differently from a team-based real-time strategy game. It is also rather common to find communities within communities (ibid.: 22): An online community grouped around the role-playing game genre

---

3 The term *community of practice* has been discussed critically (e.g., cf. Androutsopoulos 2006: 421–423). The discussion of how or whether gaming communities fit the respective definitions of *COPs* will not be a part of this article due to the limited scope and space.

4 For an overview of video game genres and titles, cf. Ensslin (2012: 45–47) or Pohlmann (2007: 9–15). The term *genre* in this context is critically discussed in Beil (2013: 39–46).

could have separate strands focusing on individual games of this genre – and mutual intelligibility of ludolects cannot be taken for granted between these sub-communities. In this matter, ludolects do not behave differently from the language of other communities that use CMC – which might not be surprising as ludolects could easily be understood as a hyponym of CMC. CMC studies have recently worked towards a demythologization of "the alleged homogeneity" (cf. Androutsopoulos 2006: 421) of the language that is used by users of the Internet and that is sometimes referred to as *Netspeak*, a term introduced by Crystal (2006). Due to the mix of media, channels and communities, there is not one systematic language on the Internet, although a number of common features can be identified, like the preference for brevity and the ability to quickly adapt to changes (cf. Marx & Weidacher 2014: 91f.). This also holds true for ludolects (cf. Ensslin 2012: 70f.).

Additionally, online games make use of the same synchronous and asynchronous modes of communication that were established during the early phases of CMC studies (cf. Androutsopoulos 2006: 420; Döring 2003: 43), either directly integrated into the *user interface* (*UI*) of the game or used independently from the game through external applications or services. Synchronous forms of communication include, for example, chat rooms with different filters and channels, e.g. teammate-only chat or chat rooms based on the area of the game a player is currently situated in, voice chat or the option to send private instant messages (also called *whispers*) to other players. Asynchronous communication happens via electronic letters or discussion boards. It is important to note, however, that gamers, in contrast to most other users of CMC, are influenced by certain constraints, mostly while using synchronous forms of CMC: When they are playing the game, they are usually multi-tasking (cf. Ensslin 2012: 70). Depending on various factors of the game (e.g., whether it is a competitively-played game), this requires more or less concentration of the player, making communication only a secondary priority. This affects various levels of language: For example, politeness strategies might be ignored, which usually has no negative consequences for the speaker, and morphological and syntactical brevity is, for obvious reasons, heavily favored by gamers in stressful situations.

Bergs adds that "a [community of practice] is defined both by (formal) membership and by shared practice, i.e. members develop similar cultural practices and meanings" (cf. 2006: 6), which is consistent with Ensslin's argumentation (see above). Within these communities, the practices form, at first, through experimentation and, when established, are maintained by socialization (cf. Döring 2003: 535; Thorne et al. 2009: 803) and, especially regarding the linguistic conventions of the group, by standardization through codification in the form of guides that can be found on the community's relevant message boards, fan pages or wikis (cf. Consalvo 2009: 309). For gaming communities, these are either guides that explicitly focus on vocabulary and terminology, or guides that focus on certain game mechanics and strategies, which sometimes are so influential or literally game-changing, that they could be considered belonging to the community's canon. However, as games are an ever-changing system and information can be rendered obsolete by a developer's software patch or update very quickly, these community guides are rarely published in print. Still, communities display much more stability than the previous lines would suggest: An overhaul of core game mechanics and respective terminology would be highly unusual.

As far as actual language use online is concerned, Bergs comes to the conclusion that "innovation is the norm" (cf. 2006: 13).[5] Other, more general observations include the overall tendency for informality and brevity by using such means as ellipses, abbreviations, and acronyms, or the ability to quickly close emerging lexical gaps with neologisms or borrowings, especially from English, if the frame language is another language (cf. Marx & Weidacher 2014: 96 f.).

Ensslin comes to similar conclusions in her analysis of the language of gamers, i.e. ludolects (cf. 2012: 64 ff.). Ludolects are informal jargons, enriching the frame language (e.g. English) with specific and, mostly, technical vocabulary to fill lexical gaps emerging through games and their mechanics and dynamics. While lexis is the most obvious level, ludolects can also demonstrate different linguistic conventions for other areas of the language, like distinctive syntactic constructions (ibid.: 68).

2.2. Introduction to League of Legends

> League of Legends is a fast-paced, competitive online game that blends the speed and intensity of an *RTS* with *RPG* elements. Two teams of powerful champions, each with a unique design and playstyle, battle head-to-head across multiple battlefields and game modes. With an ever-expanding roster of champions, frequent updates and a thriving tournament scene, League of Legends offers endless replayability for players of every skill level. Play for free. (cf. *What is League of Legends?*; my emphases, F.Z.)

5 Dittmann, for example, argues for a predominant oraliteracy on the web and analyzed French and German chat communities, which both demonstrated enormous creative potential in their language use, but with differences: The French group was more innovative at the word level, whereas the German group made use of their linguistic creativity at a more conceptual level by using actionstrips like **freu** (cf. 2001: 120).

With this description, the North American game developer and publisher *Riot Games* advertises their 2009 game *League of Legends* on its website, which might already be difficult to understand for a video game newcomer, especially the highlighted parts. *RTS*, which is short for real-time strategy (game), and *RPG*, short for role-playing game, describe the game's genre mix, which is also commonly described as *multiplayer online battle arena (MOBA)*. From 2009 onwards, various varieties of *MOBAs* have been released to the online gaming market, securing the genre's position among the most-played games in the 2010s, so far, and even challenging the position of *massively multiplayer online role-playing games (MMORPGs)* that have dominated online gaming since the mid-2000s (cf. Custer 2013; see Swoboda, this volume). In early 2014, *LoL* alone was played by 64 million players monthly and even 27 million players daily, creating a revenue of $624 million in 2013 (cf. *League of Legends*; Sherr 2014), which seems quite impressive for a game that runs on a free-to-play model.

As the game's description already states, *LoL* is a fast-paced and competitive game. The player's goal is to defeat the opposing team by destroying a central structure within their base. This involves the strategic use of the game world's environments, the abilities of the player's and teammates' champions, resources, and other elements. Most matches take at least 20 minutes and require high attention, fast reaction times, tactical thinking as well as a thorough knowledge and correct assessment of both teams' abilities. These dynamics can seem intimidating to newcomers to the game as, by now, there are over 120 champions who all differ in abilities and playstyle, especially in certain combinations within a team. So, in general comparison, *LoL* is a highly demanding game that is easy to learn, but very difficult to master.

The *LoL* community does not have the most favorable reputation when it comes to politeness and communication strategies. Making mistakes during gameplay, especially in ranked games, can result in insults or mockery, usually referred to as *flaming*, from the other players. This also illustrates the high competitive factor of the game and that, above all, successful gaming is the main priority for most *LoL* players. As a channel for communication, the game offers a textual chat interface that can be used to either message individual players, one's own team or anyone involved in the match before and during matches. However, the game is played by using the combination of the computer keyboard and the mouse, which means that, during gameplay, players use one hand for operating the keyboard (to activate abilities) and the other one for operating the mouse (for maneuvering their avatar). When sending chat messages to other players, a player has to remove their hand from the mouse to type their message with both hands. This, in turn, means that a player will have to sacrifice maneuverability and flexibility in order to communicate via the textual interface. An alternative mechanic that enables the user to communicate on a non-textual level is called *pinging*: the player can move the mouse cursor over the map, the graphical representation of the battlefield in the player's user interface, and click on certain points to send an audiovisual signal to the teammates' maps, drawing their attention to these exact locations on the battlefield.

By default, players are randomly grouped together, usually according to their skill level, which is determined by the matches they have previously played. However, players also have the option to form fixed teams with their friends or players they have previously played with before registering for a match. Playing with fixed teams enables players to use an external voice chat software like *Skype* or *TeamSpeak* to communicate and coordinate more efficiently during the game. This process is much more complicated for randomly-grouped players as they would have to spend a significant amount of time on exchanging relevant voice chat credentials or the like, which is deemed inefficient by most players for such one-time team constellations.

Before playing, players can connect to one of several regional servers, like North America, Latin America South or EU West. This way, in contrast to other games, servers are not strictly categorized by language, and players from various western European countries, for example, come together on the server EU West and, usually, use English to communicate. The game itself is officially available in at least 13 predominantly European languages including German, Spanish, Portuguese, Russian, and Korean in addition to English. When not playing the game, community members exchange thoughts on the gameplay, strategies, or well-known players and tournaments on discussion boards, wikis and fan pages, which exist in a variety of languages.

The following sums up *LoL*'s default means and constraints of communication – loosely based on the idea of *medium variables* (cf. Bieswanger 2007: 2; Herring 2007):

1. Communication during the game is optional.
2. The default means of communication is a synchronous, text-based chat with a one-way transmission process.
3. Chat messages are typed on the keyboard – one of two input devices that are used during regular gameplay. Typing messages restricts the player's in-game reaction time and maneuverability. In other words, using the chat can pose a high risk on the player's part, which the player wants to avoid as far as possible.

2.3. Working Hypothesis

Game studies as an interdisciplinary field has spawned various approaches of research on video games and its communities, as can be seen in various introductions to the field, like Beil (2013). Linguistic analyses, however, remain exotic in this context and, so far, only seem to scratch the surface of the matter. Research on online communities in CMC studies have shown major similarities to online gaming communities and one could argue for mentioning gaming communities in the same breath with the frequently-researched chat and message board communities. Then again, gamers show distinctive features: Their focus lies primarily on the respective game and playing in a successful or enjoyable way while the channels of communication, such as text and voice chat, only seem to represent a tool to reach this goal – i.e. communication constitutes a more or less desirable byproduct or necessity, especially during competitive gaming. When starting the game, the main intention of a majority of gamers is not a topic-based exchange of ideas and beliefs, contrary to chatters or forum users who choose to use the respective medium for this exact purpose.[6] As previously shown, the practices of a community are also reflected in their members' language use and, thus, a thorough linguistic analysis of the language of gaming communities is relevant.

Based on the previous research and the mechanics of the game *League of Legends*, my analysis will be based on the following working hypothesis:

Members of the English LoL community make extensive use of word-formation processes that ensure brevity.

Not only the strong focus on gameplay itself, but also the necessity to multitask for communication during gameplay require the communication to be quick and efficient as the keyboard has to be operated differently for gameplay and communication. This would most likely be achieved by the use of various shortening processes. While this is commonly found in CMC, *LoL* gamers might take this to another level, as their time constraints seem to be more critical. The gamers' lexicon, i.e. the product of word-formation processes, constitutes a convenient basis for the following analysis that will tackle the following questions:

1. Are shortening processes the most frequent word-formation processes of the *LoL* ludolect?
2. What other shortening strategies are used?

6 This does not suggest, though, that gaming communities are antisocial. Quite the opposite can actually be observed in several message boards where lively discussions of any sort take place.

The next section will address the method for scrutinizing the *League of Legend* ludolect with regards to the above-mentioned hypotheses.

3. Method

3.1. Data Collection

Thanks to the web, language data from *LoL* players is generally not particularly rare: one can find YouTube videos, message board discussions, user-written gameplay guides, etc. These sources come with different problems, however. YouTube videos are usually addressed to a certain audience and, thus, do not necessarily represent authentic gaming language data. If a video actually happens to be a recording of a spontaneously-occurring discussion or the like, this does not automatically deem them eligible for academic linguistic analysis. Data on the Internet lies in a grey area ethically: Despite its public availability and relative anonymity, it cannot be assumed that researchers have the permission to use the data without contacting the respective authors or creators of the content in question.[7] This naturally applies to message boards, chat rooms, blogs and other personal websites in the same way. Also, in this specific context, these sources would mainly comprise of metaludic discourse without time constraints, i.e. gamers discussing the game while not simultaneously playing it, which functions differently from the communication that occurs during gameplay. Obtaining data of the latter category poses more difficulties: Apart from using the language that has been programmed into the software by the developers, one would need to connect to other players and either play or observe the game as a spectator to gain access to the communication channels of the game. Then, the chat communication would need to be recorded because the messages are not saved after a match ends, which can be achieved by a third-party software running in the background. Again, the ethical code of conduct can turn this step into a tedious endeavor – if only one out of the usual ten players refused the idea of a recording, the whole session could not be recorded. Also, there are matches that seem to progress without any textual communication, especially when playing with or against experienced teams, as they are probably using a third-party voice chat software. The most productive way of data collection seems to be the recording of a steady group of experienced players during gameplay, either by being present during their game sessions or by letting them record their voice chat sessions. If only their voices are recorded

7 Marx & Weidacher (2012: 17–18), however, argue that the quotation of web contents for scientific purposes is acceptable – at least according to German law.

and not the game itself, the other – random – players would not have to be notified of any recording. However, experience shows that steady groups of gamers start to deviate from the community's regular ludolect by adding idiosyncratic elements to it, which is also observed by Ensslin, who terms this kind of behavior *buddylects* (2012: 20). This would compromise the representativeness of the data.

The compromise I have chosen for this project avoids not only the ethical discussion, but allows for the collection of representative data. As mentioned in section 2, gaming communities like the *LoL* community standardize their language by means of codification: There are several sources for dictionary-like terminology lists, i.e. glossaries that explain game-specific lexical items mainly to newcomers to the game. Usually, the glossaries are compiled by either a single experienced player or as the collaborative work of several players. They can usually be found in message boards, like the official League of Legends forum, or on web pages that are administrated by the community, like the *LoL wikia*, which is a *LoL*-themed online encyclopedia with a similar structure as *Wikipedia*. Like the game, the forum and web pages such as the *LoL* wikia are available in several languages. As these depict sources with rather anonymous multiple authorship and the objective of collecting and listing language data, versus the production of original data, privacy issues should not be of any concern. Thus, for the purpose of this case study, I have decided to build a word list of lexical items taken from said glossaries of the English *LoL* community.

In order to avoid potentially idiosyncratic variations, I have collected my data from three different sources:

1. The *LoL* wikia entry regarding the game's and community's terminology (cf. *League of Legends terminology*), which consists of the most entries by far. The wiki article is frequently updated by multiple users. The first source adds 634 items to the glossary.
2. A forum entry in the official North American *LoL* forum that was created in 2010 but has been frequently updated by the original author since then, due to numerous comments by other players (cf. Larias 2010). In August 2015, the thread consisted of over 35 message board pages. The glossary from the forum includes 123 items.
3. The terminology section of a user-written guide directed at new *LoL* players (cf. The All Tomato 2015). The guide is hosted on *mobafire.com*, which represents a well-frequented website in the *LoL* community that hosts user-written guides for various gameplay mechanics and dynamics. The terminology section of the guide consists of 95 items.

In total, the compiled glossary of lexical items of English *League of Legends* ludolect amounts to 709 unique items, which already takes into account the amount of terminological overlaps among the sources.

3.2. Analysis of Word-Formation Processes

The analysis of word-formation processes in the compiled glossary is mostly of a quantitative nature and based on a framework that Ensslin briefly presented in her work (2012: 69–73). She introduces several categories and subcategories of word-formation processes in accordance with Algeo (1999) and Shortis (2001), as seen in Table 1.

Table 1: Word-formation Processes as Suggested by Ensslin (2012) with Adjustments

Word-Formation Process	**Subcategory**
composites	compounds, affixation
conversion*	-
shortenings*	clippings, acronyms, initialisms, backformations, contractions, letter/number-homophones, phonetic spellings, word-value characters
loans	-
blends	-
neologisms	-

The ordering depicts the general frequency of the processes according to Algeo (1999).[8] This framework summarizes most word-formation processes that can be frequently found in the English language (e.g., cf. Plag 2003; Gramley 2012). However, I suggest two adjustments – which are represented by the two asterisks in Table 1: First, Ensslin mixes morphological function shifts and forms of semantic shifts in her second category, originally called *shift* (2012: 70), which seems problematic when analyzing word-formation processes and, thus, the category as such was not incorporated into my analysis and only conversions were taken into account. Additionally, the category of shortening processes is extended by four

8 Ensslin briefly discusses most of the categories and provides the reader with examples of rather general and frequent terms most gamers use to illustrate the word-formation processes (2012: 70–73). A more thorough analysis with regard to a specific gaming community is not mentioned, however.

additional subcategories based on the analysis of shortening strategies in SMS communication by Bieswanger (2007): contractions, letter/number-homophones, phonetic spellings, and word-value characters.

The items in the compiled glossary have also been categorized according to word length to receive a more thorough picture of the word-formation products.

4. Results

First, the word-formation processes are presented in a rather broad view, describing the general word-formation process. Approximately a quarter of all terms in the data (n=171) does not show any signs of morphological change when compared to the standard variety's lexicon, but has undergone semantic shifts – these tokens have been excluded from the rest of the analysis, which leaves a total of 538 tokens. As shown in Table 3, almost two thirds of all the word-formation products in the glossary are formed by shortening processes (n=354). The processes of composition and conversion can also be frequently observed (n=94 and n=60, respectively). Neologisms (n=7), blends (n=6) and combinations of more than one word-formation process (n=17) only play a marginal role in the data. Loans are only found twice in combination with a compounding process.

Table 2: Distribution of Word-formation Processes (Broad Categorization)

word-formation process	**count**	**percentage**
Shortening	354	65.8 %
Composite	94	17.47 %
Conversion	60	11.15 %
Neologism	7	1.3 %
Blending	6	1.12 %
Combinations	17	3.16 %
total	**538**	**100 %**

Figure 1: Distribution of Word-formation Processes (with subcategories)

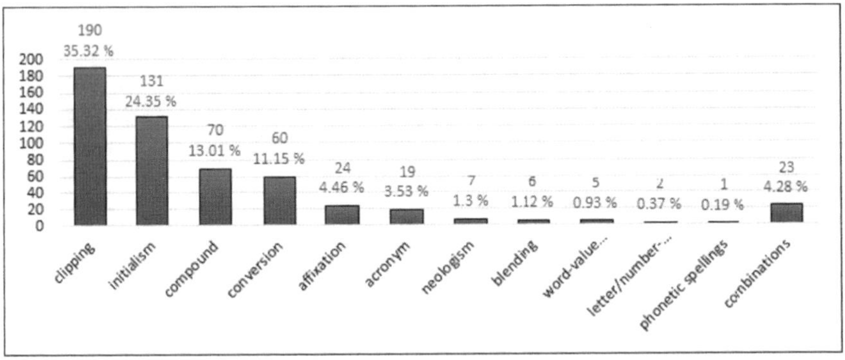

Taking a closer look at the morphological processes at work, the following can be observed (cf. Figure 1): Clippings (n=190) and initialisms (n=131) constitute by far the most frequent shortening processes and make up about one third and one quarter, respectively, of the overall word-formation products. Following this are compounds (n=70) and conversions (n=60). The other categories each make up less than 5 percent of the data. The processes of backformation and contraction could not be observed in the glossary.

In the following, examples from the data for all word-formation categories are given to illustrate the findings. The composite category consists of the processes of compounding and affixation. Compounding refers to the combination of at least two free morphemes, such as *pentakill* (referring to the elimination of all five enemy heroes in a short period of time) and *ragequit* (meaning to quit the game in anger). Affixation describes the combination of a bound and a free morpheme, like *tanky* (referring to a champion with high defensive statistics) or *debuff* (which is a negative effect that is applied to a champion). Creating a new word by changing the word class of an existing word without changing its form is called conversion and can be found in the data, as represented by the examples *carry* (which is a noun and describes a champion with the ability to 'carry the team' by winning fights) and *nerf* (which is a verb that describes a change in game mechanics that makes something less powerful). Clipping, a form of shortening, refers to the deletion of parts of the word, like the words *cap* (short for the item *Rabadon's Deathcap*) and *Ren* (short for the champion *Renekton*). Initialisms and acronyms both are abbreviations of phrases that are usually formed by using the first letters of each word within the respective phrase, with the difference that acronyms are pronounceable words. See, for example, the words *CD* (meaning *cooldown*, which is the recharging time of an ability before it can be used again) and *proc* (from *programmed random occurrence* – referring to the activation of a weapon, item or ability with a *Chance on Hit* or *Chance on Use* effect). Phonetic spellings shorten a respective word by replacing elements with non-standard spelling, e.g. *Fourchan* (short for the champion *Miss Fortune*). Letter-/number-homophones constitute a rare phenomenon in the data and are borderline cases at best as none perfectly matches Bieswanger's description (2007: 5) of the replacement of words or sequences by the use of identically-sounding letters or numbers. An example from the data is *3's* (which is referring to *Twisted Treeline*, a game mode with three players on each team) where it could refer to the similar sounding word *trees* or just the fact that three players will be playing on each team. Word-value characters, the last type of shortenings, are characters that refer to a whole word without sharing a common pronunciation. Examples include *b* (for *base* as in 'return to base') or *Q* (the first champion ability that is bound to the Q key on the keyboard). Loans are loanwords from other languages, such as *penta* (short for *pentakill*) from Greek. The process of blending combines parts of at least two words to create a new word, see *Atmallet* (a combination of the items *Atma's Impaler* and *Frozen Mallet*) or *gank* (from *gang kill*). The creation of a completely new word is defined as a neologism. Examples include the term *wombo combo* (which is when teammates effectively and consecutively chain together their abilities on enemy champions).

The mean word length of all items in the word list amounts to 5.26 characters.

5. Discussion

Overall, the large amount of shortening word-formation processes stands in accordance with the working hypothesis that the *LoL* players' ludolect emphasizes brevity. However, some details need to be taken into consideration:

The categorization of word-formation processes can become a complex matter as the word-formation process categories are, of course, not mutually exclusive and possess a certain degree of fuzziness – especially in combination with the ludolect's degree of semantic opaqueness. A finer categorization framework, possibly with a lexical-semantic perspective, could solve this problem and also account for the 171 lexical items that could not be categorized here. Most of the other complex or fuzzy cases have been grouped as *combinations*. Examples from this category include terms like *pentakill*, which could be classified as the combination of a loan, the Greek number five, and the English noun or verb *kill*, which makes it a compound. Another interesting example is the word *4Chan*, which not only constitutes a compound clipping of the champion name *Miss Fortune*, but also makes use of shortening by using a number-homophone, replacing the syllable *for* with the phonetically similar numeral *four* in its short numerical form *4*. Additionally, the syllable *tune* is replaced by the phonetically similar string *chan*, which, in combination, creates *4Chan*. This is an explicit reference to the infamous imageboard of the same name that is the source of numerous items of Internet culture. *Chan* by itself could be categorized as *phonetic spelling* according to the framework but rather emphasizes the playfulness of language as both *tune* and *chan* are four characters long. Ultimately, however, *4Chan* is significantly shorter than *Miss Fortune*.

Despite the complexity of some tokens, the majority of the lexicon's terms consist of clear-cut word-formation products: Almost half of all the analyzed terms are either clippings or initialisms that are mostly used to shorten the terms that were coined by the game developers, i.e. ludic elements such as champion, ability or item names. This is perfectly plausible as, in the heat of a match, it would cost valuable time to actually spell out the hero *Fiddlesticks* or the item *Iceborn Gauntlet*, for example. The time can be saved using the clippings *fiddle* or *fid*, or the initialisms *FS* and *IBG*, respectively. The other, more infrequent shortening processes – namely acronyms, word-value characters, letter/number-homophones, and phonetic spellings – also follow this economic pattern but seem to require more specific conditions to work, whereas the processes of clipping and creating initialisms seem to be almost universally applicable.

However, not all ludic terms are shortened, for example the term *triple kill* (which refers to one player defeating three enemy champions in rapid succession). This suggests a prioritization of certain items over others, presumably based on a concept's significance for successful gameplay and, hence, frequency. In other words, basic concepts of the game are common knowledge for a majority of the players and would not necessarily be referred to during a heavily time-constrained gameplay session. Therefore, longer terms (including composites rather than shortenings) possibly appear more frequently in metaludic discourse without time constraints, like strategic discussions on message boards, where players have the opportunity to discuss concepts that might be regarded too fundamental or irrelevant for the fast-paced in-game battlefield. This would also suggest that, during gameplay, the constraints of the communication form support the use of shortenings. These claims need to be assessed by further research, however.

Taking a look at the lexicon's items that are not shortenings of ludic terms proper (i.e. terms that have been created by the game developers), it is interesting to observe that items which seem to fulfill an alerting or commanding function are four or less characters long. While these words make up only roughly 5 percent of the lexicon, the terms seem to refer to decisive strategic elements during gameplay that need to be communicated fast. Examples for this are the terms *inc* (for *incoming*), which functions as a warning for a player that enemies are heading their way (see also Swoboda, this volume), or *mia / ss* (short for *missing in action* or *missing*, respectively – the latter seeming like a rather peculiar choice for a clipping in oral communication forms as only the fricative remains), which indicates that a champion from the opposite team has left their regular position and might prepare a *gank* (an ambush).

Shortening strategies in the *LoL* lexicon are not limited to the explicit shortening word-formation processes. The 171 terms that could not be classified by the framework introduced above consist of semantic shifting processes – at first sight, mostly semantic narrowings and metaphors. About half of them appear to be used for referencing a longer ludic term: *cow*, for example, is used to refer to the champion *Alistar* whose appearance is modelled after the mythological figure of the Minotaur. This is just one example of a plethora of creative constructions in the ludolect that could be the target of a systematic analysis.

The analysis of the word-formation processes of the *LoL* ludolect also confirms Ensslin's observations that compounds as well as conversions are frequent elements of gamer language (2012: 72–73). Examples include the compounds *soft leash* (which means to briefly draw the *aggro*/attention of a monster before moving away) and *split push* (which is a team strategy that refers to the act of simultaneously advancing on at least two of the game's *lanes*) as well as the result of conversion: *juke*. *Juke*, originating in the discipline of American football, is another word for feint, i.e. a maneuver to deceive and outsmart the enemy in order to successfully escape or retreat, and a possible usage could be the very short exclamation '*juke!*', which could translate into either '*that was a nice juke!*' or '*you need to juke now!*'.

The analyzed data only outlines the lexicon of a certain ludolect. Also, the data does not discriminate between ludic language elements, i.e. words that refer to game contents that are usually coined by the developers, and metaludic components, i.e. constructions used to speak about the game and its mechanics and dynamics that are usually coined by the players. Usually, the terms of the former category are found in the game's descriptive texts or dialogues and rather less frequently in actual metaludic discourse. While it makes sense to include both types of vocabulary in general glossaries, this does not have any implications for the actual usage of the terms. A fully-fledged corpus of in-game communication would solve these problems but is quite difficult to come by, as previously explained.

6. Conclusion

With this case study, I have presented one way of conducting linguistic research on a language variety called ludolect that is used by online video game communities. For that, relevance and importance of video games as a medium were presented at the beginning and, following this, previous academic approaches to the matter were discussed. With rising influence on society on various levels, be it economy, education or just plain entertainment, video games have increasingly garnered attention from academic circles, which becomes evident by the growing interest in the interdisciplinary area of game studies. It has also become apparent that linguistics is still nearly absent from this field, even though video games and their communities offer interesting points of departure for various linguistic projects, which can focus on the language of games itself or the language of gamers that combines the former with metaludic discourse. With only little published work at this time, the field still seems to be in its infancy, which will change, hopefully, in the future when more researchers find access to the topic – especially in the light of more digital natives entering the academic world.

The present case study has analyzed word-formation strategies of the English *League of Legends* community, based roughly on the framework that was introduced in Astrid Ensslin's *The Language of Gaming* (2012). The hypothesis that *LoL* gamers possess a distinct preference for brevity in their language, mainly due to the high pace and competitiveness of the game, was reflected in the data that was collected from three different community glossaries of *LoL* terminology. Of course, these observations should be taken with a grain of salt as the language data was collected from English terminology glossaries of the community that do not necessarily reflect the actual language use either while gaming or when discussing gameplay. For this, the quantitative analysis is insufficient and qualitative data would need to be collected, e.g. recordings of voice chat conversations between players.

The present study leaves plenty of room for further linguistic research: For one, with a revised framework, in terms of more diversified and finer categorization, comparable data could be collected from different language communities of *League of Legends*. These data could, for example, provide insight into the actual status of English within the respective communities and help to investigate whether word-formation processes that have been observed in the English data can also be found in the data of speakers of another language.[9] Additionally,

9 As mentioned in section 2, Dittmann (2001) found differences between German and French chat communities in terms of creative processes like word formation.

comparable data could be collected from communities of other games to analyze whether similarly high-paced games of a different genre, such as first-person shooters like *Counter-Strike*, show similar patterns, or, as a contrast, whether more slowly-paced games show a different distribution in word-formation processes as communication would probably be constrained in a different manner. A fully-fledged corpus would offer data that is comparable to other CMC media, like text messaging, and could illustrate whether gamers and texters use similar shortening strategies or the like. Of course, the field of word-formation as such constitutes only one of many linguistic areas that can be analyzed. The creative processes that can be observed in the present study are an interesting phenomenon and further analysis of metaphors used within the community, for example, could yield interesting results. Also, the area of pragmatics seems a potentially promising subject (see Swoboda, this volume), especially in the *League of Legends* community that has become infamous for rude behavior but is still one of the biggest and most active online gaming communities at the moment.

References

Algeo, John: *Cambridge History of the English Language*. CUP: Cambridge 1999.

Androutsopoulos, Jannis: "Introduction: Sociolinguistics and Computer-mediated Communication". *Journal of Sociolinguistics* 10 (4), 2006, 419–438.

Beil, Benjamin: *Game Studies. Eine Einführung*. LIT: Berlin 2013.

Bergs, Alexander: "Analyzing Online Communication from a Social Network Point of View: Questions, Problems, Perspectives". *Language@Internet*, 3, 2006, article 3.

Bieswanger, Markus: "2 abbrevi8 or not 2 abbrevi8. A Contrastive Analysis of Different Space and Time-saving Strategies in English and German Text Messages". In: Floyd, Simeon et al. (eds.): *Texas Linguistic Forum 50*. Texas Linguistic Forum: Austin 2007, 1–12.

BIU: *Gesamtmarkt für Computer- und Videospiele wächst 2014 um 11 Prozent*, 13.03.2015, retrieved 24.08.2015, from http://www.biu-online.de/de/presse/newsroom/newsroom-detail/datum/2015/03/13/gesamtmarkt-fuer-computer-und-videospiele-waechst-2014-um-11-prozent.html.

Consalvo, Mia: "Lag, Language, and Lingo. Theorizing Noise in Online Game Spaces". In: Perron, Bernard & Wolf, Mark J. P. (eds.): *The Video Game Theory Reader 2*. Routledge: New York 2009, 295–312.

Custer, Charlie: *The Fall of MMO and the Rise of MOBA: Using Data to Track Gaming Tastes*, 14.11.2013, retrieved 24.08.2015, from https://www.techinasia.com/the-fall-of-mmos-and-the-rise-of-moba-games/.

Crystal, David: *Language and the Internet* (2nd edition). CUP: Cambridge 2006.

Dittmann, Miguel: *Sprachverwendung im Internet. Untersuchungen zur Nutzung des Internet Relay Chat (IRC) in Deutschland und Frankreich*. Edition Indoles: Sarlat 2001.

Döring, Nicola: *Sozialpsychologie des Internet. Die Bedeutung des Internet für Kommunikationsprozesse, Identitäten, soziale Beziehungen und Gruppen* (2nd edition). Hofgrefe: Göttingen 2003.

Ensslin, Astrid: *The Language of Gaming*. Palgrave Macmillan: Basingstoke 2012.

ESA: *Essential Facts about the Computer and Video Game Industry*, 01.04.2015, retrieved 24.08.2015, from http://www.theesa.com/wp-content/uploads/2015/04/ESA-Essential-Facts-2015.pdf.

Evans, Stephen: *League of Legends Gaming Final Fills Seoul Stadium*, 20.10.2014, retrieved 24.08.2015, from http://www.bbc.com/news/business-29684635.

Gramley, Stephan: *The History of English. An Introduction*. London: Routledge: London 2012.

Herring, Susan C.: "A Faceted Classification Scheme for Computer-mediated Discourse". *Language@Internet* 4, 2007, article 1.

Larias: *Beginners Phrases and Acronyms in LoL*, 10.05.2010, retrieved 24.08.2015, from http://forums.na.leagueoflegends.com/board/showthread.php?t=110065&page=1.

League of Legends. In *Wikipedia, The Free Encyclopedia*. 17.08.2015, retrieved 24.08.2015, from https://en.wikipedia.org/w/index.php?title=League_of_Legends&oldid=676475414.

League of Legends Terminology: retrieved 24.08.2015, from http://leagueoflegends.wikia.com/wiki/League_of_Legends_terminology.

Marx, Konstanze & Weidacher, Georg: *Internetlinguistik. Ein Lehr- und Arbeitsbuch*. Narr: Tübingen 2014.

McDonald, Emma: *Top 100 Countries Represent 99.8% of $81.5Bn Global Games Market*, 23.06.2014, retrieved 24.08.2015, from http://www.newzoo.com/insights/top-100-countries-represent-99-6-81-5bn-global-games-market/.

Mueller, Saira: *League of Legends is Taking Over College Campuses across the U.S. Thanks to Scholarships*, 06.11.2015, retrieved 15.11.2015, from http://www.dailydot.com/esports/league-of-legends-college-scholarships/.

Plag, Ingo: *Word-Formation in English*. CUP: Cambridge 2003.

Pohlmann, Horst: „Überwältigt von der Spieleflut? – Genrekunde". In: Kaminski, Winfred & Witting, Tanja (eds.): *Digitale Spielräume. Basiswissen Computer- und Videospiele*. Kopaed: München 2007, 9–16.

Sherr, Ian: *Player Tally for 'League of Legends' Surges*, 27.01.2014, retrieved 24.08.2015, from http://blogs.wsj.com/digits/2014/01/27/player-tally-for-league-of-legends-surges/.

Shortis, Tim: *The Language of ICT: Information and Communication Technology*. Routledge: London 2001.

Swoboda, Birgit: "'Looks like you wiped us' – Communication in MMORPGs. A Hybrid with New Challenges and Motivations". In: Brock, Alexander & Schildhauer, Peter (eds.): *Communication Forms and Communicative Practices. New Perspectives on Communication Forms, Affordances, and What Users Make of Them*. Peter Lang: Berlin, this volume 111–129.

The All Tomato: *Strategy Guide: LoL Essentials*, 22.08.2015 (last updated), retrieved 24.08.2015, from http://www.mobafire.com/league-of-legends/build/lol-essentials-league-of-legends-new-player-beginner-guide-371292#chapter15.

Thorne, Steven L. et al.: "Second Language Use, Socialization, and Learning in Internet Interest Communities and Online Gaming". *The Modern Language Journal* 93, 2009, 802–821.

What is League of Legends?, retrieved 24.08.2015, from http://gameinfo.euw.leagueoflegends.com/en/game-info/get-started/what-is-lol/.

Wolf, Mark J. P. & Perron, Bernard (eds.): *The Video Game Theory Reader*. Routledge: New York 2003.

Birgit Swoboda

"Looks like you wiped us" – Communication in MMORPGs: A Hybrid with New Challenges and Motivations

Abstract MMORPGs (Massively Multiplayer Online Role-Playing Games) like *World of Warcraft*® are not only highly popular but also a social practice with a hybrid character apparent in the several communication forms and genres offered and used in them, like chat-channels (chat-rooms), instant messaging, message-boards, machinimas and *Let's play* videos. Furthermore, it can be observed that the motivations of the gamers lead to various styles and registers from role-playing to efficient acronymic style. Even though communication is of crucial importance to achieve goals, progress and for role-playing in MMORPGs, there are many communicative challenges for gamers, for example high-stress situations, missing paralinguistic cues and intercultural obstacles. All these factors allow for the claim that MMORPGs constitute not a new communication form but a discourse, i.e. the process of meaning-making and negotiation, with a hybrid character.

The question of how gamers communicate and overcome obstacles in MMORPGs is dealt with by drawing upon quantitative data from an online-questionnaire (n=324) and qualitative data from a self-compiled language corpus consisting of chat-logs ingame and messages from the official message-boards. This chapter shows how the technical medium and the speakers' motivations influence the language used by them.

1. Introduction

Gregory Bateson (as quoted in Pias 2007: 210) regards playing as "[...] an interchange of messages within a contextual frame [...]". Therefore, not only the action of playing and language as mediator of messages that are interchanged but also communication are essential aspects of games and gaming.[1] Huizinga (1938: 20–21) highlights that during playing, communities are formed in which in-group meanings, hence language and conventions are negotiated. This assigns a special status to interaction, communication and participation during gaming.

1 For the sake of convenience, the usual distinction between *play* (rule-unbound) and *game* (rule-bound) (cf. Rosenstingl & Mitgutsch 2009: 24) is henceforth not made in this paper anymore, but both terms used to describe the act of playing and in particular playing/gaming computer games.

Active participation and communication is intensified in computer games but especially in MMORPGs (Massively Multiplayer Online Role-Playing Games). The community in MMORPGs is of crucial importance. Traditional media like newspapers, books, TV, and radio mostly allow only for passive consumption. New media and new channels of communication allow for more interaction and participation of the audience in creating contents. In MMORPGs the potential reaches as far as offering gamers to be co-developers and co-authors of the game. The gamers do not only interact with one another, but also mentor and teach one another and, hence, create and affirm conventions in the community. They participate, shape, create and alter meanings instead of only making meaning by interpreting the existing and provided tokens (cf. Kramer 2014: 112–114). So, MMORPGs constitute a complex social practice based on communication and cooperation.

This chapter aims at shedding light on MMORPGs and their hybrid character concerning communication forms, genres, gamers' challenges and motivations.

Communication forms in MMORPGs as discussed in this paper refer to channels of communication used by gamers such as chat-channels or chat-rooms in the game (henceforth ingame), message-boards, wikis and such. In my definition, which is similar to Dürscheid's (2005), communication forms are external frames in which conventions, schemata and communication practices are created and manifested. The communication forms existing in MMORPGs are therefore, as Dürscheid (2005: 14) calls it, „medienvermittelt" (technically mediated) communication forms making use of a certain medium or as Schildhauer and Brock (Brock & Schildhauer, this volume: 28) state "technical constellation[s] which [give] rise to communicative potentials". In other words, just as the medium *telephone* is a tool for distance communication providing the communication form *phone call*, MMORPG communication forms (e.g. chat-channels) are products of the medium (Internet). The internal interaction practices and conventions (e.g. discussions, advertisements, etc.) are often referred to as genre (Gattung) or text-type (Textsorte) (cf. Dürscheid 2005). Contrary to this differentiation between genre and text-type, in which the former is based on dialogic communication and the latter based on thematic function, this paper is based on another, discourse-analytical definition of genre. According to Scollon and Scollon (2001: 35), genre refers to:

> different conventional forms of speech events. For example, jokes, lectures, business meetings, textbooks, [...] By genre we mean any speech event, whether it is spoken or in writing, which has fairly predictable sets of speech acts, participants, topics, settings, or other regularly occurring and conventional forms.

In the same vein, Widdowson (1996: 127) defines genre as "[a] type of discourse in written or spoken mode with particular features established by convention." Similarly, this paper will regard the internal characteristics and functions of communication forms as genre, in which certain schemata and conventions are used independently of spoken or written language or dialogic or monologic character. This applies to *Let's play* videos and *machinimas* (ingame movies made by gamers), which comprise certain schemata and conventions. *Let's play* videos include walkthroughs, video guides and live-streaming of gaming, i.e. texts based on different purposes and genre patterns (cf. Brock & Schildhauer, this volume: 18). For the sake of clarity in my definition, discourse refers to the process of meaning-making and negotiation in and through language (including paralinguistic cues, signs and the context) (Kramer 2014: 10–11).

This paper, however, does not only describe the communication forms and genres of MMORPGs but pays special attention to the gamers as members of a speech community and their needs, motivations and challenges. It combines the technical and formal aspects of the MMORPG setting and gaming discourse with aspects of the speakers' motivation and linguistic choices. Thereby, the chapter raises questions in how far the medium, form, genre and community influence communication in general.

Computer games and MMORPGs have been extensively discussed by many scholars recently (cf. Consalvo 2009; Corneliussen & Rettberg 2008; Rosenstingl & Mitgutsch 2009). Linguistic inquiries, however, have been rare in computer game studies, especially in the setting of MMORPGs. One can clearly resort to the by now extensive research done in CMC (computer-mediated communication) like Crystal (2006), Danet & Herring (2007), Baron (2008), and Herring et al. (2013). But while traditional CMC may look similar to MMORPG communication, they are not the same. Gamers are faced with other challenges than the "common" Internet user and they have other needs for communication. As concerns language use, works by Goffman (1967) or Harré & Langenhove (1999) on cooperation and positioning offer useful frameworks for dealing with communication and gamers' motivation in MMORPGs. Similarly, conversation-analytical approaches have been taken towards chats (cf. Beißwenger 2007) and prove beneficial.

In order to explore the topics of communication in MMORPGs, data was collected in MMORPGs and outside of them. The following section describes the data and methods of this study. Furthermore, MMORPGs as well as gamers as members of speech communities and their motivations are described in detail. Afterwards, the paper deals with the communicative setting of MMORPGs, illustrating the communication forms and the challenges, but also opportunities they offer. By drawing upon examples taken from the collected data, the following section shows how the gamers' motivations, communication forms, obstacles and challenges make interaction in MMORPG a hybrid.

2. Data and Method

This chapter draws upon a survey carried out for my PhD thesis project (Kramer 2014). Participant observation as well as a hands-on approach, i.e. active gaming and participating as a member of the community, were the basis for this research (cf. Kramer 2010, 2013; Swoboda 2015). Hence, the data was gathered in MMORPGs, ingame and from gamers. Three data sources were drawn upon to research the communication in MMORPGs: a self-compiled language corpus, an online-questionnaire and introspection. Methodological triangulation allows reassessing findings in the other data sets. The data sets and methods used are summarized in the table below. It has to be mentioned that I limit myself to written communication in my corpus. Despite the popular use of VoIP (Voice over IP) chats, i.e. communicating via headsets, I argue that written communication is still prevalent when it comes to casual gaming, playing in random groups and contacting strangers (see also Zähres, this volume). An exception to the written data are audiovisual communication genres such as *machinimas* and *Let's play* videos.

Table 1: Summary of the Data Sources and Methods Used

Data Source/Approach	Data Type	Analysis Method
online-questionnaire (n=324)	quantitative, elicited data	statistic evaluation, pragmatic frameworks
self-compiled corpus (ingame: 1,776 h/ 46,176,000 characters; outside: 300,000 characters)	qualitative, observed data	grounded theory, hermeneutic approach, pragmatic frameworks
introspection	qualitative, observed data	qualitative heuristic approach, critical incident log, discussion

First, the online-questionnaire was a voluntary survey; hence, there was no artificial sampling applied to the questionnaire. The questionnaire consisted of 50 questions comprised of three parts: gamer profile, gaming behavior and language behavior. The gamer profile surveyed general data like gender, age and nationality of the gamers. The questions about gaming behavior concerned playing time per week, self-assessment concerning gaming style and gaming behavior. The main part of the questionnaire surveyed the language behavior. The questions attempted to determine the use of stylistic features and interaction strategies, for example the use of acronyms while searching for other gamers to play with or smileys during role-playing. The participants' subjectivity and possible unawareness concerning their language use is countervailed by the corpus, which allows for testing findings of the questionnaire. All in all, 324 gamers from 42 countries participated and completed the survey.

The results were contextualized and linked to theories of pragmatics, such as politeness theory, conversational analysis and positioning theory. It provides insights into the use and frequency of stylistic features, motivations and factors which bring about linguistic choices as well as the gamers' perception of ingame communication. The results suggest ways in which gamers react when they are confronted with problems ingame and how they attempt to avoid potential arguments.

Second, the self-compiled corpus complements the online-questionnaire. It yields examples of communication in MMORPGs (chat-logs primarily recorded in *World of Warcraft*® and *Lord of the Rings Online*®) as well as outside of the games (official game message-boards and official game websites). The corpus was analyzed on the basis of Grounded Theory and a hermeneutic approach. This refers to „a cyclical process in which theoretical insights [...] are discovered in the data, those insights are then tested [...] [on] other parts of the data, which in turn produce their own theoretical insights [...]" (Hayes 2000: 184). This approach allowed context-specific observations in certain situations, testing existing hypotheses and provided real and contextualized examples.

Third, introspection was used as an approach to research the language of MMORPG gamers, due to the fact that the researcher is a member of the speech community examined. Being part of the community allows knowing the in-group workings and meanings of a speech community. A qualitative heuristic approach was followed while researching, supported by a critical incident log (cf. Bell 2006: 186–194) which allowed structuring communication situations of interest. It gives not only information on language use from an insider perspective but also provides authentic examples of real language usage rather than artificial examples. The issue of subjectivity was countervailed by testing observations in the other data sets and discussing them with other gamers.

The three data sets and types of methodology complement one another and also help to compensate for shortcomings in the other sets. The combination of the data sets makes the picture clearer, yet it is still a kaleidoscope and not exactly the whole effigy.

3. MMORPGs and Gamers' Motivation

MMORPGs have been popular games for the last years. Among them, *World of Warcraft®* is one of the most popular ones.[2] The acronym *MMORPG* stands for *Massively Multiplayer Online Role-playing Game* and describes the principal elements of this gaming genre, as in these role-playing games (RPG) a large (massive) number of gamers simultaneously play online with each other (multiplayer). While the term *role-playing* is a basic part of the acronym *MMORPG*, in what way a role of a character (*avatar*) is taken on and acted out varies from MMORPG to MMORPG and from gamer to gamer (cf. Kramer 2014: 65).

MMORPGs allow gamers to become more than mere consumers of ready-made entertainment. The gamers cooperate and communicate with one another and the game developers. Hence, they also influence and shape the games as such. This makes the gamer a vital aspect when looking at communication in the MMORPG setting.

The sender and receiver are crucial for any speech event (cf. Jakobson 1960) as they create and accept conventions and by this become a community. Of course, there is no such thing as a homogenous group of gamers and therefore not one gamer language. However, speakers and gamers in particular gather and form communities, such as parties and guilds, to play together. Here, the question arises what type of community gamers create.

The concept of *community of practice* (Eckert 2000) has already been applied to CMC contexts (e.g. Bergs 2006; Mauranen 2013) despite spatial proximity and face-to-face conversation being key elements of it (cf. Eckert 2000: 32). Even though these issues could be ignored, this paper introduces the concept of *semiotic domain* and *affinity group* by Gee (2003), as it was designed for describing gamers and the meaning-making process in games. According to Gee (2003: 17) *semiotic*

> is just a fancy way of saying we want to talk about all sorts of different things that can take on meaning, such as images, sounds, gestures, movements, [...], and not just words.

Thus, a semiotic domain is a set of practices in which practices stand for particular meanings in particular settings. Specific knowledge of a domain is needed in order to make sense of a practice. Speakers who can recognize, understand and create meanings in a semiotic domain are referred to as *affinity group*. They share the same practices and can detect others as insiders or outsiders of the group

---

2 *World of Warcraft®* had about 12 Mio. players world-wide in 2011, and has currently about 5,5 Mio. players (http://www.statista.com/statistics/276601/number-of-world-of-warcraft-subscribers-by-quarter/ [29.04.2016]).

(cf. Gee 2003: 24–30). Applying this concept would make MMORPGs a semiotic domain and the gamers an affinity group, as they can make sense of tokens unrecognizable to others. An example of this would be the ding!-sound in *World of Warcraft®* which is heard when an avatar rises in level. Many gamers started to write *ding*! into the chat-channels to let their fellow gamers know that they had a *level up*. Hence, an ingame sound was coded into an onomatopoeic expression which refers to an event in the game. A non-gamer will possibly be unable to understand what *ding!* means and activate other connotations such as the sound of a microwave or the sound of a cartoon character having an idea (cf. Kramer 2014: 173). Playing MMORPGs, therefore, also means learning to read and use tokens of the community.

Based on the results of the questionnaire (n= 324), it can be assumed that the affinity group of MMORPG gamers are a very multifaceted community. The results suggest that the common clichés of the gamer are, in fact, not more than stereotypes. Gamers are not lonely, unsocial, addicted (teenage) males but humans of both genders (88% male, 12% female) who have social ties, family and come from a wide range of professional backgrounds (cf. Kramer 2014: 128–142).

The motivations which drive gamers to play MMORPGs are as multifaceted as the gamer community itself. One of the main aspects which makes MMORPGs different to other current computer-games is the strong incorporation and linking of social and cooperative gaming. The motivations of gamers are strongly connected with one another and gamers are often driven by several desires while playing. Two crucial motivating forces in cooperative gaming in MMORPGs are achievement and progression. They are linked in a vicious circle, since in order to progress in the game, the gamer has to achieve something (fulfill quests), but to do this, they have to improve their character ingame (e.g. reaching higher levels with one's character or acquiring better gear). Moreover, ingame progress requires the help of others; therefore, gamers have to cooperate. The experiences, challenges, failure and success create a sense of community, and even friendships, and deepen existing ones in MMORPGs. This yields affinity groups with strong ties and highlights the social aspects of these games which themselves function as a strong motivation. According to the results of the questionnaire, the aspect of socializing and spending time with friends and family online in MMORPGs is an important motivation. Several participants state that playing MMORPGs with their siblings, partner and even parents is, just like any other pastime activity, an entertainment that gives them even more reason to spend time together and share a common interest (cf. Swoboda 2015: 157).

Motivations listed by other researchers are power and manipulation, representation (role-playing), escapism, immersion and entertainment (cf. Yee 2006: 202). Clearly, for some gamers achievements ingame, such as improving their characters, are more important than role-playing, exploring and creating characters with background stories, yet the social and cooperative component is a part of all these gaming motivations. Achievements on the higher levels of the game are only possible with the help of others. In order to improve one's character, materials and resources are required that other gamers can offer, and role-playing is more exciting when there is someone to perform to (cf. Swoboda 2015: 157). It could therefore be said that socializing and cooperation are the main driving forces, while achievement, progression, power, manipulation, representation, escapism, immersion and entertainment are motivations emerging from them.

The gamers in MMORPGs are not a mere audience but an active part of the community and form a participatory culture as Jenkins et. al. (2009) call it. They come from various cultural, social and linguistic backgrounds. Their motivations are not only a reason to play MMORPGs but also the cause for certain playing styles and language use. The next section on interaction in MMORPGs focuses on how the gamers' language is shaped by their motivation and the communication forms available to them.

4. Communication in MMORPGs

It is argued in this paper that MMORPGs are a hybrid when it comes to communication because of the new combination of traditional aspects such as the motivations described in the previous section. Clearly, they are not unique to the MMORPG *semiotic domain* nor new as such. Achievement, progression and creativity as apparent in role-playing are basic desires of humans. However, the combination with the communication forms and genres provided by the game and the obstacles and challenges presented in them make MMORPGs a unique area of inquiry. The following subsections describe the communication forms provided for and used by gamers, as well as challenges arising from them and the game as such.

4.1. Communication Forms and Genres

Communication forms are often differentiated by the concept of written and spoken language. The main problem with the terms *writing* and *speech* is that they denote two different concepts, namely the realization and the conception of the language used. Koch and Oesterreicher (1994) noted this differentiation in an approach in which they differentiate between *medial* („*mediale*") and *conceptional* („*konzeptionelle*") writing and speech (Schriftlichkeit und Mündlichkeit). Similarly, Halliday distinguishes between medium and mode, the first being the manifestation or production of language, the latter being the language used as such (cf. Widdowson 2002: 549–550).

It is more useful to look at the characteristics of communication forms such as the spatial and temporal dimension. All MMORPG communication forms overcome the spatial dimension: the sender and recipient do not need to be in the same place. However, some of the communication forms require the presence at a virtual locus, for example, being online ingame and logged into the same chat-channel or VoIP-chat-room. Communication forms like the say-function and the emote-function even require a certain virtual spatial presence since they are bound to locations ingame. A gamer can only "see" or "hear" emotes or utterances by other gamers who are nearby. The temporal dimension refers to the necessary temporal presence. There is almost no time delay between production and reception of language in synchronous forms of communication, unlike asynchronous communication.

MMORPGs provide gamers with several communication forms ingame and outside of it. The most commonly-used ingame communication form is the chat-channel which is comparable to a chat-room ingame. There are several chat-channels available to the gamers in MMORPGs, which have specific functions. The chat-channels are used to look for other gamers to play with (LFG-channel, looking for group), to search for items to buy or sell (trade channel) or to advertise one's own guild (general chat channel). Chitchat which has nothing to do with the game is discouraged in the general chat-channels. While the chat-channels can be used and read by all gamers on the same server, other channels are more private, like party channels (only for members of a group, i.e. party), or the guild channels for members of a guild (an association of gamer characters). While the chat-channels are – like chat-rooms – one-to-many communication forms, there is also the possibility to send a private message to one gamer, called *whispering*, which can be regarded as one-to-one communication. This is comparable to instant-messaging (cf. Swoboda 2015: 155). The aforementioned say-function is an ingame location-bound chat-channel, hence synchronous and one-to-many communication. Similarly, the emote-function, which allows gamers to utilize prefabricated animations which display emotions like laughing, dancing, fainting and others, can only be seen by characters nearby. Emotes are commonly used by role-players to let their avatars act on the screen (cf. Kramer 2014: 107).

Outside the game, most MMORPGs offer their gamers message-boards (or forums) to communicate. These can be used by the gamers to talk about the game or anything else which they are interested in. Message-boards offer the gamers a platform for casual chitchat and small-talk, which is discouraged in ingame chat-channels. They are, just like other communication forms outside the game, for example wikis and websites, asynchronous and public forms of communication. It appears that knowledge transfer very often takes place in an asynchronous setting. This is possibly because asynchronous communication allows for preparing texts, which can hence be structured appropriately for other gamers to provide condensed information. The only private asynchronous communication form is the ingame mail, comparable to e-mail. It is often used to send goods or money from one character to another almost like mail-order trade.

These communication channels are medially written forms of communication. There is only one type of medially spoken communication form in MMORPGs, namely VoIP. VoIP-chats require the gamers to have the respective software (e.g. teamspeak, Ventrilo, etc.), a voice-chat server or gamer's PC acting as such, headphones and the presence of the speakers. It is commonly used by guilds and friends playing together, particularly when it comes to demanding ingame encounters like raids (undertakings requiring more than five players). But clearly VoIP-chats also fulfill a social function (see Kramer 2014: 79).

Let's play videos add a visual component to the audio input VoIP provides. They can be regarded, like *machinimas*, as a genre. In these videos, gamers play and comment on game content and give advice to other gamers on how to master certain ingame challenges. Some videos contain background music, cut-scenes and other stylistic devices of film making. Other videos are live streams which feature gamers during a live playing session. They provide the audience with live footage and commentary of games. This is comparable to sitting next to a friend watching him or her playing a game. These videos partly fulfill a social function (playing and experiencing games together) and partly a mentoring function (providing help, solutions and guidance to other players). They are an essential element of the participatory culture.

Machinimas, while also videos, fulfill a different function than *Let's play* videos. *Machinimas* (a combination of the words *cinema* and *machine*) are ingame movies in which the ingame environment and avatars are used for making movies. They include all elements which are vital for traditional movie-making, such as narration, screenplay, scene cutting, background music and so on.

The following table sums up the communication forms and genres of MMORPGs and their characteristics.

Table 2: Communication in MMORPGs

	Name	Sender	Recipient	Type	Privacy	Location
Communication Form	chat-channels (general, trade, LFG, etc)	one	many	synchronous	public	ingame
	party-channel	one	many	synchronous	open to group members	ingame
	guild-channel	one	many	synchronous	open to guild members	ingame
	whisper, tell or private message	one	one	synchronous	private	ingame
	say-function	one	many	synchronous	public (location bound)	ingame
	emote	one	many	synchronous	public (location bound)	ingame
	VoIP	one	one/many	synchronous	open to channel users	ingame/ outside game
	mail	one	one	asynchronous	private	ingame
	message-board	one	many	asynchronous	public	outside game
	wiki	many	many	asynchronous	public	outside game
	website	one	many	asynchronous	public	outside game
Genre	*Let's play* videos	one/ many	many	synchronous/ asynchronous	public	outside game
	machinimas	one	many	asynchronous	public	outside game

4.2. Obstacles and Challenges

The communication characteristics provide the gamers with different possibilities and challenges. For example, the privacy of one-to-one communication can be an advantage when gamers do not want to harm their reputation by asking a question. However, information gathering by asking a single person, for example where a certain quest objective is located, can be slow and unsuccessful. One-to-many communication, for instance asking a question in the general chat-channel, can provide more and faster replies than privately whispering to individuals. The use of wikis, websites or *Let's play* videos for solving problems poses even less of a risk of harm to the gamer's reputation since they – though public – guarantee privacy to the users. One more communicative aspect influencing the language of gamers is the possible time lag between production and reception. Asynchronous forms of communication such as message-boards do not require the presence of the interlocutors during production of speech, hence it could take some time until the interlocutor reads a question on a messageboard and answers it (cf. Swoboda 2014: 155).

Another challenge, but also opportunity, to the gamers is the absence of paralinguistic cues just like in CMC communication in general. In normal face-to-face conversations, facial expressions, gestures and voice quality help interlocutors to interpret the utterances of the other speaker. Yet, most MMORPGs communication forms are medially written; hence, these cues are missing. In order to compensate for these missing paralinguistic cues, gamers utilize stylistic features like smileys to add meaning to their written conversations (cf. Dittmann 2001: p. 72).

Furthermore, opportunities and challenges are posed by the fact that, for many MMORPG gamers, English has become a lingua franca ingame. One reason for this is the technical setup of these games. MMORPGs are separated into region servers and language servers based on the region the gamer is in. Gamers have to play on the servers of their region. In most cases, the following region servers are provided: United States, Europe, Asia and Pacific. The language servers refer to the prevalent language used on the respective server; hence, it is expected to use the server language in the chat-channels and support is only given in this language. Normally, English, German, French and Spanish language servers are offered to the gamers. In addition to this, *World of Warcraft®* also has Italian and Russian servers. The 324 gamers of my study come from 42 countries, are native speakers of 36 different languages and speak, in total, 31 languages as foreign or secondary languages. It comes as no surprise that no game can offer a language server for every language; hence, many are forced to play on English servers. According to my data, 291 (89.8%) of 324 gamers play on English language servers. However, only 126 (39%) regard themselves as native speakers of English. Thus, the majority of gamers on English language servers are non-native English speakers, yet use English to communicate with one another. The prominence of English as the most frequent foreign language among the gamers (197) combined with the fact that 291 gamers play on English language servers, allows for the conclusion that English is used as a lingua franca by many gamers. Yet, this does not allow for any conclusions on the gamers' proficiency in English. The participants name several degrees of proficiency ranging from beginner level to native-like competence. Hence, not all gamers are equally skilled in English and yet they are forced to use it in order to play with one another (cf. Kramer 2013: 47–48).

High-stress situations are another factor which crucially influences the gamers and their language.[3] Many ingame encounters are complex, attention-demanding, time-intensive and put enormous pressure and stress on the gamers. The gamers are required to be able to multitask and deal with several different inputs simultaneously. This also influences their gaming styles and language use. More often than not, it is a matter of ingame life or death; hence, there is not much time for long-winded explanations. Typing *inc* for *incoming* in order to warn other gamers of approaching danger is by far quicker than typing "Watch out! There are enemies arriving!" This is also linked to what Huizinga (1938: 27–30) refers to as *holy earnestness*. Games cause strong emotions like sympathy, excessive joy but also earnestness about the outcome. They are not just games but a serious matter. That is why the high-stress situations as well as the desire for progression and achievement are treated by gamers with such seriousness, which strongly influences their language use.

A final factor which has to be kept in mind when dealing with language in MMORPGs, even though not necessarily valid for every gamer, is the role-playing aspect. Paradoxically, while MMORPGs have the term role-playing in their name, role-playing is not mandatory. Yet, it is an aspect which can influence linguistic choices and lead to the intentional omission of stylistic features, like smileys, as they are often frowned upon by strict role-payers. At the same time, it can also cause gamers to use specific politeness or impoliteness and positioning strategies because they are part of the enacted character. Other examples of language used for role-playing are the use of dialects and accents or the use of a certain register (cf. Swoboda 2015: 157). This can also be observed when looking at machinimas. Machinimas such as *War of the Ancient – The Well of Eternity*[4] are narration-based and completely set in the gameworld also concerning language, while other machinimas, often music videos, break the story frame and use stylistic features of gamers' language.[5]

Gamers face numerous communicative challenges and obstacles in MMORPGs. The communication and its technical setup provide different opportunities such as differences between production and reception time (asynchronous/synchronous communication) and the factor of direction (one-to-one/one-to-many communication). Additional obstacles for gamers to overcome are the absence of

---

3 See also Zähres, this volume, on word formation patterns in the MMORPG *League of Legends* under the influence of such circumstances.

4 https://www.youtube.com/watch?v=P0iKFASurHk (15.6.2015).

5 E.g. Oxhorn music videos: https://www.youtube.com/watch?v=iEWgs6YQR9A&list=PLDD56D144C835BD93 (15.6.2015).

paralinguistic cues in the mainly written medium and the fact that most gamers use English as a lingua franca. Yet MMORPGs require gamers to cooperate, and, hence, communicate with one another to achieve goals. The goals become congruent with the gamers' motivations, namely progressing, achieving, socializing, role-playing and exploring. All these manifold factors motivate linguistic choices taken by gamers and make communication in MMORPGs a hybrid.

5. Interaction in MMORPGs

In order to illustrate the hybrid character and exceptional position of communication in MMORPGs, some examples of interaction are discussed here in more detail. The first example belongs to the genre or habitus of *Looking for group-sequences* (LFG) which can take on different forms in MMORPGs, namely conventionalized schemata. As mentioned before, it is often crucial in MMORPGs to join together for certain quests or undertakings, hence gamers ask in the public channels for help and companions. Conventionalized schemata are fundamental structures of interaction since they organize the course of actions but also categorize which actions are appropriate or not. They provide the speaker with secure pathways through interactions. The following example illustrates a LFG-sequence in the public chat-channel in *World of Warcraft*®:

Example (1)

LFG SoO normal 2DD and tank

Here, a gamer of *World of Warcraft*® is looking for a group (*LFG*), in particular two damage dealers (*DD*) and a *tank* (a class who can take a lot of damage) for the raid *Siege of Orgrimmar* (*SoO*) in normal mode. This paraphrase is definitely a long-winded sentence compared to the acronymic way, hence using initialisms serves the function of efficiency. This is supported by the results of the questionnaire, which show that acronyms are the preferred way of asking for help in MMORPGs. 79% (257 of 324 gamers) rate acronymic *LFG*-sequences as appropriate, and only 11% as inappropriate. They are efficient, fast and provide the gamers with the exact quest objective (*SoO*) and what tasks they are expected to fulfill, in this case being a damage dealer or a tank. Furthermore, acronyms and neologisms do not only speed up conversation and nourish the gamer's strife for efficiency but can also be regarded as in-group markers and positioning moves because they allow the gamers to position themselves actively as part of their community. If gamers do not know what *DD* is, they are exposed as *noobs*, newcomers to the game, and clearly not taken along to such a demanding undertaking. Hence, in-group markers like acronyms and neologisms allow the gamers to separate the wheat from the chaff, the pro-gamers (professional gamers) from the noobs. Clearly, gamers will be more willing to help an old hand in gaming rather than having to deal with a newcomer who will probably need additional explanation during the quest. Therefore, *LFG*-sequences combine technical features of the communication form (chat) and the gamer's motivations (efficiency) as they provide clear structure, information transmission, positioning as part of the fast in-group communication (cf. Kramer 2014: 151–153).

Acronyms and neologisms are not only used in ingame chats but also in message-board conversations, wikis, *Let's play* videos and *machinimas*. The reasons for using these stylistic elements also in communication forms and genres which do not call for speed or offer paralinguistic cues is the desire to show knowledge of the insider code, efficiency and gamer's pride. Speaking the language of a community is always a crucial aspect to be accepted by other members of the respective community.

Smileys or emoticons are another example of MMORPG interaction. Smileys are commonly known and used in MMORPG and online communication. The questionnaire participants state that they use smileys especially when whispering or messaging friends.6 Based on these results, it could be said that the less familiarity a situation has, the fewer smileys the gamers use. Like facial expressions, smileys convey information and fulfill several functions which help the interlocutors to interpret utterances. Smileys can fulfill a back-channel function; by using them, the speaker can display attention to the interlocutors and encourage them to continue talking. Furthermore, they can be used to convey closeness through sympathy and compassion but also distance through antipathy. The possible reasons to use smileys range from creativity, efficiency, compensation for missing extra-linguistic features to conveyance of additional information (cf. Swoboda 2015: 161). The following example shows how smileys are used in MMORPGs:

Example (2)

Looks like you wiped us (: so one last chance where you either do what we say or I'll kick you out, I'm afraid S:

Here, a gamer warns another gamer who caused the death of all party members (*wipe*) by a beginner's mistake that he/she will be removed from the group (*kicked*) if he/she does not shape up. The use of the positive smiley *(:* attenuates the harsh comment. The second smiley *S:* conveys the mixed feelings of the speaker if not

---

6 46% often, 26% always, 16% occasionally, 8% not very often, 3% not at all, 1% did not answer the question.

even a certain confusion caused by the malpractice of the other gamer. The results of the questionnaire show that smileys are commonly used as means of mitigation in difficult situations like wipes or arguments. Generally, it can be said that gamers react more positively to requests when a smiley is used. They appear to be aware of this, and, hence, use smileys for this purpose. This means that the concepts of efficiency and rapport are both taken into consideration by the gamers. They consider how to overcome the technical obstacles of the communication form (missing paralinguistic cues) as well as how to establish rapport and convey extra-linguistic information (cf. Swoboda 2015: 161).

6. Conclusion

This paper demonstrates the numerous challenges and obstacles gamers are faced with while gaming and the motivations and desires which drive them. The gamers are confronted with the technical challenges of these games and their communicative settings. While the communication forms are not new, like chat-rooms, instant-messaging, message-boards, videos and so on, they are uniquely combined in MMORPGs. Each communication form provides technical particularities which have to be dealt with, like the aspect of direction (one-to-one/one-to-many), time (synchronous/asynchronous), and privacy. Each has its pros and cons concerning communication. Game-specific particularities like location and server-language also influence the language of the gamers, for example the use of English as a lingua franca. They can be obstacles but also provide opportunities to the gamers.

Additionally, the gamers' goals and motivations influence their language use, for example the need and desire to be efficient and fast in order to save ingame lives and achieve something, but also to display their knowledge of the in-group code and their involvement with the community. Progression, achievement and socializing are directly linked to ingame cooperation and, therefore, also to interaction. In order to play MMORPGs, one has to interact and cooperate with other gamers and, thus, gamers alter their language use to serve their needs.

Gamers are well aware of the different options they have in the several communication forms and they make best use of the linguistic faculties and the arsenal of interaction strategies available to them. When communicating with one another, they consider the technical and conversational challenges of the games as well as their motivations and goals. Role-players who are motivated by creating background stories of their characters use another register than gamers motivated by progression and achievement. Role-players do not use smileys, acronyms or neologisms but make use of a certain register and accent. Progression-driven gamers orient towards efficient and fast language use based on acronyms and neologisms. Both extreme gamer types are driven by the desire to be part of a community and display their membership to other gamers, no matter in which communication form they communicate.

This article demonstrates that, while the separate communication forms (e.g., chat-rooms, message-boards, video, instant-messaging, etc.), stylistic features (e.g. acronyms, neologisms, smileys, etc.) and motivations (e.g. achievement, rapport, membership, etc.) are not new or unique, their combination as manifested in MMORPGs is a special hybrid of the present time. Furthermore, since MMORPGs are not only played, as clichés indicate, by young, male gamers, but rather by men and women of all age-groups, social and linguistic backgrounds, it could be claimed that looking at this communication setting provides us with interesting insights about communication in general. Hence, it could be very insightful to invest more time into researching communication in computer-games and MMORPGs. It is not game over yet.

References

Baron, Naomi: *Always on. Language in an Online and Mobile World.* Oxford University Press: Oxford 2008.

Beißwenger, Michael: *Sprachhandlungskoordination in der Chat-Kommunikation.* De Gruyter: New York 2007.

Bell, Judith: *Doing your Research Project, a Guide for First-time Researchers in Education, Health and Social Science.* Open University Press: New York 2006.

Bergs, Alexander: "Analyzing Online Communication from a Social Network Point of View. Questions, Problems, Perspectives". *Language@internet* (vol. 3/article 3), 2006, http://www.languageatinternet.org/articles/2006/371 [25.03.2016].

Brock, Alexander & Schildhauer, Peter: "Communication Form. A Concept Revisited". In: Brock, Alexander & Schildhauer, Peter (eds.): *Communication Forms and Communicative Practices. New Perspectives on Communication Forms, Affordances, and What Users Make of Them.* Peter Lang: Berlin, this volume 13–43.

Consalvo, Mia: "Lag, Language, and Lingo. Theorizing Noise in Online Game Spaces". In: Perron, Bernard & Wolf, Mark J. P. (eds.): *The Video Game Theory Reader 2.* Routledge: New York 2009, 295–312.

Corneliussen, Hilde & Rettberg, Jill W. (eds.): *Digital Culture, Play and Identity. A World of Warcraft Reader.* MIT Press: Cambridge, MA 2008.

Crystal, David: *Language and the Internet.* CUP: Cambridge 2006.

Danet, Brenda & Herring, Susan (eds.): *The Multilingual Internet. Language, Culture, and Communication Online.* OUP: Oxford 2007.

Dittmann, Miguel: *Sprachverwendung im Internet. Untersuchungen zur Nutzung des Internet Relay Chat (IRC) in Deutschland und Frankreich*. Edition Indoles: Sarlat 2001.

Dürscheid, Christa: „Medien, Kommunikationsformen, kommunikative Gattungen". *Linguistik online* 22(1), 2005, 1–16.

Eckert, Penelope: *Linguistic Variation as Social Practice*. Blackwell Publishers: Malden 2000.

Gee, James P.: *What Video Games Have to Teach us about Learning and Literacy*. Palgrave Macmillan: New York 2003.

Goffman, Erving (ed.): *Interactional Ritual*. Anchor Books: New York 1967.

Harré, Rom & Langenhove van Luk (eds.): *Positioning Theory*. Blackwell Publishing: Oxford 1999.

Hayes, Nicky: *Doing Psychological Research. Gathering and Analysing Data*. Open University Press: Buckingham 2000.

Herring, Susan et al. (eds.): *Pragmatics of Computer-mediated Communication*. de Gruyter Mouton: Berlin 2013.

Huizinga, Johann: *Homo ludens. Vom Ursprung der Kultur im Spiel* (20th edition). Rowohlt Taschenbuch Verlag: Hamburg 1938.

Jakobson, Roman: "Linguistics and Poetics". In: Seboeck, Thomas (ed.): *Style in Language*. MIT Press: Cambridge, MA 1960, 350–377.

Jenkins, Henry et. al.: *Confronting the Challenges of Participatory Culture. Media Education for the 21st Century*. The MIT Press: Cambridge, MA. 2009.

Kramer, Birgit: "L2P n00b, the Language of MMORPGs". In: Swertz, Christian & Wagner, Michael (eds.): *Game\\Play\\Society. Contributions to Contemporary Computer Game Studies*. Kopaed: München 2010, 135–146.

Kramer, Birgit: "I'm by Default Polite – Politeness and Positioning in MMORPGS". *Discourse and Interaction* 6(1), 2013, 41–53.

Kramer, Birgit: *L2P n00b!! – The Pragmatics of Positioning in MMORPGs*. (Dissertation). University of Vienna: Vienna 2014.

Mauranen, Anna: "Hybridism, Edutainment, and Doubt. Science Blogging Finding its Feet". *Nordic Journal of English Studies* 12(1), 2013, http://ojs.ub.gu.se/ojs/index.php/njes/article/view/1795 [25.03.2016].

Oxhorn music videos: https://www.youtube.com/watch?v=iEWgs6YQR9A&list=PLDD56D144C835BD93 [15.6.2015]).

Pias, Claus: „Kommentar zu Gregory Bateson: Eine Theorie des Spiels und der Phantasie". In: Pias, Claus & Holtorf, Christian (eds.): *Escape! Computerspiele als Kulturtechnik*. Bohlau Verlag GmbH: Köln 2007, 208–213.

Rosenstingl, Herbert & Mitgutsch, Konstantin: *Schauplatz Computerspiele*. Lesethek Verlag: Wien 2009.

Scollon, Ron & Scollon, Suzanne: *Intercultural Communication. A Discourse Approach*. Blackwell Publishing: Oxford 2001.

Statista, the statistics portal: "Number of World of Warcraft Subscribers from 1st Quarter 2005 to 3rd Quarter 2015 (in mill.)". http://www.statista.com/statistics/276601/number-of-world-of-warcraft-subscribers-by-quarter/ [29.03.2016].

Swoboda, Birgit: "GTFO!! – Positioning as Interaction Strategy in MMORPG Communication". *Comunicação e Sociedade* 27, 2015, 151–166.

War of the Ancient - The Well of Eternity (https://www.youtube.com/watch?v=P0iKFASurHk [15.6.2015].

Widdowson, Henry G.: *Linguistics*. OUP: Oxford 1996.

Widdowson, Henry G.: "Skills and Knowledge in Language Learning". In: Byram, Michael (ed.): *Routledge Encyclopedia of Language Teaching and Learning*. Routledge: New York 2002, 548–553.

Yee, Nicholas: "The Psychology of Massively Multi-user Online Roleplaying Games. Motivations, Emotional Investment, Relationships and Problematic Usage". In: Schroeder, R. & Axelsson, A. (eds.): *Avatars at Work and Play. Collaboration and Interaction in Shared Virtual Environments*. Springer-Verlag: London 2006, 187–207.

Zähres, Frederic: „"pentakill inc" – A Case Study of Shortening Processes in Ludolects". In: Brock, Alexander & Schildhauer, Peter (eds.): *Communication Forms and Communicative Practices. New Perspectives on Communication Forms, Affordances, and What Users Make of Them*. Peter Lang: Berlin, this volume, 89–109.

Ina Batzke

„*Der Gläserne Mensch*“ 2.0? Self-Tracking and the Quantified Self Movement as New Communicative Practices

Abstract While traditionally human beings used pen and paper to 'self-track' themselves, contemporary digital self-tracking uses wearable technology to record, analyze and share various pieces of personal data to discover previously unknown patterns and gain a quantitative insight into daily life. While in the beginning the focus of participants was on monitoring one's own health and fitness, soon the need grew to share and discuss the recorded data sets both online and offline. As a result, digital self-tracking was formalized as a social movement in 2007, when a blog eventually enabled makers and users to collaborate around the globe. The blog and its practices became known as the Quantified Self (QS) movement. In addition to self-monitoring and recording of data, the focus of participants of the movement has shifted towards a social and communicative dimension, as data is collected and discussed among peers and in social networks, blogs and chat rooms. After investigating the general human motives behind self-tracking, this article will conceptualize both traditional self-tracking and the concepts behind the QS movement as communicative practices, and thus reveal characteristic communicative differences between the factors involved in both.

1. Introduction: Tracking Oneself?

> I got up this morning at 6:10 a.m. after going to sleep at 12:45 a.m. I was awakened once during the night. My heart rate was 61 beats per minute – my blood pressure, 127 over 74. I had zero minutes of exercise yesterday, so my maximum heart rate during exercise wasn't calculated. I had about 600 milligrams of caffeine, zero of alcohol. And my score on the Narcissism Personality Index, or the NPI-16, is a reassuring 0.31. (Wolf 2010a: n.p.)[1]

This account given by technology-savvy journalist and Quantified Self (QS) founder Gary Wolf, presented during a 2010 TED talk on the QS movement, is probably the most convenient way to make the idea of 'self-tracking' graspable to an unfamiliar audience. Generally, self-tracking is defined as the "regular collection of any data that can be measured about the self such as biological, physical, behavioral or environmental information" (Swan 2009: 519). In today's context,

1 All quotes from blogs and other websites are reproduced in their original version and have not been edited.

self-tracking furthermore always stands in close relation to modern tracking technologies such as smartphone applications and wearable gadgets, which enable their users to simultaneously monitor, record, document and analyze multiple aspects of personal daily life. Clipped onto trouser pockets, worn on wristbands or hung from necklaces, such devices measure – among other things – how many steps one takes, how many stairs one climbs, how many hours one sleeps or what one's heart rate is.[2] In the majority of cases, the recorded data is subsequently synced to websites or mobile apps in which graphs are generated and daily averages are calculated.

Even though the degree to which users integrate self-tracking devices into their daily lives varies greatly, their increased general popularity is undisputed and they "seem[…] to constitute the 'new hype'" (Lomborg & Frandsen 2015: 1) in the versatile and fast-growing market of digital mobile services and technologies. A 2013 Pew Research Center survey on self-tracking practices found that seven in ten U.S. adults already self-track personal data, with "weight, diet or exercise routines [being] the most frequently tracked" (Fox & Duggan 2013: n.p.). While according to Fox and Duggan's study many Americans still use traditional methods such as pen and paper or spreadsheets for tracking, another study from 2014 estimates that one in ten Americans owns a technological device to track and subsequently record and share his or her personal data on a regular basis (cf. Rettberg 2014: 61). After the advent and continuous development of wearable computers and wireless communications, the idea of tracking oneself thus seems to have become the logical next step in the ever-increasing 'amalgamation' between technology and human beings.

Given this enhanced diffusion of self-tracking technologies, a refined understanding of this phenomenon and an evaluation of its potential for future processes becomes imperative. Self-tracking has accordingly already attracted much attention from both public opinion makers and researchers,[3] particularly due to its possible potential for "improving life conditions through preemptive action on health, and as a tool of user empowerment vis-à-vis health-care professionals and private and public institutions" (Lomberg & Frandsen 2015: 1). It has been considered for its innovativeness from a health and surveillance perspective (cf. Patrick et al. 2008;

2 A comprehensive list of possible measurement functions and the appropriate devices can be found in the Quantified Self Guide; it currently lists 505 tools, retrieved 18.09.2015, from http://www.quantifiedself.com/guide.

3 In the academic discourse on ways in which human beings can record, monitor and communicate specific features of their lives, "self-tracking" is also referred to as "self-logging", "personal analytics" or "personal informatics".

Swan 2009; Whitson 2013), and a rich body of literature is beginning to emerge that examines the social, cultural and political dimensions of the phenomenon of self-tracking.[4] Until now, however, there has been no sustained examination of the communicative importance of self-tracking and the QS movement, particularly with regard to the "spreading out of self-tracking cultures and practices from the purely personal into multiple social domains" (Lupton 2014a: 4).[5]

The processes involved in self-tracking are, however, obviously of a communicative nature. Although we naturally might not think of quantitative data in terms of communication,[6] a closer examination of modern digital self-tracking through a communicative lens immediately reveals that it comprises at least three communicative dimensions: Firstly, quantitative data sets are recorded and processed by an application and then communicated to the user (1st dimension). Secondly, self-tracking devices and applications forward the collected data sets to other users (2nd dimension). Eventually, the collected data is the means for further communicative processes such as discussions, chats and challenges (3rd dimension). It is particularly the presence or absence of the 2nd and 3rd dimension that, as will be shown, not only differentiates traditional self-tracking processes from the QS movement, but also has great influence on the communicative practice itself. After investigating the general human motives behind self-tracking, this article will therefore conceptualize both traditional self-tracking and the concepts behind the QS movement as communicative practices, reveal characteristic communicative differences between the factors involved in both and evaluate their potential for future (online) communication processes.

4 See, e.g., Lupton (2012a, 2013a, 2013b, 2014a), Nafus (2014), Nafus & Sherman (2014), Pantzar & Ruckenstein (2014), Ruckenstein (2014), and also Whitson (2013).

5 Lomborg & Frandsen's (2015) article "Self-tracking as communication" is the only available study that approaches self-tracking from a communication studies perspective. While it usefully conceptualizes self-tracking as a communicative phenomenon for the first time, it does not differentiate between self-tracking and the QS movement, even though – following the argumentation of this article – a clear differentiation is necessary, particularly when looking at the communicative features of both phenomena.

6 Following Jensen (2013) and Austin (1962), this article is based on the assumption that digital data are performative, i.e. both vehicles of information and sources of meaning that construct and act on reality, and thus can be understood as communication as well be communication.

2. Self-Tracking – A General Introduction

The slogan of the modern self-tracking community – 'self-knowledge through numbers'[7] – already hints at the general motivation of acquiring data on aspects of a person's daily life by means of technology: It goes beyond simply collecting data or "personal informatics" (cf. Elsden & Kirk 2015), in that the data is used to "reflect, learn, remember and [...] improve" (Wolf 2010a: n.p.). Monitoring features of one's life and reflecting upon them in the quest for self-knowledge are, however, not new cultural practices and have not always depended on technology. Traditional self-tracking practices, for example, include centuries-old strategies such as diary keeping or journaling. Already in the first century AD, the Roman philosopher Lucius Annaeus Seneca tracked "the food he ate and what he dreamt at night" (Weintraub 2013: n.p.). Similar self-tracking practices are also documented for the 15th and 16th century, where Sanctorius of Padua weighed himself for thirty years before and after meals to study the energy expended by a living organism. The most famous "early-selftracker" (Rettberg 2014: 10) is however probably the American Founding Father and polymath Benjamin Franklin: In Chapter IX of his autobiography, he presents his "Plan for Attaining Moral Perfection", for which he consistently recorded his performance on thirteen virtues, such as frugality, cleanliness and overindulgence, believing it would keep him virtuous. He tracked his process by using a little book with thirteen charts:

> I rul'd each page with red ink, so as to have seven columns, one for each day of the week, marking each column with a letter for the day. I cross'd these columns with thirteen red lines, marking the beginning of each line with the first letter of one of the virtues, on which line, and in its proper column, I might mark, by a little black spot, every fault I found upon examination to have been committed respecting that virtue upon that day. (Franklin, quoted in Bennett 1997: 277)

Naturally, his goal was to live as long as possible without having to put any marks on his chart. While initially he found himself putting more marks on the pages than he ever imagined, after a while he wrote in his autobiography he "had the satisfaction of seeing them diminish" (ibid.: 41).

Self-tracking thus certainly existed already well before the age of technology and its historical predecessors showcase many significant commonalities with contemporary practices: All self-trackers, whether historical or contemporary, apparently share a strong interest in knowing and recording, and believe firmly that 'knowledge' can be represented as numbers, graphs and statistics. The satisfaction

---

7 The slogan is, e.g., used as a sub-title in the logo of the QS collaboration, retrieved 18.09.2015, from http://www.quantifiedself.com.

in tracking one's data, which is particularly obvious in Franklin's journal, has survived and is still present in contemporary self-tracking practices: Still positing the truth in numbers, self-trackers believe that "gadgets can help them organize torrents of personal data that can help us turn us all into happier, healthier, wealthier and more productive human beings" (Hill 2011: n.p.). Interestingly, the data that is measured is also still similar to historical self-tracking data and focusses mainly on bodily functions: The common tracking domains of the most wide-spread applications, devices and projects are health, fitness, mood, location, efficiency and social behaviour. Finally, the quantification of the self also still shows significant "commonalities with the time-honoured tradition of journaling and the care of the self as an ethical practice of reflection detailed by Foucault (1988)" (Walz & Deterding 2015: 345).

What is, however, clearly different when it comes to digitized self-tracking is the complexity, the simultaneity, the precision and the amount of the data collected, as well as the ways in which it is presented back to the tracker. This only developed in the beginning of the twenty-first century,[8] with the advent of smartphone apps and wearable self-tracking monitors such as Apple Watch, Nike+, Pebble, Fitbit, Jawbone and QardioCore. Contrasting such new devices and their utilization to traditional self-tracking methods, it is firstly particularly the idea that technology can be a "neutral, objective observer that can alleviate the uncertainty of human perception" (Rettberg 2014: 74) that seems to be alluring to many modern self-trackers. Furthermore, instead of leaving it up to the tracker to decide what is worth recording, the tracking process is now automated, enabling incredibly precise details and thus larger data sets. Lastly, the now possible transfer of collected data to online services has added a social aspect to self-tracking that is in accordance with Web 2.0 trends and has led to another surge of interest in personal tracking and data analysis. Nowadays, users can select from a variety

8 According to Riphagen et al., the history of digitized self-tracking via wearable sensors in combination with wearable computing and wireless communication began in the 1970s, in the form of 'sousveillance'. In contrast to 'surveillance', 'sousveillance' means *to bring any means of observation down to the personal level*, "either physically (mounting cameras on people rather than on buildings), or hierarchically (ordinary people doing the watching, rather than higher authorities or architectures doing the watching)" (Mann 2012: n.p.). Sousveillance must, however, strictly be regarded as a countermovement to the "surveillance society" (Mann et al. 2003: 332), and recorded data only for the purpose of protest; neither the personal level nor a communicative level could be found in these early techniques.

of websites, apps and gadgets that serve as tools for self-quantifying – and that arguably convinces them to use self-tracking. As again stated by Gary Wolf:

> Millions of us track ourselves all the time, but something changes when we digitize this self monitoring. We step on a scale and record our weight. We balance a checkbook. We count calories. But when the familiar pen-and-paper methods of self-analysis are enhanced by sensors that monitor our behavior automatically, the process of self-tracking becomes both more alluring and more meaningful. Automated sensors do more than give us facts; they also remind us that our ordinary behavior contains obscure quantitative signals that can be used to inform our behavior, once we learn to read them. (Wolf 2010b: n.p.)

In short, the digitization of self-tracking and quantification has enabled new kinds of data accumulation and record keeping, "detailing and chronicling the minutiae of our lives at an unprecedented level of granularity" (Whitson 2013: 168). The process of gathering personal data is now automated and feedback can be received almost simultaneously. In addition to that, a connection of self-tracking gadgets to social media networks and the Internet allows users to share and transmit what was previously private and personal. It is particularly this added social and public dimension that differentiates what is defined as digitized self-tracking from the QS movement:

3. Self-Tracking vs. the Quantified Self Movement

In order to investigate self-tracking as a communicative practice, it is important to differentiate between the ways in which modern self-tracking devices are employed by users. A first important distinction is the scope in which self-tracking is utilized: While traditional self-trackers tended to collect data in only one or two dimensions of their lives and for a short time, technical advance now enables contemporary users to track countless phenomena and store them for longer periods. The general trend thus seems to grow towards tracking various data dimensions in order to triangulate results and gain a holistic measurement of one's body and behavior patterns. A second main distinction lies in the motivation behind self-tracking: In general, more and more self-trackers do not only collect data about themselves as a way of recording and remembering characteristics of their daily lives, but take an approach which is more specifically goal-oriented, seeking to "reflect on and make meaning out of the information they choose to collect" (Lupton 2014a: 3). After data collection, self-tracking practices therefore "typically incorporate organization, analysis, interpretation and representation of the data (such as producing statistics or graphs and other data visualisations) to make sense of them, and efforts to determine how these data can offer insights for the user's life" (ibid.).

Apart from such a trend towards triangulation and an increased goal-orientation, the most important distinction, however, revolves around the question of whether self-tracking devices are implemented not only in the private, but also in the public sphere: While many self-trackers use the data only for themselves and understand self-tracking as an intimate practice, others have started to exchange and discuss it with other users – such self-trackers usually describe themselves as participants in the QS movement. As it is particularly this distinction between private and communal[9] or QS self-tracking that is highly relevant when looking at self-tracking as a communicative practice, both practices and their respective differences will be characterized briefly:

3.1. Private Self-Tracking

Private self-tracking relates to "self-tracking practices that are taken up voluntarily as part of the quest for self-knowledge and self-optimisation and as an often pleasurable and playful mode of selfhood" (Lupton 2014b: n.p.). When self-tracking is portrayed or advertised in the media, this mode is often the one presented, "with regular references to the 'narcissism' or 'self-experimentation' that self-tracking supposedly involves" (Lupton 2013a: n.p.).[10] The private self-tracking mode is also often articulated when the general self-tracking phenomenon is defined: The Oxford English Dictionary for example defines "self-tracking" as

> [t]he practice of systematically recording information about one's diet, health, or activities, typically by means of a smartphone, so as to discover behavioural patterns that may be adjusted to help improve one's physical or mental well-being. ("self-tracking")

For the general public, private self-tracking can therefore be understood as the underlying or primal concept of self-tracking in general. Accordingly, the phenomenon of self-tracking is often equated with private self-tracking also in the scholarly literature. While there are in general only few explicit definitions of

---

9 The terms 'private' and 'communal' were first used by Deborah Lupton, who presents a total of five self-tracking modes in her paper called "Self-tracking modes: Reflexive self-monitoring and data practices" at the *Imminent citizenships: Personhood and identity politics in the informatic age,* workshop on 27 August 2014 in Canberra.

10 In a June 2014 announcement, Apple's Senior Vice President of Software Engineering Craig Federighi, for example, introduced the new app Health by bragging how it would "monitor all of *your* metrics that *you're* most interested in" (Federighi, quoted in Eveleth 2014: n.p., my emphasis, I.B.).

self-tracking, the ones which are, in fact, available study self-tracking as "a practice of collecting, accumulating and making visible everyday habits and bodily reactions in order to reflect upon and regulate these" (Lomborg & Frandsen 2015: 2–3; also cf. Choe et al. 2014; Ruckenstein 2014; Swan 2009). Focusing often on personal health management, the research literature thus neglects dimensions of self-tracking that go beyond a private practice and self-optimisation.

Research investigating the motives of self-trackers in general has indeed found that many are involved in self-tracking for private and personal reasons. According to the 2014 Pew Research Center study, only 34 per cent of trackers share their data or notes with another person or group, either online or offline (Fox & Duggan 2013: n.p.). This correlates with another study by Li et al. (2010), who found that reasons for engaging in self-tracking were "natural curiosity, interest in data, discovery of new tools, suggestion from another person, and trigger events" (2010: 560), such as problems in relationships, weight or sleep patterns.[11] For all private self-trackers, the emphasis on personal experience is thus the common denominator. The incentive for self-tracking is to utilize the data one collects to optimize and improve one's life and eventually achieve self-awareness. The 'knowledge' contained in the collected data is understood as enabling private self-trackers to "achieve better health, higher quality sleep, greater control over mood swings, improved management of chronic conditions, less stress, increased work productivity, [or] better relationships with others" (Lupton 2014a: 6). Private self-tracking is motivated and undertaken for purely personal reasons. Accordingly, the tracked data is mostly kept private.

3.2. Communal Self-Tracking or the Quantified Self Movement

While self-tracking, if only on account of the 'self' in its name, is thus often conceptualized as an individualistic or private practice, the advent of wireless communication has added another dimension to its conceptualization: its connection to Social Media and the World Wide Web. Many of the contemporary self-tracking devices let users share their progress, location or other captured data, either on established Social Media platforms such as Facebook, Twitter and

11 Li et al. (2010) differentiate between three distinct groups of private self-trackers: The first group monitors mainly health-related data such as food consumption, physical activity, weight or mood patterns. A second group tracks work-related data, such as productivity and cognitive performance. A third group is comprised of trackers who are eager to find new life experiences through self-tracking and who are mainly involved in experimenting with the data recorded.

Instagram, or via newly-created online forums and applications. Many tools have established their own social medium where users can add friends, share their data, and communicate with and challenge other users. As a result, people share self-tracking data about themselves with other users on a daily basis, and "many self-trackers view themselves as part of a community of trackers" (Lupton 2014: 8; also cf. Boesel 2013; Lupton 2013a; Nafus & Sherman 2014; Rooksby et al. 2014).

The most public face of communal self-tracking is the QS website (http://www.quantifiedself.com). This community of self-trackers was founded in 2007 by Gary Wolf and Kevin Kelly of *Wired* magazine. Indeed, particularly Gary Wolf has contended from the beginning that self-tracking need not be a purely individualistic enterprise:

> [...] self-tracking culture is not particularly individualistic. In fact, there is a strong tendency among self-trackers to share data and collaborate on new ways of using it. (Wolf 2009: n.p.)

He continues by stating that "[t]he excitement in the self-tracking movement right now comes not just from the lure of learning things from one's own numbers but also from the promise of contributing to a new type of knowledge, using this tool we all build" (ibid.).

In the beginning, the key component of this 'movement' was particularly the QS website where participants can engage with and learn from other self-trackers. Over time, however, other websites and blogs were created that recycled the QS excitement and also connected self-trackers in a social and public sphere. In general, it can thus be stated that the drive towards 'sharing your numbers' in contrast to pure '(self-) knowledge through numbers' matches the overall interest in content creation and sharing personal details and experiences with others "that underpins many activities on Web 2.0 social media platforms" (Luton 2014: 8; also cf. Beer 2013; John 2013). The focus on personal motivation and individual benefit, which has been described as typical of the private self-tracking practice, is, however, also still apparent in communal self-tracking practices. While the name of the movement alone, Quantified *Self*, again refers to this private dimension, the community "largely refers to [...] learning from others' data or self-tracking or data visualisation methods *so that one's own data project may be improved*" (ibid., my emphasis, I.B.). The QS movement is, therefore, sometimes also referred to as "Quantified Us" (cf. Jordan & Pfarr 2014: n.p.), as a way of emphasizing how data produced by self-trackers may be usefully incorporated into large data sets to "get more meaning out of our data" (Ramirez 2013: n.p.). Even the conceptualization of "Quantified Us", however, still focuses firmly on a private agenda, as the pooled data should be used to further one's own interests and goals (cf. Luton 2014: 8).

To conclude, in contrast to private self-tracking, communal or QS self-tracking involves a drive towards sharing and discussing private data sets with other users, and thus contains a stronger social or communicative dimension than private self-tracking.

4. Self-Tracking and the QS Movement as Communicative Practices

After this introduction on both historical and contemporary executions of self-tracking has clearly pointed to distinct differences between various practices, the remainder of this article will now conceptualize traditional, private and communal/QS self-tracking as successive, but incommensurable communicative practices. In order to gain a first fundamental understanding of the communicative factors involved in self-tracking, it indeed makes sense to go back to Lucius Annaeus Seneca, Sanctorius of Padu and Benjamin Franklin, and thus the 'diary-like' historical form of self-tracking: Looking at the medium – communication form – genre trias as presented in the opening article (Brock & Schildhauer, this volume), one would probably intuitively allocate traditional self-tracking 'diaries' to *communication form*, as it arose out of a "technical constellation" (Schildhauer 2016: 30) that is indeed remarkably similar to that of writing a personal letter: The *medium* pencil and paper enabled the use of the *semiotic system* of the alphabetic writing system, which taken together enabled diary-like self-tracking as one of the many semiotic potentials this technical constellation has in the first place. While medium and semiotic system are thus the same for personal letter and diary-like self-tracking, the other two factors that comprise the communication form differ significantly: *potentially*, private self-tracking could have been 1:many and distant communication. In contrast to the personal letter, which resulted from distant 1:1 or 1:many communication, cultural practice and conventions however led Seneca, Sanctorius and Franklin to opt for a diary like form, as the diary has traditionally been understood as a daily record that is kept *private*. The genre patterns of the diary, then, restricted the initial potential (it was not fully exploited) and rather drove the self-trackers to opt for private communication (which was still distant – in a temporal way).

In conclusion, particularly conventional provisions were the organizing, if not determining force that specified the communicative factors involved in diary-like self-tracking:

Figure 1: Traditional, Diary-like Self-Tracking

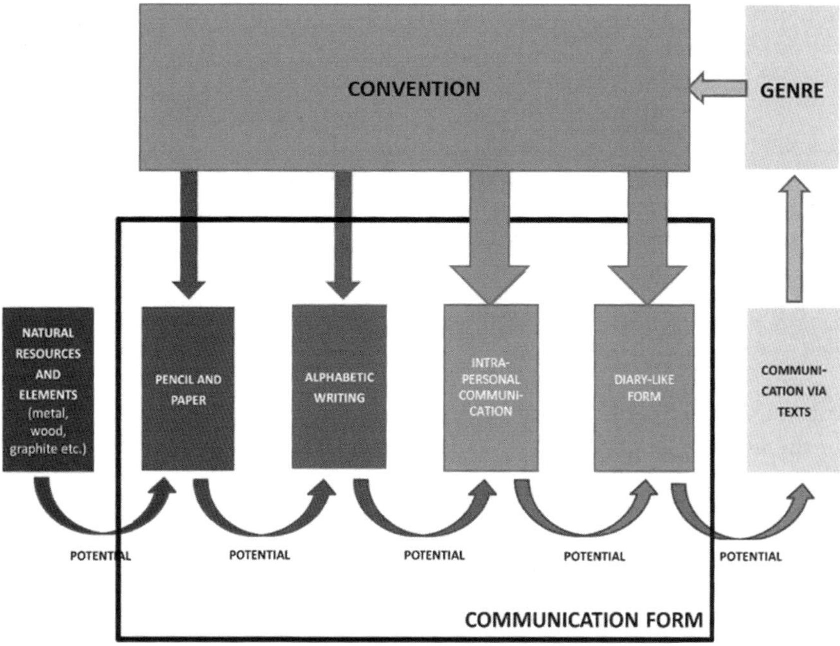

Starting off from this conceptualization of traditional self-tracking, it is now possible to trace how the introduction of new 'tools' – in this case the digitization of self-tracking – influenced this traditional communicative practice and the composition of the communication form. Conceptualization of both private and communal / QS self-tracking are here based on one premise: Self-tracking technologies and devices are defined as *media* and thus replace pen and pencil. In contrast to pen and pencil, and also dependent on the particular type of device, they accordingly enable a diverse but interrelated set of potentials, including

- the accumulation of a tracking log into a digital system,
- the possibility of interacting with analysis features that are integrated into the interface of the tracking device,
- the sharing of tracking activities and communicating about self-tracking with others.

These activities are central for the following conceptualizations as they are fundamentally communicative, although in very different ways, representing at once processes of conveying information about oneself to others and to a system, of constituting and performing oneself, and of upholding a set of social relations in a particular way. While the third bullet point only becomes relevant when considering communal self-tracking activities, the other two potentials are also relevant when conceptualizing 'private' self-tracking as a communicative practice.

Contrasting 'private' self-tracking to traditional, non-digitized self-tracking, it is firstly notable that modern self-tracking technologies and devices comprise software and specific programming for data tracking that not only *enable* the semiotic system, situational factors and genre patterns, but indeed *specify* and determine all these factors.[12] When one, e.g., tracks a run, the self-tracking device 'responds' to the bit trail and makes sense of the data. The data points collected on pace and geo-location are processed and selected by the system. Then the system determines the semiotic system for its output, e.g. layout, text size, parameters, visualization type etc. Ranging from general numeric plots of exercise activity over an extended period to more fine-grained visualization of, for instance, routes or the user's pulse during one exercise session, different devices offer different outputs of the accumulated input. The visualizations and tracking methods offered by self-tracking devices thus function as a mirror for the self, a means of communicating with the self, which is however not created by the self, but by a system – in stark contrast to traditional diary-like self-tracking methods. While one device might offer several sets of potentials a user can choose from, programming indeed leads to a "much narrower set of potentials than in the case of pencil and paper" (Brock & Schildhauer this volume: 35).

The same observation can only be confirmed when looking at the next dimension, the situational factors: With private self-tracking devices that do not understand self-tracking as a social activity, communication is always 1:1 (system to user). Taking up once again the example of tracking a run, the user firstly 'speak[s]' into the system (cf. Jensen 2013), which then imprints the activities as digital bit trails and feeds those back to the user. Notably, it seems that the social convention that self-tracking is a highly intimate activity has still influenced the make-up of private self-tracking devices, even though the technical medium has taken over most of the factors:

---

12 Seen through a communicative lens, modern self-tracking technologies devices are to traditional, diary-like self-tracking what Twitter or Facebook messaging are to the personal letter.

Figure 2: 'Private' Self-Tracking

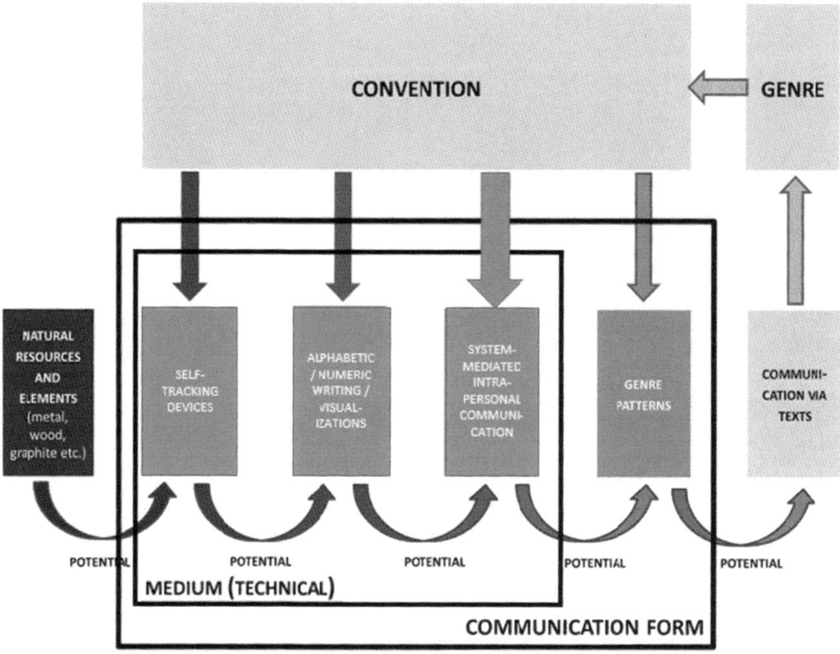

Fully neglecting the social convention that self-tracking is a private activity indeed only occurred with the transition from private to communal / QS self-tracking. Since the advent of the QS movement in 2007, self-tracking devices and technologies such as Endomondo, Garmin Connect, Strava or Apple+ have embedded key functionalities from social media for networking, sharing, liking and commenting that are further shaped by the users' communicative practices online. These advancements of the *medium* involved in communal / QS self-tracking have accordingly also influenced the structure of the associated communication form. It seems that communal / QS self-tracking technologies have fully pushed back the force and importance of the social convention that self-tracking is a private affair, and instead have extended its influence on the communication form as a whole: While particularly social conventions determined the communication form of the traditional self-tracking and still had an influence on digitized but private self-tracking, now it is the medium itself which is not only a factor in the communication form, but it "encompasses the majority of factors which make up the communication form" (Brock & Schildhauer this volume: 34):

Figure 3: Communal or QS Self-Tracking

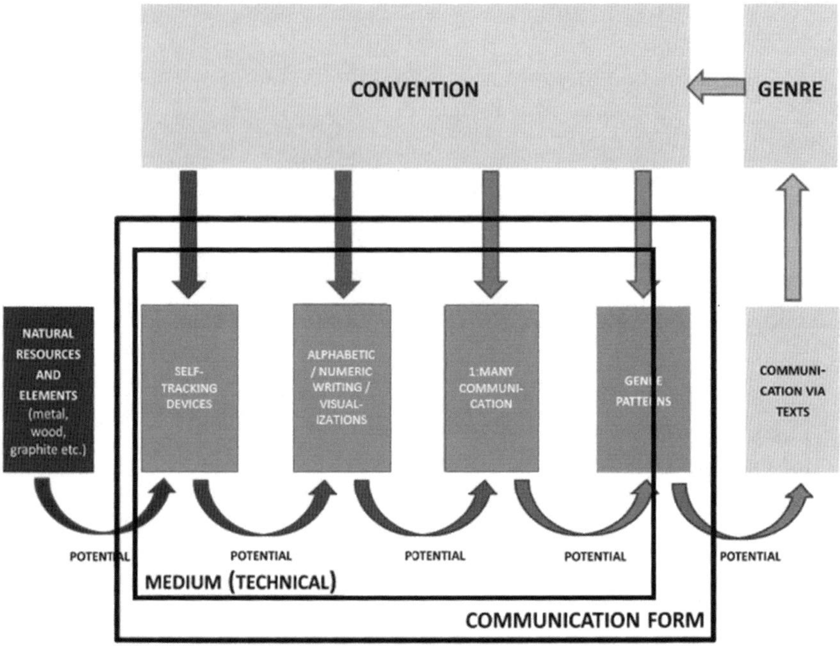

Under the lens of sociality, communal self-tracking in the context of the QS movement has predominantly become a means of achieving a common social practice and a shared understanding of the situation at hand, "of maintaining social order and thus finding meaning and pleasure in a sense of belonging" (cf. Carey 1992; Vordere et al. 2006). That is to say, the practice of communicating with others implies an ongoing negotiation of what is appropriate, relevant and expected to be communicated in a given context and with a given set of people. Instead of only communicating data back to the creator, self-tracking devices now not only enable but encourage communication to other users. It is therefore particularly the situational factor in the technical constellation which marks progress from private to communal / QS self-tracking: Influenced by the technical medium, it has changed from a system-mediated intrapersonal form to 1:many communication. In the process, the traditional notion of the private aspect of self-tracking has been further backgrounded and seems to not influence the communicative form of self-tracking any more. Quite on the contrary, the traditional convention of self-tracking as a private activity has been challenged by the idea that self-tracking may very well be a public activity, which in turn might become a convention over time.

What can be traced in these three conceptualizations of self-tracking as a communicative practice is thus a mutating degree of influence that both medium and conventions have on the communication form and practice as a whole. While traditional self-tracking processes were highly dependent on social conventions that understood recording one's own data as something private, the digitization of self-tracking – and thus the introduction of a technical medium into the process – had a noteworthy impact on all other factors of the communication form: Even though being conventionally understood as a private affair, it seems that new self-tracking technologies (*media*) not only converted self-tracking into a 1:many communication process, but also enlarged its influence on the actual output in many ways: Self-tracking devices determine where the data can be shared, what can be commented on and what form communication should assume (e.g. Likes, Shares, Comments, Challenges). Moving from private, digitized self-tracking to communal / QS self-tracking, the factor *media* hence amplified its influence on the other factors, instead of merely enabling them. At the latest with communal / QS self-tracking, the technical medium has taken over the influence that *conventions* have on the communication form.

5. Conclusion and Outlook

Following this argumentation and conceptualization of self-tracking as a communicative practice, both in its traditional and contemporary facets, the development from a conventional, non-technological activity to a highly medium-mediated, restricted practice connects remarkably well to the idea that media increasingly shape and frame the communicative processes and discourses of personal and public communication. It seems that the introduction of modern technology into a communication process that is conventionally understood as private and interpersonal can change its form to a public, 1:many communication. This is indeed in line with other observations about contemporary technologically-mediated communication practices. Within the last two decades, many users of online services have become accustomed to sharing a certain level of private information: Personal communication through Facebook, Twitter or other social media website seems to become less and less about 1:1 communication, but now involves the sharing of private photos, statuses, and likes that are communicated 1:many (cf. Marche 2012). Also other activities that were formerly considered 'private' are nowadays openly discussed online, may they be medical conditions, banking operations or sexual preferences. Standard personal information, such as full name, date of birth, phone number, address, password etc., is stored without questioning with online service providers. It seems that users have come to accept this as a trade-off to using online services in the first place.

The shift of influence away from social conventions to online opportunities thus seems to determine 21st century communication practices. Notably, this hypothesis seems to be valid not only for online, but also for offline lifestyles: Communal self-tracking in the form of QS has recently spread from a pure online movement to include meet-ups or conferences offline, where self-trackers engage face-to-face with others. Such 'QS meetings' have spread internationally to include "more than 100 groups in 30 countries with approximately 20,000 participants" (Nafus & Shermann 2014: 1787). Following this development, it indeed seems valid to propose that self-tracking in its evolution from traditional to communal is an perfect example of how media become increasingly important for "the construction of everyday life, society and culture as a whole" (Krotz 2009: 24), both online and offline.

References

ABIResearch: *Wearable Computing Technologies*, retrieved 18.09.2015, from https://www.abiresearch.com/market-research/product/1015644-wearable-computing-technologies/.

Austin, John Langshaw: *How to Do Things with Words*. Clarendon Press: Oxford 1962.

Beer, David: *Popular Culture and New Media. The Politics of Circulation*. Palgrave Macmillan: Houndmills 2013.

Bennett, William John: *Our Sacred Honour. Words of Advice from the Founders in Stories, Letters, Poems, and Speeches*. Simon & Schuster: New York 1997.

Boesel, Whitney Erin: *What Is the Quantified Self Now?*, retrieved 11.03.2015, from http://thesocietypages.org/cyborgology/2013/05/22/what-is-the-quantified-self-now/#more-15719.

Brock, Alexander & Schildhauer, Peter: "Communication Form. A Concept Revisited". In: Brock, Alexander & Schildhauer, Peter (eds.): *Communication Forms and Communicative Practices. New Perspectives on Communication Forms, Affordances, and What Users Make of Them*. Peter Lang: Berlin, this volume 13–43.

Buchanan, Kathryn & Lockton, Dan: *Understanding Human Connectivity and the Quantified Self. Working Papers of the Sustainable Network*, retrieved 29.08.2015, from http://research.danlockton.co.uk/Understanding%20human%20connectivity%20and%20the%20Quantified%20Self%20-%20Buchanan%20and%20Lockton.pdf.

Burger, Harald: *Mediensprache. Eine Einführung in Sprache und Kommunikationsformen der Massenmedien. Mit einem Beitrag von Martin Luginbühl.* de Gruyter: Berlin & New York 2005.

Carey, James W.: *Communication as Culture. Essays on Media and Society*. Routledge: New York 1992.

Christakis, Nicholas A. & Fowler, James H.: *Connected. The Surprising Power of Our Social Networks and How They Shape Our Lives*. Little, Brown and Company: New York 2011.

Choe, Eun Kyoung et al.: *Understanding Quantified-selfers' Practices in Collecting and Exploring Personal Data*, retrieved 29.08.2015, from https://faculty.ist.psu.edu/choe/download/CHI-2014-Choe-QuantifiedSelf.pdf.

Dürscheid, Christa: „Medienkommunikation im Kontinuum von Mündlichkeit und Schriftlichkeit. Theoretische und empirische Probleme". *Zeitschrift für Angewandte Linguistik* 38, 2013, 37–56.

Dürscheid, Christa: „Netzsprache – ein neuer Mythos". In: Beißwenger, Michael & Hoffmann, Ludger & Storrer, Angelika (eds.): *Internetbasierte Kommunikation. Themenheft der Osnabrücker Beiträge zur Sprachtheorie* 68: Duisburg 2004, 141–157.

Dürscheid, Christa: „Medien, Kommunikationsformen, kommunikative Gattungen". *Linguistik Online* 22, 2005, S. 3–16.

Elsden, Chris & Kirk, Dave S.: "A Quantified Past: Remembering with Personal Informatics". *Proceedings of the 2014 Companion Publication on Designing Interactive Systems*. ACM: New York 2014, 45–48.

Eveleth, Rose: *How Self-Tracking Apps Exclude Women*, retrieved 11.03.2016, from http://www.theatlantic.com/technology/archive/2014/12/how-self-tracking-apps-exclude-women/383673/.

Fox, Susannah & Duggan, Maeve: *Tracking for Health*, retrieved 29.08.2016, from http://www.pewinternet.org/2013/01/28/tracking-for-health/.

Hill, Kashmir: *Adventures in Self-Surveillance, aka the Quantified Self, aka Extreme Navel-gazing*, retrieved 11.03.2016, from http://www.forbes.com/sites/kashmirhill/2011/ 04/07/adventures-in-self-surveillance-aka-the-quantified-self-aka-extreme-navel-gazing/.

Jensen, Kim B.: "How to Do Things with Data. Meta-Data, Meta-Media, and Meta-Communication". *First Monday* 18(10), 2013, n.p., retrieved 20.05.2016, from DOI 10.5210/fm.v18i10.4870.

John, Nicholas A.: "Sharing and Web 2.0. The Emergence of a Keyword". *New Media & Society* 15(2), 2012, 167–182, retrieved 29.08.2016, from DOI 10.1177/1461444812450684.

Jordan, Matthew & Pfarr, Nikki: *Forget the Quantified Self. We Need to Build the Quantified Us*, retrieved 11.03.2016, from http://www.wired.com/2014/04/forget-the-quantified-self-we-need-to-build-the-quantified-us/.

Krotz, Friedrich: "Mediatization. A Concept with which to Grasp Media and Societal Change". In: Lundby, Knut (ed.): *Mediatization*. Peter Lang: New York 2009, 21–40.

Li, Ian & Dey et al.: "A Stage-Based Model of Personal Informatics Systems". *Proceedings of the SIGCHI Conference on Human Factors in Computing Systems*. CHI: Atlanta 2010, 557–566.

Lomborg, Stine & Frandsen, Kirsten: "Self-Tracking as Communication". *Information, Communication & Society* 19(7), 2015, 1–14.

Lupton, Deborah: *Self-Tracking Modes. Reflexive Self-Monitoring and Data Practices*, retrieved 29.08.2016, from DOI 10.2139/ssrn.2483549.

Mann, Steve: "Eye am a Camera: Surveillance and Sousveillance in the Glassage". *Time* 2 Nov. 2012, retrieved 11.03.2016, from http://techland.time.com/2012/11/02/eye-am-a-camera-surveillance-and-sousveillance-in-the-glassage/.

Mann, Steve et al.: "Sousveillance. Inventing and Using Wearable Computing Devices for Data Collection in Surveillance Environments". *Surveillance & Society* 1(3), 2013, 331–355, retrieved 29.08.2016, from http://www.surveillance-and-society.org/articles1(3)/sousveillance.pdf.

Marche, Stephen: *Is Facebook Making Us Lonely*, retrieved 29.08.2016, from http://www.theatlantic.com/magazine/archive/2012/05/is-facebook-making-us-lonely/308930/.

Nafus, Dawn & Sherman, Jamie: "This one Does not Go up to 11: The Quantified Self Movement as an Alternative Big Data Practice". *International Journal of Communication* 8, 2014, 1785–1794, retrieved 29.08.2016, from http://ijoc.org/index.php/ijoc/article/viewFile/2170/1157.

Patrick, Kevin et al.: "Health and the Mobile Phone". *American Journal of Preventative Medicine* 35(2), 2008, 177–181, retrieved 29.08.2016, from DOI 10.1016/j.amepre.2008.05.001.

Ramirez, Ernesto: *How Can We Get more Meaning out of Our Data?*, retrieved 11.03.2016, from http://quantifiedself.com/2013/08/how-can-we-get-more-meaning-out-of-our-data/.

Rettberg, Jill Walker: *Seeing Ourselves through Technology*. Palgrave Macmillan: New York 2014.

Robertsson, Lukas: *Quantified Self: An Overview & the Development of a Universal Tracking Application*. (Master's Thesis) University of Umea: Umea, Sweden 2014.

Rooksby, John et al.: "Personal Tracking as Lived Informatics". *Proceedings of the 32nd Annual ACM Conference on Human Factors in Computing Systems*. CHI: Toronto 2014, 1163–1172.

Ruckenstein, Minna: "Visualized and Interacted Life. Personal Analytics and Engagements with Data Doubles". *Societies* 4(1), 2014, 68–84, retrieved 29.08.2016, from DOI 10.3390/soc4010068.

Schmitz, Ulrich: *Sprache in modernen Medien. Einführung in Tatsachen und Theorien, Themen und Thesen*. Erich Schmidt Verlag: Berlin 2004.

"self-tracking, n." Def. 1. Oxford Dictionaries Online, OED, n.d., retrieved 28.09.2015, from http://www.oxforddictionaries.com/definition/english/self-tracking.

Swan, Melanie: "Emerging Patient-Driven Health Care Models. An Examination of Health Social Networks, Consumer Personalized Medicine and Quantified Self-Tracking". *International Journal of Environmental Research and Public Health IJERPH* 6(2), 2009, 492–525.

Swan, Melanie: "Sensor Mania! The Internet of Things, Wearable Computing, Objective Metrics, and the Quantified Self 2.0". *JSAN Journal of Sensor and Actuator Networks* 1(3), 2012, 217–53.

Vorderer, Peter et al.: "Motivation". In: Bryant, Jennings & Vorderer, Peter (eds.): *Psychology of Entertainment. Lawrence Erlbaum Associates Publishers*: London 2006, 3–18.

Walz, Steffen P. & Deterding, Sebastian: *The Gameful World. Approaches, Issues, Applications*. The MIT Press: London 2015.

Weintraub, Karen: "Quantified Self. The Tech-Based Route to a Better Life?", retrieved 11.03.2016, from http://www.bbc.com/future/story/20130102-self-track-route-to-a-better-life.html.

Whitson, Jennifer R.: "Gaming the Quantified Self". *Surveillance & Society* 11(1/2), 2013, 163–176, retrieved 29.08.2016, from http://ojs.library.queensu.ca/index.php/surveillance-and-society/article/view/gaming/gaming.

Wolf, Gary: "The Quantified Self." TED. Lecture. 2010a.

Wolf, Gary: "The Data-Driven Life". New York Times, 2010b, retrieved 11.03.2016, from http://www.nytimes.com/2010/05/02/magazine/02self-measurement-t.html?_r=1&pagewanted=al.

Communication Forms and Their Use from a Diachronic Perspective

Peter Schildhauer

Changing Potentials and their Use: The Case of Blogs

Abstract This paper investigates the development of selected potentials provided by the blog communication form (chronology, participant structure, embedding images and widgets) from the beginnings of blogging in the late 1990s to 2012. This diachronic perspective reveals that the potentials of the blog communication form did not develop along the lines of a steady increase; particularly the advent of blog systems around 2000 entailed significant restrictions to the bloggers using them. By drawing on an analysis of the diachronic blog corpus DIABLOC, the potentials are contrasted with their actual use in the personal weblog, the prototypical blog genre. The comparison shows that there are often immense discrepancies that suggest complex interrelations between potential and use.

1. Introduction

If those websites of the late 1990s that explicitly called themselves *weblog* are to be included in our survey, then blogging as a communicative practice looks back on a tradition of roughly 20 years. During this time, a number of medial innovations have occurred. One of the most important of these developments was certainly the spread of blog software around the beginning of the new millennium, mainly led by *Blogger*.[1] Until then, blogs (or *weblogs*, to be precise) had mostly been coded by hand; the authors had known HTML and updated the source code of their website with every new post. The principal task of early blog software was to relieve blog authors of the business of coding. However, it is apparent that blog software today wants to do more than that. In 2015, for instance, *WordPress* released its 4.2 version with a "new and improved Press This" feature, promising: "Sharing your favourite videos, images, and content has never been this fast or this easy." Users are encouraged to "make sure the theme looks great" with a *Customizer* tool and to try out "more intuitive" plugins, among other features.[2] There appears to be a tremendous growth of possibilities along the lines of *faster – better – new*. These observations lead to the key questions of this article:

1 Blogger was launched in August 1999 and had a decisive impact. It was, however, not the first blog software available, as blogging pioneer Dave Winer, for instance, had already released the software *Frontier* (see Schildhauer 2016: 73).

2 https://codex.wordpress.org/Version_4.2 (last access 15 March 2016).

(1) To what extent can we describe these developments as a steady expansion of possibilities – towards an *anything goes*?
(2) To what extent are these potentials typically used on blogs – or, in other words: *Everything done*?

Besides these empirical questions, I would like to pursue another, more principal one here:

(3) What do the results of (1) and (2) tell us about the theoretical concepts of *communication form* and *communicative practice*, which are at the centre of this volume?

The following section introduces the background, both theoretical and methodological, of this article. Section 3 contrasts selected potentials and their use in personal weblogs and section 4 discusses these results in the light of questions (1) to (3).

2. Background

2.1. Blog Communication Form

In contrasting communicative potentials and their use, questions (1) and (2) directly lead to the concepts that are at the core of this volume: communication form and communicative practice. This article follows the conceptualisation of *communication form* that Brock & Schildhauer suggest:[3]

> Communication forms typically answer communicative needs. They are factors which influence the *form* of the *communication*, and they arise out of human practice. They are clusters of technical and communicative constellations with certain potentials, which are commonly restricted by conventions. (Brock & Schildhauer, this volume: 32)

Using the example of *Twitter*, the authors suggest that computer hardware, general software and the *Twitter* software play a decisive role in this "cluster of technical and communicative constellations". The blog communication form is digital just as *Twitter*. However, it is (a) more complex and (b) more diverse.

Considering (a), complexity of the blog communication form, I have shown elsewhere (Schildhauer 2016: 95) that several layers should be taken into account:

3 For this reason, I will skip the conventional overview of research on that concept here, and refer the interested reader to Brock & Schildhauer (this volume) for a critical discussion of several research strands dealing with the communication form concept.

Figure 1: Complexity of the Blog Communication Form

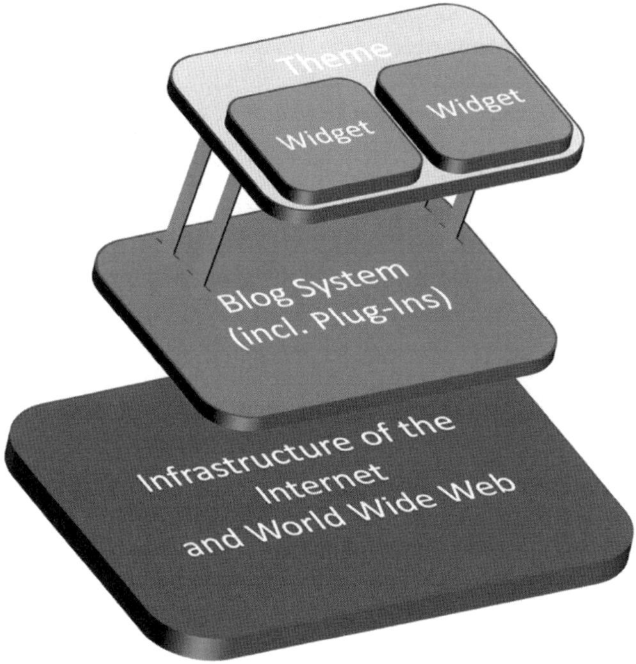

Those early weblogs mentioned above that were coded by hand made use of the first layer only (infrastructure and World Wide Web). If authors use specific blog systems such as *Blogger*, *WordPress* and others, then this constitutes a second layer based on the first one. *Blog system* is used here to denote certain platforms that influence the way blogs are created in various ways, e.g. by the amount of server space each user is offered and the extent to which additional modules such as plug-ins and widgets can be implemented. Most importantly, blog systems provide a specific *blog software,* a software package for creating and managing web-based content with a pronounced focus on blogs.

The third layer takes into account that most blog software works with prefabricated *templates* or *themes* that provide specific potentials concerning the design of the blog. As some *themes* modify the interface of the underlying blog-software, layer 3 may exert an influence on layer 2. Finally, the *theme*-layer often determines to what extent *widgets* can be implemented (layer 4), which enrich the functionality of the blog by, for instance, displaying the author's latest *tweets* in the sidebar.

Sufficient programming skills provided, a blog could be maintained with the author resorting to layer 1 only, of course. In fact, blogger Rebecca Blood stated in 2004: "And me? I still handcode my site, though doing so is more difficult to justify with each new technological advance." (2004: 55) Other bloggers might (also today) use blog software but refrain from implementing widgets, for instance. Therefore, Figure 1 displays the degree of complexity that the blog communication form can maximally *take* if all the potentials provided are used.

As far as (b), diversity, is concerned, there is a vast number of blog systems to be taken into account: *Blogger*, *Tumblr*, *WordPress.com* and *WordPress.org*, *TypePad*, *LiveJournal* and *MovableType* are just a few of the more common providers of blog software. The picture gets more diverse with a diachronic perspective because blog systems which are outdated or not in use anymore such as *pMachine*, *Greymatter*, *Frontier* and *Radio Userland* have to be included as well. All of these systems provide a solution for blogging without a need for knowledge of HTML, but they may also differ in the potentials they provide concerning, for instance, interaction with other blogs, privacy options etc. (Schildhauer 2016: 73). In order to make statements about potentials and their use in blogging, it is, therefore, necessary to abstract away from this heterogeneity and offer a description of shared or rather general features. In Schildhauer (2016: 74), I have suggested one way of doing so by grouping blog systems in terms of how accessible they are to lay bloggers (see Figure 2).

Figure 2: Blog Systems along the Accessibility Scale

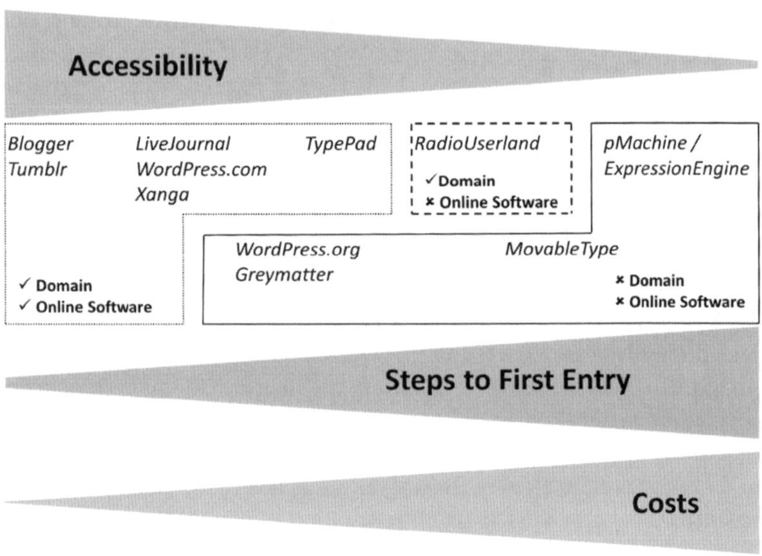

Highly accessible systems such as *Blogger* and *WordPress.com*

- offer online software (no download necessary),
- provide a domain (e.g. *example.wordpress.com*) and server space (storage space for the blog and associated files),
- are free of charge[4] and
- offer a quick way to the first post (only 5 steps for *Tumblr*).

Usually, this grouping according to accessibility coincides with common potentials that are offered by the respective blog systems during a certain period of blog history. In the following sections, therefore, this dimension of accessibility will provide a reasonable degree of abstraction from the actual range of blog systems that still allows for detailed descriptions of potentials and their use.

In sum, whenever I refer to the *blog communication form* in this article, I denote an abstraction concerning the wide range of blog systems and, usually, also concerning the (potential) complexity of the communication form outlined above.

2.2. The Genre Personal Weblog and the Diachronic Blog Corpus

A similar abstraction is needed when the actual use of the potentials provided by the blog communication form is investigated: Blogging as a practice has established many different forms such as personal blogging,[5] corporate blogging,[6] science / research blogging[7] and many more. Here, I will focus on personal blogging as the prototypical blogging practice (Mauranen 2013: 7).

In doing so, I take a *genre* perspective as defined in Brock & Schildhauer (this volume): Genre is an abstraction from actual communicative practice, a grouping of texts according to certain similarities. There is a consensus among text and media linguists that these groupings exhibit a prototypical structure with more and less typical members of a genre category.[8] Genres acquire labels by the communities dealing with them.[9]

Blog itself constitutes such a label and is often used as an umbrella term for the blogging practices (or rather, the visible results of these practices) listed above. This label is a clipping from *weblog*, a compound of *web* and *logbook*, which was

4 Some accessible systems such as *WordPress.com* are free for some basic functionalities but charge their users for additional options and plugins.

5 See, e.g., Lomborg (2009, 2014); Schildhauer (2013, 2014, 2016).

6 See Puschmann (2010).

7 See, e.g., Efimova (2009); Fritz (2011); Mauranen (2013); Puschmann & Mahrt (2012).

8 See, e.g., Brock (2013); Luginbühl (2014); Sandig (2000).

9 See, e.g., Miller (1984); Miller & Shepherd (2004, 2009); Luginbühl (2014).

coined by Jorn Barger in 1997 to characterise his own website and which was soon extended to denote other sites that also presented dynamic content in a reverse chronological order. While these *weblogs* overwhelmingly presented commented lists of hyperlinks from the growing World Wide Web, the focus shifted somewhat to sharing and reflecting on personal experiences in the years around the millennium. These sites were soon labelled *personal weblog* – a new genre category was born (Schildhauer 2016: 251).

My analysis of the personal weblog genre is based on a diachronic blog corpus (DIABLOC). It was compiled manually by use of the Internet Archive.[10] The corpus contains blog-pages, i.e. the homepages of blogs. They can be reached by entering the blogs' URLs into the address bar of a browser. For each blog-page, the DIABLOC comprises a link to the original page on the Archive, a text file of the posts, and a pdf file for multimodal analysis.11 For every blog-page, I used the earliest version available that was archived with sufficient quality. The structure of the corpus and its size are summed up in Table 1. This corpus was enriched by adding approx. 100 essays by bloggers and other documents12 to capture the wider discourse of the blogging community.[13]

Table 1: DIABLOC Overview

				Blog-Pages	**Posts**	**Word Forms**
DIABLOC	**Part I** *Weblogs*		1997–2000	30	775	ca. 34,075
	Part II *Personal Weblogs*	**II.A**	2002–2005	100	1091	ca. 224,025
		II.B	2006–2008	100	786	ca. 211,420
		II.C	2009–2012	100	901	ca. 302,017
			Total:	330	3,553	ca. 771,537

Part I contains 30 of the earliest weblogs (1997–2000). In order to compile these texts, I used two lists created by core members of this first blogging community: Jessie James Garret's listing of "ye olde school"-weblogs as well as Cameron

10 www.archive.org.

11 For a complete list of the DIABLOC URLs, please see Schildhauer (2016: ch. 11).

12 Cited as "corpus extension" in the following.

13 See Schildhauer (2016: ch. 2); Schildhauer (2014: ch. 4) for more on the design and the compilation of the corpus.

Barrett's blog roll on his weblog *Camworld*, which the author used to collect "other sites like his" (Blood 2000: n.p.).[14]

Part II assembles 300 blog-pages of the genre *personal weblog*. These texts were compiled by using the oldest blog directory available, the Globe of Blogs.[15] This directory was founded in 2002 and contains a system of categories authors can use (and modify) in order to classify their blogs. One meta-category (i.e. non-topical) is termed *personal weblog*. I entered the list pages contained in this category via the Internet Archive. The prospective corpus texts were put to several tests in order to ensure the validity of each text for the respective period.

2.3. Methodology

As far as the corpus just outlined is concerned, this study made use of common media linguistic methods of genre description (see, e.g., Luginbühl 2014), with a slightly more pronounced focus on descriptive statistics. The frequency of a feature was interpreted as an indicator of prototypicality, while standard deviations can be seen as a reflection of the variation scope of a genre category. The source code of the blog-pages was also used for analysis: The use of blog software, for instance, leaves traces in the source code; the use of widgets can also be analysed with more certainty when the source code is taken into account.[16]

While these methods are suitable for question (2) above – the *use* of potentials – the potentials *themselves* are more difficult to grasp. If we assume that there may be a discrepancy between potential and actual use, then potentials cannot be reconstructed by investigating blogs. Consider the following example: As will be shown later, reverse chronological order is almost the exclusive structural principle in the DIABLOC corpus. If we attempted to reconstruct potentials from use only, we would have to conclude that the blog communication form exclusively allowed for reverse chronology. However, this is not true for every period in blogging history (see 3.2).

The data for the reconstruction of the blog communication form (and its change over time) were, therefore, mainly gained from *blogging guides* such as *We blog: Publishing Online with Weblogs* (Bausch et al. 2002). These books provide guidance on how to set up a blog, and give an overview of different functionalities – i.e.

14 These sources were triangulated with Blood (2000) and several others (e.g. Barrett 1999a/b; Rosenberg 2009; Winer 2001).

15 www.globeofblogs.com.

16 For a more detailed description of the source-code-approach, see Schildhauer (2014: 131–133).

what potentials the blog software in question offers its users. Because guides like these usually take some time to react to innovations, were scarce in the first years of the new millennium, and do not cover each blog system in equal detail, this study additionally resorted to *online tutorials* as well as *FAQ*- and *help*-sites of the respective blog systems – accessed via the Internet Archive in order to ensure the validity for the corpus period in question.[17]

In other words, these sources were collected according to the principle of *theoretical sampling* established in *Grounded Theory* (see, e.g., Glaser & Holton 2004). Additionally, the analysis followed the *Grounded Theory* methods of *open* and *selective* coding. Thereby, data sheets were created for each corpus period. These sheets contain categories and their respective features for several typical blog systems and, thereby, provide a detailed picture of what can be considered the state of the art of the blog communication form in a certain corpus period.

2.4. Research on the Blog Communication Form

Research on the blog communication form as defined in 2.1 appears to be scarce, particularly when the standards outlined in 2.3 above are taken into consideration: The seminal studies carried out by Susan Herring and her team (Herring et al. 2004, 2005, 2006; Herring & Paolillo 2006) focus mainly on features of actual *use*, even though Herring et al. (2005: 164) use the term *socio-technical format*, which is close to the communication form concept. Puschmann (2010: ch. 2.2) applies Herring's (2007) classification scheme to blogging "on a global level" (Puschmann 2010: 25). While the *medium factors* of Herring's scheme could be used to describe communication forms as understood here, Puschmann (2010: 25) emphasizes the "dimension of practice". This becomes most apparent when he states concerning *anonymous messaging* that "many blogs are written under a pseudonym" instead of focusing on the potentials offered by blog software. Meiler (2013) provides an explicit attempt at describing the blog communication form, and also uses data on current software developments. However, Meiler's analysis almost exclusively draws on a collection of blogs, i.e. examples of actual use of the blog communication form. This results in confounding the levels of communication form and genre. For instance, he raises the question of how prototypical the implementation of the comment function on actual blogs is and *whether a blog can only be a blog if its posts can*

17 Please see the *Corpus* section of this article for a comprehensive list.

be commented on (Meiler 2013: 75). Here, the analytical focus clearly switches from considering what is *offered* by the blog communication form (potential) to the extent to which these potentials are actually *used* on blogs, i.e. if users actually tick the box "allow comments on this post" before publishing (genre). It is exactly this distinction which will be explored in the next section.

3. Results: Contrasting Potentials and their Use

3.1. General Use of Blog Software

As stated above, a blog is, essentially, not different from other web-based documents: It is an HTML document that is turned into a structured amalgam of language, image etc. only by means of a browser "translating" the HTML commands. In principle, a blog can therefore be maintained with nothing more than a simple text editor used to write the HTML-code, which is apparently the common way of keeping a blog in period I:

Figure 3: Blog Systems in the DIABLOC

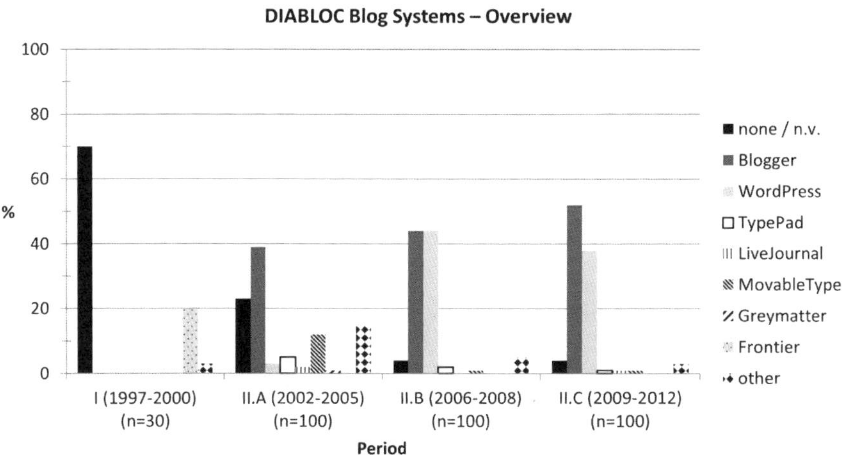

In 70% of the cases, the source code does not provide any evidence for the use of blog software in that period; another 20% used the *Frontier* software mentioned above and 10% other software packages. This picture changed profoundly in the following periods, with the fraction "no software detected" declining to almost as little as 4% in periods II.B and II.C.

At the same time, Figure 3 indicates that *the* blog software used by personal bloggers was *Blogger*, followed by *WordPress* in II.B and II.C.[18] It is certainly no coincidence that these systems are listed among the most accessible ones in above: While period I-bloggers were IT-*aficionados* with a high degree of know-how, the "mini-boom in weblog services" (Rosenberg 2009: 112) around the beginning of the new millennium attracted blog-authors-to-be from all fields of life. Technical knowledge was no precondition for blogging anymore (Schildhauer 2016: 110–111). It is likely that personal weblog authors typically just want(ed) to blog without facing the challenge of overcoming several technical obstacles – which is exactly what *Blogger* and *WordPress* (especially the online version *WordPress.com*) have always offered.[19]

3.2. Reverse Chronological Order

One of the most salient features of blogs appears to be the reverse chronological order – the newest-post-on-top principle. Indeed, this structural principle is dominant in the DIABLOC as well:

Table 2: Reverse Chronology in the DIABLOC

Period	**Reverse Chronology**				**Total (valid cases)**[20]	
	No		**Yes**			
I	20.0%	(6)	80.0%	(24)	100%	(30)
II.A	1.1%	(1)	98.9%	(92)	100%	(93)
II.B	0.0%	(0)	100.0%	(97)	100%	(97)
II.C	0.0%	(0)	100.0%	(98)	100%	(98)

If we consider the periods after 2000, i.e. II.A to II.C, there is only one exceptional case, namely the personal weblog *august dreams*, which published each new entry

18 *WordPress* was only launched in 2005 and, therefore, did not leave any traces in period II.A.

19 In Schildhauer (2016: 97–100), I have shown that new functionalities usually originate in less accessible systems as something to try out (and play with) for more experienced users. It is only when they have been tested, and somewhat established, that features are taken up by more accessible systems. This is particularly true for the comment function, but also for several others.

20 Naturally, I had to exclude personal weblogs with only one post as well as blogs without timestamp from this survey. In these cases, it could not be determined whether the respective blog followed reverse chronology.

on a separate page.[21] As stated above, this picture could lead us to the conclusion that there was no other way for the authors than to follow the principle of reverse chronology.[22] This is, however, only partly true.

Let us consider what happens *backstage* when a blog system is used for publishing a new post: Whenever an entry is produced and a user hits the "publish"-button, the entry is, first of all, stored in a database. In a very purist sense, the *backstage blog* is a program script with commands that the blog software uses to assemble the HTML document that can be displayed by the browser. This script contains database queries that retrieve posts from the database and place them in the basic layout of the blog. Every database query can apply certain criteria to widen or narrow down a search, for instance in order to display posts only of a certain category on a specific page of the blog.

What is more, the queries can also specify the way the output is presented. Reverse chronology is also based on such a command: The entries are sorted according to their record number in the database, in descending order. Entries that were added last to the database are, thereby, presented first (Puschmann 2010: 55–56). Therefore, it is not only a *deliberate* decision to use this particular ordering algorithm, but it would be very easy to use several other ordering principles such as straight chronology (ordering according to ascending record number).

In period II.A, however, the most accessible systems, i.e. those most widely used by DIABLOC authors, did not provide any other option besides reverse chronology. *MovableType*, on the other hand, allowed its users to overwrite the default setting of the attribute *sort_order* and, thereby, to choose from a whole range of imaginable ordering algorithms.

In period II.B, reverse chronology remained the default setting but many blog systems started to offer additional options. For instance, at the end of II.B, all systems except *Blogger* offered *sticky posts* that remain on top even if new content is added. In II.C, some plugins for *WordPress* allowed for choosing any order of posts, for instance alphabetically. In II.C, the latest, there were also several *WordPress* themes that made use of these different sorting options, for instance by displaying posts on the blog's homepage according to their topical category (Schildhauer 2014: 162).

---

21 This blog was run by the system *Diaryland*, which appears to be a host for sites that follow the "traditional" diary way of thinking in *pages* rather than *posts* on one and the same (dynamic) page.

22 See Herring et al. (2005: 145) and Puschmann (2010: 33; 55–56), who suggest such an explanation.

It becomes apparent that the potentials of following other structural principles besides the reverse chronology were rather limited in II.A, but widened afterwards even in the "less daring" accessible systems such as *Blogger*. But why was the reverse chronology so firmly established in the communication form itself in period II.A and why did it continue to be *the* structural principle even when circumventing it became easier?

In period I, most authors did not use any blog software but hand-coded their weblog. Consequently, they were free to choose how to arrange content on their website. These first-generation bloggers were faced with a crucial problem: They wanted to present dynamic, up-to-date content and neither erase less up-to-date content nor flag everything *new* with *This-is-new* buttons (Rosenberg 2009: 25–27). Some chose to publish a new page for each chunk of new content, providing access to all pages in the navigation bar (for instance, *Windowseat*). This can be labelled the *page-paradigm* and continues traditions from offline practices such as diaries.

Many others, however, resorted to a principle that can be labelled the post-paradigm, namely assembling all posts on one page, with the newest on top. This principle had been already been used as early as 1993 by Tim Berners-Lee, the founding father of the World Wide Web, on his *What's New* site (Rosenberg 2009: 9). Berners-Lee had taken his readers and contemporary technology into account: In general, it is easier to just check for new content on top of a page; additionally, in those early years, sites took so long to load that also from this perspective it was reasonable to present everything new on top – to be displayed first.

As this structural principle was also employed by the leading figure of the first blogger generation, Dave Winer, on his weblog *Scripting News*, we can assume that it was soon perceived as an established *convention* that narrowed down the range of potentials that were actually available. Apparently, the designers of the first blog systems, who were bloggers themselves, took up this established practice and implemented it as a default option (sometimes as the *only* option, as shown above) in their blog software. Even when the potentials were widened again in II.B and II.C, blog-authors probably simply followed a convention that had imprinted itself so much on the *genre patterns* (i.e. cognitive schemata governing text production, see Brock & Schildhauer, this volume) that other options were not even considered and, consequently, the effort of searching for the button or command to change the default setting not made.

3.3. Language and Image

As shown in the introduction, current blog systems advertise the ease with which users can share any sort of content, i.e. language, image, sound, and video. From the perspective of a complex communication form, three aspects play a decisive role in this respect:

- *Bandwidth* as a measure of the total amount of data drawn from a user's server account (usually measured per month). An image of, say, 1 MB, takes 5 MB of bandwidth if it is viewed five times per month. This becomes particularly important when a blogger does not use the most accessible systems, but ones like *WordPress.org* and others that do not provide server space. In these cases, server space has to be rented from a provider, who usually offers a limited amount of bandwidth only; if that amount is used up, either transmission speed is reduced considerably or the entire website is shut down for the rest of the month.
- *Storage space* is a relevant factor also for bloggers using the most accessible systems. An external provider rents a limited amount of storage space to a client just as a blog system such as *Blogger* sets clear limits to the amount of data a user can upload and, therefore, display on a blog. In II.C, for instance, *Blogger* offered image hosting in cooperation with *Picasa* with a maximum storage space of 1 GB per blog.
- *Transmission speed*: The larger (and more numerous) the files to be displayed on a blog, the longer the site takes to show fully. While the importance of this factor certainly decreased with the advent of broadband transmission, it was certainly something to take into account in period II.A:

Example 1: Considering Transmission Speed

> To those of you on dial-up: I'm sorry. I'm sure the loading time is horrible. I think this shot is worth the wait, though, especially since calling myself an amateur photographer is, at best, a stretch.
>
> (*(sometimes) cynical nature*, II.A)

Besides these mainly infrastructural constraints, it is also important to consider the specific potentials provided by the blog system (and software) itself. In general, there appears to have been a steady trend towards increased options from II.A onwards. In II.A, all systems except blogger enabled uploading image files, but only few accessible systems offered thumbnails before II.B. Thumbnails are small-sized versions of an image that are only enlarged when a reader clicks on them. They have a considerable influence on the demand for bandwidth (decreased) and transmission speed (increased).

Still in II.C, *Blogger* only offered very restricted possibilities regarding the positioning of images within a post (only left, right, and centre). *WordPress*, on the other hand, provided a higher degree of flexibility with a drag-and-drop approach and a tool for editing images (e.g. cropping). *WordPress* became also more flexible concerning other file types such as *pdf* when the file manager was introduced in II.C. Videos, however, needed (and still do at the time of writing) an additional *WordPress*-plugin – or a detour to Youtube. Embedding the Youtube hyperlink allows to display the video on the blog-page without wasting bandwidth and storage space. *Tumblr*, founded in 2007, provides a very easy approach to multimodal elements: *Tumblr* users can choose among various entry types that differ regarding the modality that is focused on (language, image, audio, or video).

Intuitively, it can be assumed that these increased potentials led to an increase of the use of images in blog posts. Indeed, the DIABLOC data indicates that this was the case:[23]

Table 3: Use of Images in Blog Posts

Period	**Images per Posting and Blog-Page**				
	Min.	**Max.**	**Mean**	**σ**	**N (of total)**
I	0.00	1.00	0.06	0.21	30 (30)
II.A	0.00	2.22	0.33	0.51	100 (100)
II.B	0.00	10.67	1.05	1.78	100 (100)
II.C	0.00	12.00	1.95	2.12	100 (100)

Table 3 shows that the number of images per posting increased steadily. While the use of images appears to have been an exception in period I, the mean value rose to about two images per post in period II.C. However, despite these developments that indicate an increasing importance of images on personal weblogs, there are apparently blog-pages in each period whose posts do not contain any image, as indicated by the minimum values in Table 3.

Obviously, not all bloggers used the growing potentials concerning the use of images and rather followed an established convention of a mainly language-based

23 These figures were calculated as follows: In a first step, a mean value of images per post was determined for each blog-page in the corpus. These values were then, in a second step, used to calculate mean values for the individual corpus periods. The same procedure was followed for Table 4 (length of posts).

blogging practice. This assumption is supported by data concerning the mean length of blog-posts, i.e. the number of word forms per post:[24]

Table 4: Length of Blog Posts

Period	Post Length (Word Forms)				N
	Min.	Max.	Mean	σ	(of total)
I	7.00	1796.00	208.40	403.05	30 (30)
II.A	1.00	916.00	239.40	190.76	100 (100)
II.B	39.71	929.70	269.50	182.30	100 (100)
II.C	9.00	1965.00	433.67	375.85	100 (100)

These data clearly show that the average length of blog-posts measured in number of word forms increased from period I to II.C. They allow for the conclusion that blogging, despite the increase of image use, remained a rather language-based practice. However, Table 4 also indicates that there are blogs with very short posts in terms of word count.[25] In period II.C, there are some personal weblogs in which language is merely used to briefly introduce the images to come. Apparently, language recedes to the background in these cases.

In general, however, personal blogging remained a practice in which language played a key role. Images were often used in an illustrative way (Stöckl 2004: 254), supporting the verbal text and/or providing proof of the post's authenticity (Holly 2009: 399; Steinseifer 2011: 184).

3.4. Participant Structure

In terms of participant structure, the blog communication form has always provided a potential that Meiler (2013: 83) represents as follows (here given in a modified way):

---

24 Elsewhere (Schildhauer in press), I have argued that the increase in post length might be due to a process of functional differentiation between blogs and social network sites such as *Facebook* and *Twitter*: Studies on these platforms indicate that they have increasingly been used for sharing web sources as well as brief updates. These uses had formerly been typical of personal weblogs, and they receded with the advent of social network sites. At the same time, sharing and reflecting on personal experiences in longer (language-image) posts appears to have remained a typical thing to do on personal weblogs (and less so on social network sites).

25 The very low minimum of 1.00 in II.A is an exceptional case: One personal weblog in the DIABLOC contains a greeting post saying no more than *Hello*.

Table 5: Participant Structure (Meiler 2013, modified)

Producer (Blog Author)	**Recipient (Reader)**
1 : n	n · (1 : 1)
*n : n	n · (*n : 1)
1 : *n	*n · (1 : 1)
*n : n	*n · (n* : 1)

Meiler's notation differentiates between *1* (one person only), **n* (some) and *n* (many). In the recipient column, Meiler takes into account that, actually, it is always one recipient viewing one post at a time: *(1 : 1)* and *(*n : 1)*. This reception process can, of course, take place various (**n*) or many (*n*) times.[26]

Let us have a closer look at the producers' side first. In period I, weblogs could, in principle, be maintained by various (**n*) authors – provided all of them had access to the blog domain in order to make changes to the website. This potential of multiple authorship was also provided by blog-systems all along the accessibility scale as early as II.A. The least accessible systems, e.g. *pMachine* and *ExpressionEnginge*, offered a complex set of access and editing permissions in order to smoothen the processes of collaborative writing in teams. From II.B onwards, *WordPress* has offered a comparable set of tools.

As Table 6 shows, only a small percentage of DIABLOC-blogs in each period were actually composed by multiple (i.e. **n*) authors.[27]

---

26 Meiler's notation is reproduced here because of its heuristic value. Of course, it is impossible to determine at what point **n* (some) turns into *n* (many). At the same time, it appears intuitively plausible that there are limits to the number of authors (*1* and **n*, e.g. manageability of a group blog, number of possible accounts) while the audience could, potentially, be the mass audience of all Internet users. I have modified Meiler's notation as follows: He gives *n · (1 : *n)* and **n · (1 : *n)* for the second and fourth recipient line. His aim is to show that the *one* recipient taken into account by the other notations might get in contact with *some* (instead of *one*) authors at a time in case the respective post was written by multiple authors. His original notation, however, reads "one author communicates with a few readers at a time" and therefore denotes the exact opposite of what he intended. Therefore, I noted *n · (*n : 1)* and **n · (*n : 1)*, which reads "many (or a few) times, some (more than 1, less than many) authors communicate with one reader at a time".

27 Coding was based on author signatures in the timestamp as well as metadata on profiles and *about* sites. In case of pseudonyms, I assumed one pseudonym to relate to one author each. If none of these indicators could be found, the blog was coded *0* and not included in the descriptive statistics.

Table 6: Multiple Authorship

Period	Multiple Authorship				Total (valid cases)	
	no		Yes			
I	85.7%	(24)	14.3%	(4)	100%	(28)
II.A	97.8%	(89)	2.2%	(2)	100%	(91)
II.B	94.8%	(92)	5.2%	(5)	100%	(97)
II.C	92.8%	(90)	7.2%	(7)	100%	(97)

In period I, *Memepool* was a weblog project with contributions by 31 authors, who compiled news from the World Wide Web. Similarly, *Need to Know* and *Linky & Dinky* contained contributions from multiple authors. Even though single authorship was typical of period I, there still seemed to be more scope for variation than in period II. The slight increase in multiple authorship blogs from II.A to II.C may have been related to the extension of multiple authorship options in accessible blog systems. *Hello Interloper* (II.C) was maintained by a couple and *Flying Confessions* (II.B) contained contributions from as many as eleven authors. Additionally, the practice of *guest blogging* spread in period II: Bloggers were invited to publish posts on other blogs, usually related to their particular fields of expertise. This happened, for instance, on *Jenn's Travel Closeup* (II.B). Usually, these posts were published by the blog's owner but flagged as guest posts.

As far as the readers' perspective is concerned, potentially a world-wide audience (i.e. *n*) could be reached in every corpus period. In fact, it is more interesting to investigate to what extent this immense circle of potential readers could be limited (to **n*).

If the high amount of blogs is taken into consideration that we could theoretically read every day then it appears counter-intuitive to investigate limitations of readership – blogs are there, they are available to all of us. In fact, Puschmann (2010: 31) claims by drawing on Herring's (2007) classification scheme that the "facet of private messaging does not apply to blogs." However, it was possible to protect websites by setting a password already in period I. Additionally, experienced authors of websites could make changes to a file named *robots.txt*, thereby preventing crawling software from indexing the site for search engines. In other words: Even in those early years both visibility and access to a weblog could be limited considerably.

In period II.A, *Blogger* allowed setting a blog on *private*, which entailed that the blog did not appear on *Blogger*-internal lists and, most likely, was not indexed by search engines either. At the beginning of II.B and probably even earlier, *LiveJournal* offered a variety of privacy options, for instance protecting specific entries by setting a password or making them visible to a selected audience only. The same has been true for *TypePad* and *WordPress* from II.B onwards. In II.C, at least a minimal set of privacy options can be considered the standard for every blog-system. By then, *Blogger*, too, had increased its privacy options.

However, to what extent these options were and are actually used is hard to tell, especially by relying on corpus analysis. The personal weblogs collected for this study, for instance, had to be visible in the first place – otherwise they would not have been collected. Additionally, they had been registered on a public directory with the aim of increasing visibility and readership. Consequently, it is highly unlikely even to find blogs with individual password-protected posts. As a matter of fact, there is none in the DIABLOC.

The participant structure becomes more complex as soon as the comment function is taken into account. Before the comment function was introduced by the pioneering system *MovableType* in 2001, commenting had only been possible by external systems developed by hackers which were neither particularly stable nor easy to use (Blood 2004: 55). In II.A, nearly all blog-systems had already established the feature, with *Blogger* following in 2004 (Meiler 2013: 75). In general, bloggers have since then been able to decide whether to allow comments for individual posts or not. In fact, the comment function was established as a key feature of the personal weblog practice immediately after it had been introduced: In each period, more than two thirds of the DIABLOC sites allowed comments to their posts.

3.5. Modularity

The aspect of modularity grasps the scope which a communication form provides for its own extension, modification and complementation by adding additional modules to the original software core. As far as blogs are concerned, there are two types of modules: *Plug-ins*, on the one hand, are pieces of software that add some specific functionality but usually do not show on the surface of the blog. One typical example is the plug-in *Akismet* – a spam filter for comments. On the other hand, there are *widgets*, which have a graphic output interface. They appear as small modules either in the sidebar or in the footer of a blog-page and are used for various purposes such as displaying the latest comments, showing the author's biography and contacting the author via a form (see example 2). Due to their actual appearance *on-stage* of the blog-page, I will focus on widgets here.

Example 2: Widgets in Asian Polyglot (II.C)

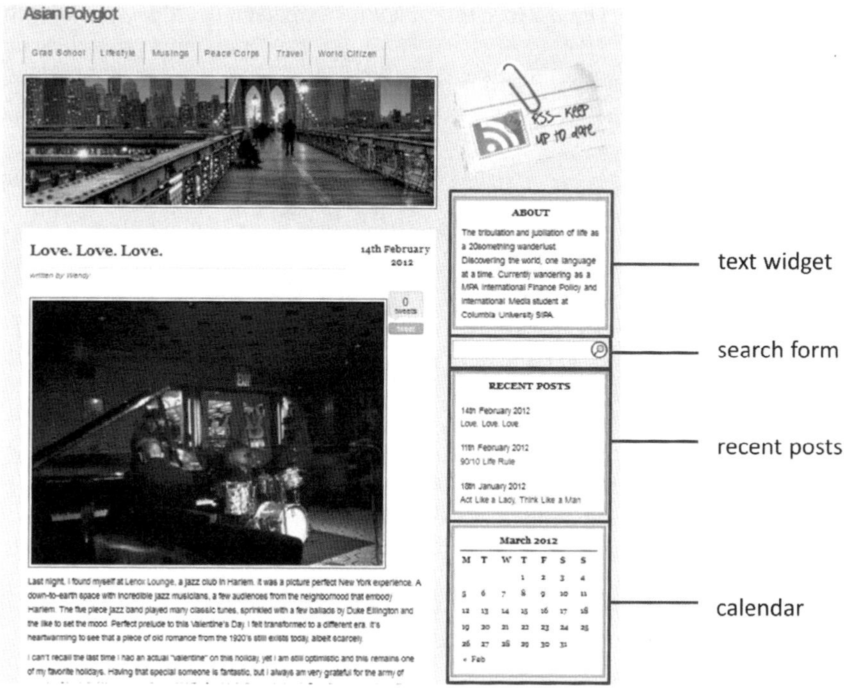

The idea of widgets goes back to Apple's early graphic operating systems and, therefore, is older than the World Wide Web itself. However, it was only reluctantly transferred to blogs. In II.A, only the rather less accessible system *pMachine* offered widgets, which were called *pBlocks* – small boxes appearing in the sidebar displaying text and pictures, even in randomised order.[28]

In II.B, the accessible systems started delivering some widgets as part of their core software package; the users could then decide to place them in the sidebar or not.[29] *WordPress* and *MovableType*, for instance, offered a search box and a calendar (among others). Additionally, users were free to develop their own widgets as snippets of code that could be added to the blog's source code. Soon, these "home-made"

28 Actually, *pBlocks* could do even more: For instance, they could be programmed to change the blog's background colour in a randomised way.

29 The choice of widgets was (and still is) restricted by the theme of a blog – while the design of some themes allows a high number of different widgets, other themes are more restrictive.

widgets could be found on forums where other users evaluated them. From II.B onwards, *Blogger* has offered a widget that is still in frequent use today: It connects a blog with the image-hosting-platform *Flickr* and displays pictures that the user has uploaded there. In II.C, *Blogger's* standard widgets were comparable to those of *WordPress*: among others, calendar, search box, text widgets, categories/labels. The standard widgets were added by drag-and-drop in a user-friendly way. It is probably because of this easy handling that widgets soon became so popular that some blogging guides warned against their exaggerated use:

Example 3: Considering Exaggerated Widget Use

> When people start mentioning how long it takes for your blog to load or that your blog 'looks funny', it's probably time to take a hard look at those widgets, especially the custom ones, and see what you truly need to have and what is just blog bling.
> (Hussey 2011: 161)

Indeed, this development is also reflected in the DIABLOC:[30] There is a considerable increase of blogs containing widgets from 1% in II.A to 93% in II.C.[31] Additionally, the number of widgets per blog-page shows a significant increase:

Table 7: Use of Widgets in the DIABLOC

Period	Widgets per Blog-Page				N
	Min.	Max.	Mean	σ	(of total)
I	0.00	0.00	0.00	0.00	30 (30)
II.A	0.00	1.00	0.01	0.01	100 (100)
II.B	0.00	24.00	4.95	6.36	100 (100)
II.C	0.00	84.00	14.52	12.91	100 (100)

30 Not every additional module that appears on a blog-page is, in fact, a widget (some features might have been hand-coded by designers or implemented by the blog-system as such). Therefore, I investigated the source code where widgets are usually activated by commands such as *register.widget* and the like. It is likely that some widgets could not be detected by this method. Still, this approach provides a sound picture of what was typical on personal weblogs.

31 The one widget in period II.A is the search engine of a webring. It can, therefore, be considered a third-party embedding and nothing that was offered by the blog-system itself.

At the same time, we can observe a phenomenon similar to the use of images discussed above: There are some blogs in each period that do not make use of the provided potential at all (7% even in II.C).

Considering the question of what kind of widgets were actually used on personal weblogs, it can be stated that the DIABLOC sites typically implement widgets that are offered by the blog-systems together with the core software. Text widgets (e.g., presenting the author's biography) could be detected on almost two thirds of the blog-pages in II.C, followed by category clouds (45% in II.C) and search boxes (30% in II.C).

4. Conclusions: *Anything Goes – Everything Done?*

This paper analysed selected aspects of the blog communication form. The results were contrasted with what bloggers typically make of these potentials. In this respect, the paper focused on the genre *personal weblog* and its immediate ancestor, the *weblog*, under the assumption that *genre* is an abstraction from actual communicative practice. The paper took a diachronic perspective, focussing on the following research questions:

(1) To what extent can we describe the development of the blog communication form as a steady expansion of possibilities – towards an *anything goes*?
(2) To what extent are these potentials typically used on blogs – or, in other words: *Everything done*?

As far as (1) is concerned, it can be stated that we cannot describe the development of the blog communication form as a steady expansion of potentials. Regarding the reverse chronological order, for instance, the blog communication form was most restrictive in the years after the beginning of the new millennium – provided that authors used rapidly spreading and accessible blog software. In the early years of blogging, when authors mainly coded their sites by hand, they had only been restricted by the functionalities of the HTML-standard. Back then, authors could have chosen literally *any* way of presenting their content. A similar state was only reached again in period II.C – at least for some blog-systems. In any case, reverse chronology remained the default option.

At a first glance, the potentials concerning participant structure have remained stable, with only the handling of multiple authors and limited audiences becoming more easy. At a second glance, of course the comment function meant an enormous growth of the interactive potential of the blog communication form, leading to participant constellations that are potentially more complex than *1 : n* or *n : n*.

The aspects of *embedding images* and *embedding widgets* can be considered closest to a *steady expansion*. With decisive infrastructural improvements, factors restricting the use of images on blogs such as *bandwidth*, *storage space* and *transmission speed* became less important, without, of course, losing their significance entirely. At the same time, the handling of images (layout options, cropping etc.) was developed steadily in blog-systems all along the accessibility scale. Similar observations could be made concerning widgets.

Regarding (2), it can be stated that the extension of potentials does not necessarily entail their actual use. This becomes most apparent when the reverse chronological order is considered, which has remained *the* dominant, if not *exclusive* structural principle despite the availability of other options. Similarly, personal weblogs have typically been *personal* in the original sense of the word from II.A onwards, with only some DIABLOC texts exhibiting evidence of multiple authorship. The potentials concerning images and widgets were apparently taken up more enthusiastically by bloggers. However, this paper has shown that, even among the blogs of the last corpus period (2009–2012), there were some not at all using the potentials provided. These considerations lead to a more general question pursued by this paper:

(3) What do the results of (1) and (2) tell us about the theoretical concepts of *communication form* and *communicative practice*, which are at the centre of this volume?

Generally, this paper has shown how useful it is to keep both concepts clearly distinct. Only then does it become possible to uncover the interesting relations between potentials and their actual use. In several cases discussed above, there were clear contrasts between these two aspects – either in individual cases (bloggers not using images and/or widgets in II.C), or even as a general phenomenon (reverse chronology).

Naturally, the question arises *why* these contrasts can be observed. One possible answer certainly lies in the aspect of *convention* that Brock & Schildhauer (this volume) stress. It is suggested as a factor restricting communicative potentials of a communication form. For instance, the discussion of reverse chronology above has shown that this structural pattern had started to emerge as a conventional (since reasonable and efficient) way of presenting dynamic content on the web. We can assume that this convention was re-enforced by the fact that the accessible blog-systems offered reverse chronology as the *only* option in II.A: What bloggers got to know as typical personal weblog was a website that, among others, presented dynamic content in reverse chronological order. This, in turn, certainly contributed to the formation of *genre patterns* (Brock & Schildhauer, this volume), i.e. cognitive schemata guiding the production of personal weblogs in general and individual posts in particular. Both conventions and genre patterns can be considered to change more slowly than, say, the infrastructural and software aspects of the blog communication form. This is, at least, suggested by the data discussed in this paper.

A similar persistence of convention and genre patterns probably plays a role in the continuing focus on verbal language in personal weblogs. We can assume that particularly some personal weblogs continued genre patterns and conventions of early (personal) weblogs, or even stereotypical notions of language-based offline diaries.[32]

Additionally, author demographics and, thereby, competences and ambitions concerning web design may play a role. It is likely that authors of personal weblogs are typically those who just want to blog and probably cannot compete with the blogging pioneers of the 1990s in terms of IT-competence. Naturally, these authors are less likely to look for ways of changing default settings concerning chronological order and of embedding additional widgets.

Apparently, there are many and complex relations between communication forms and communicative practices, which media linguistics is just about to uncover. Therefore, what will become of the personal weblog in the light of the current "faster, better, new" – remains to be seen.

Corpus

Cited Blogs

Period I:	*Camworld*	http://tinyurl.com/camworld-weblog
	Linky & Dinky	http://tinyurl.com/linkydink
	Memepool	http://tinyurl.com/memepool
	Need to Know	http://tinyurl.com/ntk-weblog
	Scripting News	http://tinyurl.com/scripting-weblog
	Windowseat	http://tinyurl.com/window-weblog
Period II.A:	*(sometimes) cynical nature*	http://tinyurl.com/cynical-pb
Period II.B:	*Jenn's Travel Closeup*	http://tinyurl.com/jenn-pb
	Flying Confessions	http://tinyurl.com/confe-pb
Period II.C:	*Asian Polyglot*	http://tinyurl.com/asian-pb
	Hello Interloper	http://tinyurl.com/helloint-pb
	Rebelle Fleur	http://tinyurl.com/fleur-pb

32 See, e.g., Kitzmann (2004: 30); Serfaty (2004: 28).

Blogging Guides

Period II.A	Bausch, Paul et al.: *We blog: Publishing Online with Weblogs.* Wiley Pub: Indianapolis 2002. Blood, Rebecca: *The Weblog Handbook: Practical Advice on Creating and Maintaining Your Blog.* Perseus: Cambridge (MA) 2002. Stauffer, Todd: *Blog On: The Essential Guide to Building Dynamic Weblogs.* Osborne: Berkeley, Calif. 2002.
Period II.B	Hayder, Hasin: *WordPress Complete: A Comprehensive, Step-By-Step Guide on How to Set Up, Customize, and Market Your Blog Using WordPress.* Packt Publ.: Birmingham 2006. Lee, Wei M.: *The Rational Guide to Google Blogger.* Rational Press: Rollinsfold 2006. Stauffer, Todd: *How to Do Everything with your Web 2.0 Blog.* McGraw-Hill: New York 2008. Yang, Jonathan: *The Rough Guide to Blogging.* Penguin: London 2006.
Period II.C	Cole, Allan: *Build Your Own Wicked WordPress Themes.* SitePoint: Collingwood 2010. Hussey, Tris: *Using WordPress.* Que.: Indianapolis 2011. Frankemölle, Gabi: *Weblog mit WordPress 3: Das grosse Buch.* Data-Becker: Düsseldorf 2010. White, Charlie & Biggs, John: *Bloggers Boot Camp: Learning How to Build, Write, and Run a Successful Blog.* Focal Press: Waltham, MA 2011. Wright-Porto, Heather: *Beginning Google Blogger.* Springer: New York 2010. Wright-Porto, Heather: *Creative Blogging: Your first Steps to a Successful Blog.* Springer: New York 2011.

FAQ-Sites and Tutorials

PyraLabs: *How To*, 2002, retrieved 20.05.2016, from http://tinyurl.com/pyra02.

Coggins, S. A. M.: *Web Logs How Tos Index*, 2004, retrieved 20.04.2016, from http://tinyurl.com/coggins04.

Improbulus: *Display links to your posts via Blogger Backlinks, Icerocket Link Tracker etc.*, 2005, retrieved 20.04.2016, from http://tinyurl.com/improb05.

LiveJournal: *State of the Goat 2012*, 2012, retrieved 20.04.2016, from http://tinyurl.com/ljrel12.

WordPress Codex: *WordPress Features*, 2005, retrieved 20.04.2016, from http://tinyurl.com/wpcod05.

SixApart: *MovableType: Features*, 2003a, retrieved 20.04.2016, from http://tinyurl.com/sixap03a.

Six Apart: *TypePad Personal Weblogging Service: Features and Pricing*, 2003b, retrieved 20.04.2016, from http://tinyurl.com/sixap03b (20.04.2016).

Tumblr, Inc.: *Tumblr is the easiest way to express yourself*, 2009, retrieved 20.04.2016, from http://tinyurl.com/tumbab09.

Tumblr, Inc.: *About us*, 2010, retrieved 20.04.2016, from http://tinyurl.com/tumab2010.

Cited Bloggers' Reflections

Barrett, Cameron: *Anatomy of a Weblog*, 1999a, retrieved 20.04.2016, from http://tinyurl.com/barrett99a.

Barrett, Cameron: *More About Weblogs*, 1999b retrieved 20.04.2016, from http://tinyurl.com/barrett99b.

Blood, Rebecca: *Weblogs: A History and Perspective*, 2000, retrieved 20.04.2016, from http://tinyurl.com/blood2000.

Blood, Rebecca: "How Blogging Software Reshapes the Online Community." *Communications of the ACM* 47 (12), 2004, 53–55.

Winer, Dave: *The history of weblogs*, 2001, retrieved 20.04.2016, from http://tinyurl.com/winer01.

References

Brock, Alexander: "On the Corruption of Text Types. The Cases of Comedy and Readers' Commentaries in Online Newspapers". In: Ammermann, Anne et al. (eds.): *Facets of Linguistics*. Peter Lang: Frankfurt am Main 2013, 63–74.

Brock, Alexander & Schildhauer, Peter: "Communication Form. A Concept Revisited". In: Brock, Alexander & Schildhauer, Peter (eds.): *Communication Forms and Communicative Practices. New Perspectives on Communication Forms, Affordances, and What Users Make of Them*. Peter Lang, Berlin, this volume 13–43.

Efimova, Lilia: *Passion at Work. Blogging Practices of Knowledge Workers*. Dissertation. Universiteit Utrecht: Enschede 2009.

Fritz, Gerd: „Texttypen in wissenschaftlichen Blogs. Eine exemplarische Analyse am Beispiel des Language Log". In: Fritz, Gerd & Gloning, Thomas (eds.): *Digitale Wissenschaftskommunikation – Formate und ihre Nutzung*. Gießener Elektronische Bibliothek: Gießen 2011, 205–287.

Glaser, Barney G. & Holton, Judith: "Remodeling Grounded Theory". *Forum: Qualitative Social Research* 5(2) 2004, retrieved 20.04.2016, from: http://www.qualitative-research.net/index.php/fqs/article/view/607/1316.

Herring, Susan et al.: *Bridging the Gap. A Genre Analysis of Weblogs,* 2004, retrieved 20.04.2016, from http://tinyurl.com/herrscheidt04.

Herring, Susan et al.: *A Longitudinal Content Analysis of Weblogs. 2003–2004,* 2006, retrieved 20.04.2016, from http://tinyurl.com/herring2006.

Herring, Susan: "A Faceted Classification Scheme for Computer-Mediated Discourse". *Language@Internet* 4, 2007, retrieved 22.09.2016, from http://www.languageatinternet.org/articles/2007/761.

Herring, Susan & Paolillo, John C.: "Gender and Genre Variation in Weblogs". *Journal of Sociolinguistics* 10(4), 2006, 439–459.

Herring, Susan C. et al.: "Weblogs as a Bridging Genre". *Information Technology & People* 18(2), 2005, 142–171.

Holly, Werner: „Der Wort-Bild-Reißverschluss. Über die perfomative Dynamik audiovisueller Transkriptivität". In: Linke, Angelika & Deppermann, Arnulf (eds.): *Oberfläche und Performanz. Untersuchungen zur Sprache als dynamischer Gestalt.* Niemeyer: Tübingen 2009, 389–406.

Kitzmann, Andreas: *Saved from Oblivion. Documenting the Daily from Diaries to Web Cams.* Peter Lang: New York 2004.

Lomborg, Stine: "Navigating the Blogosphere. Towards a Genre-based Typlogoy of Weblogs". *First Monday* 14(5), retrieved 20.04.2016, from http://tinyurl.com/lomborg2009.

Lomborg, Stine: *Social Media, Social Genres. Making Sense of the Ordinary.* Routledge: New York 2014.

Luginbühl, Martin: *Medienkultur und Medienlinguistik. Komparative Textsortengeschichte(n) der amerikanischen „CBS Evening News" und der Schweizer „Tagesschau".* Lang: Bern 2014.

Mauranen, Anna: "Hybridism, Edutainment, and Doubt: Science Blogging Finding Its Feet". *Nordic Journal of English Studies* 13(1), 2013, 7–36.

Meiler, Matthias: „Kommunikationsformenadressen oder: Prozeduren des Situationsvollzugs am Beispiel von Weblogs". *Zeitschrift für Angewandte Linguistik* 59(2), 2013, 51–106.

Miller, Carolyn: "Genre as Social Action". *Quarterly Journal of Speech* 70, 1984, 151–167.

Miller, Carolyn & Shepherd, Dawn: *Blogging as Social Action. A Genre Analysis of the Weblog,* 2004, retrieved 20.04.2016, from http://tinyurl.com/miller04.

Miller, Carolyn & Shepherd, Dawn: "Questions for Genre Theory from the Blogosphere". In: Giltrow, Janet & Stein, Dieter (eds.): *Genres in the Internet. Issues in the Theory of Genre.* Benjamins: Amsterdam 2009, 263–290.

Puschmann, Cornelius: *The Corporate Blog as an Emerging Genre of Computer-mediated Communication. Features, Constraints, Discourse Situation.* Universitätsverlag Göttingen: Göttingen 2010.

Puschmann, Cornelius & Mahrt, Merja: "Scholarly Blogging. A New Form of Publishing Online or Science Journalism 2.0?". In: Tokar, A. et al. (eds.): *Science and the Internet.* Düsseldorf University Press: Düsseldorf 2012, 171–181.

Rosenberg, Scott: *Say Everything. How Blogging Began, What it's Becoming, and Why it Matters.* Three Rivers Press: New York 2009.

Sandig, Barbara: „Text als prototypisches Konzept". In: Mangasser-Wahl, Martina (ed.): *Prototypentheorie in der Linguistik. Anwendungsbeispiele – Methodenreflexion – Perspektiven.* Stauffenburg Verlag: Tübingen 2000, 93–112.

Schildhauer, Peter: „Blogs in der Krise? Zum Einfluss Sozialer Netzwerkseiten auf die Textsorte Personal Weblog". In: Eckkrammer, Eva Martha et al. (eds.): *Medienlinguistik 3.0. Formen und Wirkung von Textsorten im Zeitalter des Social Web.* Frank & Thimme: Berlin, in press.

Schildhauer, Peter: "The Textual Functions of Personal Weblogs. Stability, Diversity, and Change". In: Ammermann, Anne et al. (eds.): *Facets of Linguistics.* Peter Lang: Frankfurt am Main 2013, 117–130.

Schildhauer, Peter: *Textsorten im Internet zwischen Wandel und Konstanz. Eine diachrone Untersuchung der Textsorte Personal Weblog.* Dissertation. Martin-Luther-Universität, Halle-Wittenberg. Retrieved 20.04.2016, from http://tinyurl.com/schild2014, 2014.

Schildhauer, Peter: *The Personal Weblog. A Linguistic History.* Peter Lang: Berlin 2016.

Serfaty, Viviane: *The Mirror and the Veil. An Overview of American Online Diaries and Blogs.* Rodopi: Amsterdam 2004.

Steinseifer, Martin: „Die Typologisierung multimodaler Kommunikationsangebote. Am Beispiel der visuellen Aspekte seitenbasierter Dokumente". In: Habscheid, Stephan (ed.): *Textsorten, Handlungsmuster, Oberflächen. Linguistische Typologien der Kommunikation.* de Gruyter: Berlin & New York 2011, 164–189.

Stöckl, Hartmut: *Die Sprache im Bild – das Bild in der Sprache. Zur Verknüpfung von Sprache und Bild im massenmedialen Text.* de Gruyter: Berlin & New York 2004.

Jana Pflaeging

Changing Potentials and Their Use: The Case of Popular Science Journalism

Abstract Ever since its first publication in 1888, the *National Geographic* magazine has grown into one of the most widely circulating popular science magazines on the market. Concomitant with broader socio-cultural developments, the *medial*, i.e. material-technical and institutional, setting for publishing the magazine has changed decisively over time. By comparing print issues from 1915 and 2015, I illustrate that it is not *convention* alone that determines how text producers make use of communicative potentials afforded by a given medium. In *commercial* press communication especially, also *production costs, individual decision-making, conscious pattern embedding* or even *coincidence* factor into making concrete choices from a range of potential ones. I draw on the notion *communication form* to describe MAGAZINE ARTICLE linguistically as a more abstract socio-cognitive category that reflects communicative *practices* and map out its diachronic sub-differentiation on a more specific genre-level.

1. Introduction

Today, the *National Geographic* magazine is one of the most prominent and, at the same time, most traditional popular science magazines on the market. First published in 1888 as an *academic* journal of the *National Geographic Society*, it took its editors only about ten years to realize that the *Society*'s initial dictum "to increase and diffuse geographic knowledge" (NGM 1888/Jan: i) could only be achieved if large *popular* audiences were reached (Lutz & Collins 1993: 22). Based on the assumption that "people would read about geography only if it was presented in a light, entertaining way" (Abramson 2010: 42; cf. Foster 2012; Wilson 1983), editors began to "'sugarcoat the pill'" (Abramson 2010: 42).

As we leaf through the pages of the January 1915 issue of the *National Geographic* magazine, we find altogether 88 "beautiful, instructive, and artistic illustrations" (NGM 1915/Mar: 319) showing Dutch dikes, Blackfeet Indians, and horse markets in Warsaw published in black and white as part of *Feature Articles*. Browsing through the January 2015 issue, we look at pigment murals in ancient caves, into the eyes of red-eyed tree frogs, and onto the bustling market squares of Lagos Island. While the magazine has always been dedicated to "themes of exploration and education" (Davies 2005: 52; cf. NGM Media Kit 2016), the communicative *practices* to present them have changed against the background of transforming socio-historical contexts and medial *affordances*.

By investigating print issues from 1915 and 2015, I trace the diachronic development of the communication form MAGAZINE ARTICLE[1] and associated genres that magazine editors employed in particular, such as *Feature Article, Your Shot* or *Visions of Earth*, and identify costs, individual decision-making & coincidence, commercial success, convention and innovation as mechanisms that factor into making concrete choices from what a medium potentially affords.

2. Theoretical Considerations

2.1. Communication Form | Early and Recent Conceptualizations

Ever since it was first sketched out in Gülich & Raible's volume on *Textsorten* (1972), and elaborated by Ermert (1979) in his study on types of LETTERS, *communication form*[2] has grown into a widely debated and diversely conceptualized term in text and media linguistics. While Ermert's (1979) early suggestion to chart *forms* of communication that operate – compared to genres – on a more abstract level of categorization still persists, there have been at least three important adaptations as (media) linguists continue to broaden and diversify their research interests and objects:

Multimodality and Spatiality | Raised awareness and consideration of the natural multimodality of communicative exchanges has led scholars to explicate the descriptive categories for 'sign system' as language, image, sound, and mode of perception as visual, auditive and tactile sensual impressions (Domke 2014: 26; see also Stöckl 2012). The observation that communication forms may also differ in the ways they are bound to space and time resulted in establishing further criteria for their description (see Domke 2010: 269; this volume).

Mediality | Listed as one criterion among many in Ermert's model, the central role of the medium in giving rise to communication forms in the first place

1 Throughout this contribution, I use small capitals to denote examples of communication form and italics to highlight the genre-status of a communicative pattern.

2 The original expression *Kommunikationsform* (Ermert 1979: 55) is typically translated as *communication form*, but the term *communicative form* is also in use (cf. Bateman 2016).

has been given emphasis.[3] Bittner (2003: 297) and Brinker et al. (2014: 142), for instance, characterize the choice of a medium as an obligatory decision, which, then, strongly determines the situational constellation of communication forms. Stöckl (2012: 19–20), too, lists oral/written, synchronous/asynchronous, bi-/uni-directional, public/private, live/non-live and recipient constellations as defining criteria of communication forms and stresses that they are medium-based.

Culturality | Emphasis on the cultural embeddedness of communication has led to a rather prominent conceptualization of communication forms as medium-based cultural practices („medial bedingte kulturelle Praktiken", Holly 2011: 155; see cross-references in Domke 2014; Meiler 2013; Pentzold et al. 2013). While the term *practice* could appear to blur the line between *potentiality* and communicative *use*, it is the closeness of communication form to concrete media *pratices* (cf. Bittner 2003: 298) that seems central to the notion.

2.2. Modelling Communication Form | An Infographic Suggestion

Terminological clarity, especially in the case of communication form, is most likely achieved if the notion is established in contrast to immediately neighboring concepts. Proceeding inductively from concrete text exemplars via genre to communication form, affordances and, eventually, to medium, I will build my discussion, somewhat eclectically, on the valuable suggestions other scholars have already made. In order to accentuate the holistic nature of communicative processes and the juxtaposition of its individual components, I have created an

3 A comparably strong foregrounding of the concept's medial dimension is suggested by Schildhauer (2014: 28; 2016). In his extensive study of personal weblogs, he adopts the term to grasp the medial-technical constellations the *genre* is based on, not least to avoid the highly polysemous concept medium. In Schildhauer (2016: 30-31), communication form is defined "in a simplistic manner as a technical constellation which gives rise to communicative potentials. Potentials include the semiotic systems available for message production, the possible number of participants and the extent to which distance in space and time can be bridged." His terminological choices suit the strong and probably rather prescriptive connection between medial-technical constellations and the potentials they offer. In that sense, medium and communication form might appear to fall together. In anticipation of the vast range of (constellations of) *potentials* that sheets of paper, a printing press and an editorial office evoke, I consider it best to keep the medial level separate and describe its repercussions on the level of affordances, communication form, and genre.

infographic model (Figure 1) of communication form and related concepts. It is meant to complement (and hopefully benefit) the lively discussions that continue to shape media linguistics as an emerging area of research.

❶ **text exemplars** | We encounter texts as concrete physical entities materialized as graphite, writing or printing inks applied to paper, or as red-green-blue-colored dots that are back-lit and projected onto a display screen. They result from communicative processes of text production in which a participant's cognitive knowledge of genre, communication form, affordances and medium is deployed. Playing by the rules, or breaking them, results in textual embodiments of conformity or non-conformity, and allows drawing lines between tradition and innovation. With that we blend over to text reception, where concrete texts could be seen as the starting point of communicative processes. Not only do they form the basis for ad-hoc text comprehension, they also constitute a frame of reference for establishing socio-cognitive devices in the minds of recipients.

❷ **genre** | Text exemplars show specific constellations of features, e.g., with regards to their multimodal structure, their topical, situational, and functional organization (see, e.g., Adamzik 2004; Brinker et al. 2014; Stöckl 2016). Communicative patterns that turn out to be successful in fulfilling communicative needs in certain socio-cultural contexts tend to recur, should the need arise again in similar situations (see, e.g., Miller 1984). As we re-produce and re-encounter such concrete textual patterns, they leave imprints in a text producer's and recipient's mind. On the basis of perceived similarities between feature constellations of individual patterns, i.e. a "patterning of patterns" (Bateman 2014: 241), genres assume shape as prototypically organized socio-cognitive "device[s] for sensemaking" (Lomborg 2014: 3; see Sandig 2000; Swales 1990).

Thus, genres are *reflections* of communicative practices, but not practices themselves (see also Brock & Schildhauer, this volume: 19). This distinction is a fundamental one that reaches beyond negotiating the conceptual borders of text exemplar and genre. It introduces a general differentiation between "cognition, in terms of socially negotiated and mentally anchored categories of classification and systematization of experiences in the social world, and actual, practical, instances of sensemaking in everyday life" (Lomborg 2014: 33). These assumptions entail two essential points: Firstly, genres are knowledge *available* for text production and, consequently, bear an *experience-based potentiality* for concrete action in communicative exchanges. I will argue below that the same holds true for communication form. This brings us to: Secondly, if we subscribe to a socio-cognitive take on genre and highlight the emergence of such mental categories on the basis of perceived patterns in communicative exchanges, then judgements concerning the exact make-up of perceived patterns reside with the recipients and their perception of communicative exchanges. Grasping genres as essentially *unspecific* ethno-categories has recently gained momentum in linguistics (see Adamzik 1995, 2004; Luginbühl & Perrin 2011; Luginbühl 2014; Schildhauer 2014, 2016; Pflaeging 2015, 2016) and is also central to this contribution. I am aware of the fact that an ethno-categorical take on genre could, in some cases, lead to placing genre-patterns at a communication-form level. What is, in my view, in the tradition of early and many recent approaches to communication form could, indeed, be seen as the flaw of a decidedly practice-based approach. However, for those many cases in which more abstract patterns show a salient sub-differentiation into much more enriched genre-patterns, communication form seems a useful distinctive category to work with in linguistics.

Figure 1: Multimodal Model of Medial and Socio-cognitive Potentiality and Communicative Practices

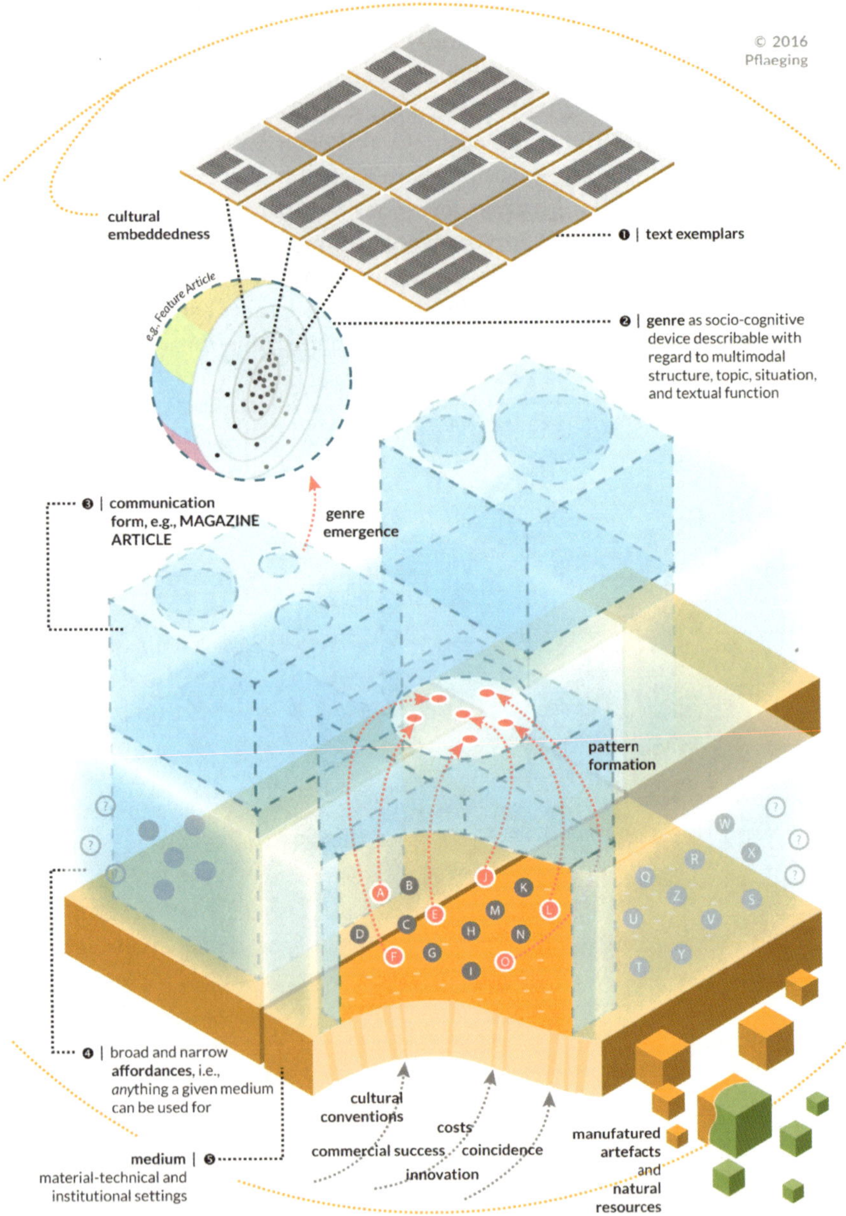

❸ **communication form** | While linguistic conceptualizations of communication form differ in quantity, hierarchization and emphasis of features, there are essentially three general descriptive dimensions that run like a golden thread through the history of the term: (1) modes and codes of sign perception and systematization, (2) spatial constellations, including questions of co-presence, reciprocity or modes of address, and (3) temporal constellations, including questions of temporariness or persistence of communicative exchanges (Holly 2011: 151; see also Luginbühl 2015: 13; Pentzold et al. 2013: 84). By applying these analytical criteria to concrete communicative practices, communication form serves to outline decidedly abstract text types or under-determined classes (Adamzik 2004: 100; see also Heinemann & Viehweger 1991). They first and foremost serve *heuristic* purposes in linguistics.

The notion communication form has been developed to classify, systematize and typologize communicative use on a fairly high level of description. Any endeavor to arrive at such generally applicable linguistic categories, then, involves abstracting away from concrete communicative *practice*. Even though the resulting categories are abstract and cognitive in nature, they *reflect* concrete use and naturally remain closely connected to it.[4] The assumption that scholars of the 'cultural practice'-strand (cf. Brock & Schildhauer, this volume) actually consider this cognitive dimension to be the result of a more complex process seems to be substantiated in Meiler (2013: 62). He grasps communication form as mental dispositif that results from stabilizing patterns of medial constellations for establishing communicative situations (Meiler 2013: 59). Since they are thought to assume shape *only* in communicative *practice* (Pentzold et al. 2013: 85), the cognitive dimension necessary to grasp communication form as concept of medial *potentiality* („Konzept medialer Ermöglichungen", Pentzold et al. 2013: 85) may easily appear backgrounded.

While the respective terminological choices *could* seem unfortunate as the lines between *potential* and concrete *use* appear to blur, I agree in emphasizing the important role of concrete *practices* in charting more abstract typologies as part of linguistic analysis. Not only can such a *practice*-based modelling of communication form be seen in the linguistic usage of everyday sorting terms („Sortierbegriffe", Dimter 1981; see also Holly 2011: 147) as communication- form labels. It can also

4 This could possibly explain why scholars like Holly (2011), Meiler (2013), Pentzold et al. (2013), or Domke (2014) have conceptualized communication forms as medium-based cultural practices. Consequently, their definition could result from a *metonymical* simplification of a complex process that comprises a realization of cognitive patterns in text production, and a cognitive patterning on the basis of concrete text exemplars. Labeling such cognitive abstractions *practices* is, essentially, taking the (potential) *result* and source of reflection to be the cognitive reflection itself.

be traced back to early conceptualizations. According to Ermert (1979: 60), for instance, the communication form NEWSPAPER ARTICLE is characterized by monologic communication in institutional settings by means of a written code and a medium not accessible to the general public. It features a periodical, temporally and spatially indirect – and hence non-acoustic and non-visual – contact between participants, who are share an indefinite and impersonal degree of familiarity. The medial basis on which his conceptualization of NEWSPAPER ARTICLE grounds is likely to comprise paper, a printing press, and editorial staff. That communication forms outlined for this specific medial basis are essentially practice- and experience-based measures is, then, supported by two observations: First, NEWSPAPER ARTICLES can appear non-periodically (cf. a non-periodical publication of MAGAZINE ARTICLES in the early days of the *National Geographic Magazine*) or could theoretically be produced and received by a single participant. And, second, we are able to name further broad *forms* of communication in relation to this medium, such as BOOK, or LETTER.[5] If we assume that linguistics aims at enriched descriptions of communicative *practice* (cf. Adamzik 1995: 24), then communication form could be even more decidedly anchored in everyday life by making it more flexible in, firstly, *what* criteria it comprises, secondly, in *how* particular criteria are weighted, and thirdly, *how* both selection and weighting of criteria change over time:

Firstly, functionality, for instance, is traditionally used to distinguish between genres and communication forms. While, according to Holly (2011: 157), some communication forms may *appear* to be "'[o]ne-trick-ponies'", he argues that they generally possess a distinctively large functional range. Genres, in contrast, are said to be functionally more specific (see also Brinker et al. 2014: 142). Recent studies, however, have argued for a multi-functionality of genres (see, e.g., Askehave & Swales 2001: 204; see also Brock & Schildhauer, this volume). Holly (2011) actually considers the existence of mono-functional communication forms, and Brinker et al. (2014) speak of dominant text functions – among less dominant ones. Functionality might serve as a distinguishing feature for many, but not for all cases. This is why current conceptualizations seem too rigid to grasp the complexity of communicative reality they try to systematize. It could, thus, be argued that communication forms are categories with a less complex intension, in contrast to genres, which have an enriched intension that applies to a smaller number of texts only (cf. Ziegler 2002: 24).

5 The latter aspect also suggests establishing an even more abstract level of potentiality for the purposes of grasping *any*thing that can possibly be done with a medium, namely *affordances* (see below).

Secondly, the *typicality* of feature constellations that results from abstracting away from concrete us is traceable in early as well as recent conceptualizations. Applying his matrix (cf. semantic notations) of communication form-features to a selection of communicative phenomena, Ermert (1979: 60) encloses some of the plusses and minuses in brackets, and thereby makes judgements on typicality; Schmitz' (2004: 58) list of communication forms uses the same of indicating typicality. In a similar fashion, Holly (2001: 153), specifies the code-dimension of Email and Letter with „Schrift" and adds „(Grafik, Bilder)" in brackets.

Thirdly, if we subscribe to grounding communication form on everyday use, it seems plausible that it is also an essentially dynamic notion that organically (re) evolves against the background of general socio-historical developments and technological progress (cf. Bittner 2003: 299). This means that communication forms can undergo change, e.g., a sub-differentiation on a genre-level based on a re-routinization of concrete communicative *practices* they abstract away from (Pentzold et al. 2013: 86; see also Holly 2011; Domke 2014: 26; Meiler 2013). Furthermore, the number of communication forms that builds on a medium can increase or decrease; a communication form may even migrate from one medium to another as in the case of Magazine Article which is still published in print but also in online environments (cf. Stöckl 2012: 19; Holly 2000: 84). This suggests that socio-historical and technological changes are, to a certain extent, *medial* changes. As I will argue below, they can be consciously induced by participants with the intention to achieve their communicative goals by inscribing new *affordances* into a medial basis.

❹ **affordances** | The assumption that, in some cases, one medium gives rise to a number of different communication forms, in my view, suggests establishing an even wider space of *potentiality* on a higher level of abstraction – while containing communication form and genre as less abstract *potentiality spaces*. In contrast to these levels however, this mapping of *potentiality* is less determined by (a reflection of) patterns of typical use; it rather orientates towards *any*thing that can *possibly* be done with a given medium. In order to grasp these phenomena, I draw on the concept of medial *affordances* as coined by the psychologist James Gibson (1979). Subsuming human beings under the wider label *animal*, he conceptualizes affordances as "what [the environment, J.P.] *offers* the animal, what it *provides* or *furnishes*" (Gibson 1979: 127, emphases in the original). The term affordances, in essence, refers to all (inter)actions a medium can be employed for from the perspective of a living creature that engages in its use. It comprises those activities we know and have names for (e.g. folding, holding, turning, burning a piece of paper; cf. Brock & Schildhauer, this volume), extends into the area of known but unlabeled actions, and even to hypothetical ones which remain disclosed until uncovered by creativity or coincidence. Following this *broad* notion of affordances, what can be done with an object is solely determined by the object's properties in relation to the natural capacities of its user.

For media linguists and semioticians (see, e.g., Eisenlauer 2016; Kress & van Leeuwen 2001; Luginbühl 2015; Pentzold et al. 2013) interested in the dynamics of technology-based communication, not only Gibson's publications, but also Hutchby's work on "Technologies, Texts and Affordances" (2001) has been influential. By addressing some idiosyncrasies of human interaction with (technological) media, he (somewhat implicitly) sketches out what is, in my view, a *narrow* reading of affordances factoring in *conventionality* and *human agency*:

Firstly, Hutchby stresses the role of fundamental socio-cultural *conventions* such as trends, norms, taboos (Hutchby 2001: 448), which determine, i.e. disclose or constrain, the range of an object's *possibilities* for action from a human perspective. It is essentially this very basic bi-dimensional take on *affordances* that blends smoothly into media linguistic theorization (see, e.g., Pentzold et al. 2013: 86) and allows placing the concept above more specific cognitive patterning of communicative practices, such as communication form or genre.

Secondly, Hutchby stresses that *affordances* can be of many types including those of *materials* that exist as natural resources, but also those of *artefacts*, i.e. objects manufactured by humans to serve specific purposes. As part of this manufacturing process, they can be consciously "designed into the artefact" (Hutchby 2001: 449) in anticipation of a desired functionality. This assumption points to the fundamental dynamics of medial-technical development in the light of changing socio-cultural contexts and communicative needs and practices. The patterning of communicative choices from a range of currently describable affordances that are then patterned as genres, and generalized as communication forms is clearly a driving force of these changes (cf. Pentzold et al. 2013: 86). In addition, however, it seems plausible to assume the *broader* framework of all possible and even hypothetical affordances mentioned above as a room for other kinds of creative and coincidental innovations, which can then be more purposefully built into a medium.

❺ **medium** | As we have just seen, affordances are closely linked to a *medium* as it is media that offer potentials for action. In the widest sense, medium can be described as a *mediating vehicle* in communication, which serves to enhance, produce, store and/or transmit signs (cf. Holly 1997, 2000; Ziegler 2002: 21); media are tools for bridging temporal and spatial distances, and, essentially, the gaps between one brain and another (cf. Holly 2011: 144).[6] Depending on the specific

6 By arguing that „[k]ein Hirn greift unmittelbar auf ein anderes zu" (2011: 144), Holly promotes a rather essentialistic understanding of the concept *medium* and *mediality*.

research objects and interests of certain academic disciplines, mediating vehicles have been attested at different levels of abstraction (cf. Burger & Luginbühl 2014: 2), and various dimensions of mediality have been foregrounded. Consequently, medium has evolved into a highly polysemous term.

In an endeavor to systematize the 'terminological chaos' („begrifflich[es] Chaos", Posner 1985: 258), Posner suggests six distinct readings of the term: At the center of the analytical attention are concrete text exemplars that (typically) reflect both the *potentiality* of conventionalized communicative patterns (culture-related), socially-conditioned styles (sociological) and systematized multimodal resources for meaning-making (code-related), as well as the *reality* of the perceptive qualities (biological) of the technical (technological) and/or material (physical) devices used for actualization (cf. Posner 1985: 258, translations acc. to Brock & Schildhauer, this volume: 14; see also Stöckl 2012: 16–17).

Figure 1 accounts for all of these readings that refer to components of a complex mediating process from sender to recipient. On closer inspection, however, the infographic indicates that I consider genre, communication form, and affordances as phenomena that are distinct from medium, even though they play their part in a more complex process of *mediating* information. In order to outline a narrower definition of *medium*, I follow a general tendency in media linguistics to foreground the *material-technical* side of mediality (cf. Burger & Luginbühl 2014; Holly 2000; Luginbühl 2015; Stöckl 2012). Modelling the particular case of commercial press communication, however, seems to require a more pronounced account for mass media institutions and their influence on *how* communication takes place. I follow Stöckl (2012) – and, in fact, a broader tendency in media linguistics to study processes of mediatization and media logics (see Androutsopoulos 2014 for an overview; Pflaeging forthcoming on mediatization and popular science journalism) – in complementing a *material-technical* dimension with a *sociological* one.

So, even though all dimensions of mediality experience some degree of foregrounding over the course of a communicative exchange, I consider those two as basic components of a medial basis, which then generally affords text production by means of specific modes, or sign repertoires (cf. Holly 2000; Stöckl 2012) in certain communicative temporal and spatial situations (cf. Brinker et al. 2014: 141; Domke 2014). As indicated above, these possible constellations, then, constitute communicative potentials (affordances), which form the basis of specific feature constellations (communication forms) at a lower level of abstraction. Figure 1 is

---

This is in contrast to Dürscheid (2005: 14), for instance, who assumes face-to-face communication to be *im*mediate communication.

meant to illustrate that the number of communication forms afforded by a medium as well as the number of media that can serve to afford one communication form may vary and could range from one to many (cf. Stöckl 2012: 19).

The juxtaposition of the two dimensions material-technical and sociological medium furthermore allows granting *human agency* (Hutchby 2001: 445; see also Luginbühl 2015) an important position. So, even though every thought and idea that experiences realization is in some way shaped by the potentials afforded by a medium chosen for realization (cf. Burger & Luginbühl 2014: 3), media (i.e., technical transmission devices and/or deeply ingrained processes at institutions) do not completely determine communicative practices (Luginbühl 2015: 14): First of all, there is always room for making communicative choices from the potentials media afford. Furthermore, human agency is observable in people consciously adapting media in such a way that medial affordances change in accordance with the intentions communicants (i.e., both individuals and institutionalized groups) have in mind. The metaphor A Medium Is A Text, as suggested by the sociologists Grint & Woolgar (1997), vividly illustrates these processes of *interpretation* and *creation*, which are considerably relevant in the light of modeling diachronic developments of medial landscapes and associated communicative practices. So, besides drawing on natural resources as vehicles for communication, medial resources and their affordances have been culturally shaped and re-shaped in processes of intentional adaptation as long as mediated communication exists (see Figure 1). These shifts and changes, then, may also lead to a re-modelling of *potentiality* constellations in the sense of communication forms and genres in the minds of linguists and non-linguists.

3. Diachronic Perspectives on Popular Science Journalism

In the following, I will sketch out the journalistic practices of the popular science magazine *National Geographic* over a period of 100 years of its publication history by analyzing an exemplary set of five 1915 and 2015 issues. For each data set, I will first provide a brief account of relevant medium-related aspects which comprise both the material-technical tools employed for text production (*physical* and *technological*), and the institutional setting (*sociological*) of publishing the magazine. Based on these constellations, I will point to general *affordances* to characterize the communicative potentials that arise from the respective medial 'set-ups'. As a second step, I will chart how these potentials are *used* in the popular science journalism of the magazine at the said points in time. In particular, my interest is in describing the diachronic development of the communication form

MAGAZINE ARTICLE and associated genres such as *Feature Article*, and later *Your Shot* or *Visions of Earth*, as realized in the magazine.

3.1. 1915: Visual Ventures and Breaking up the Gray

Medial Foundations, Communicative Potentials

The material-technical set-up available to the editors of the *National Geographic* magazine by 1915 had resulted from a number of revolutionary developments in photography and printing over the course of the 19th century. The invention of photography and swift progress in photographic reproduction itself had made printing of multimodal pages possible. The introduction of half-tone printing in the late 1880s (Mott 1957: 153; cf. Johnson & Prijatel 1999: 65; Tausk 1988: 10), however, solved the technical (and financial) difficulties publishers were facing when trying to simultaneously print photographs and text. It afforded a quick and less expensive reproduction than established wood engraving by re-photographing an image on a "sensitized [metal, J.P.] plate through a fine screen, and acid baths would remove or reduce the printing points of the whites in order to make a plate by 'automatic' process." (Mott 1957: 153) The plates could then be mounted on a wooden block and printed simultaneously with letter types (Newhall 1989: 259). Color printing had been technically possible since the 1860s (Johnson & Prijatel 1999: 71), but processes of color subtraction in half-tone printing made the reproduction of color photographs easier.

Fueled by the ongoing industrial revolution, the publishing industry strove for increasing the time- and cost-efficiency of printing processes for commercial press publications. Originally produced by hand from cloth, paper could be made from wood at significantly reduced prices from the mid-19th century onwards (Johnson & Prijatel 1999: 66, 71; Mott 1957; Tausk 1988: 27). Also, a monotype composing machine became a time-saving improvement as it helped to cast types automatically in lines. Printing presses, as well, experienced great improvement over the course of the 19th century. By 1871 already, a web perfecting printing press had complemented and succeeded earlier rotary (1847) and steam-powered presses (1822), and now allowed for "simultaneously printing both sides of a continuous roll of paper" (Johnson & Prijatel 1999: 71).

However, while material-technical innovations and their affordances quickly spread in the publishing industry, they cannot directly be assumed to be the material-technical set-up of a specific publication. Even though many commercial publishers kept improving their financial situation by incorporating advertisements into their newspapers and magazines, both funding as well as time was needed to modernize printing offices, to train employees, and to cultivate communicative patterns which would then be recognized, and demanded by an audience (Tausk 1988: 41–42).

Marked by Gilbert Grosvenor's employment as editor in 1899, the *National Geographic* magazine turned from academic publishing for a niche audience to a *popular* science journalism targeting larger and more heterogeneous reader groups. The Washington-based printing house *Judd & Detweiler* began working for the *National Geographic Society* in 1901 (Zimmermann 2013). In contrast to earlier printers, their material-technical equipment was able to meet the requirements of steadily growing circulation numbers and afforded color reproduction (Judd & Detweiler 1968). Furthermore, Grosvenor "opened the organization's photographic laboratory to do the *Society's* own film and print processing and to begin experimenting with new techniques." (Abramson 2010: 133) On the one hand, this points to the interplay between material-technical equipment and institutional (or sociological) constellations in forming a medial basis. On the other hand, it aptly illustrates how human agency may lead to medial adaptations by intentionally inscribing new (specialized) affordances into a medial basis whose general potentials for text production are inherently wide.

Communicative Use

Around 1900, the *National Geographic* magazine was "tall-octavo in size" (Mott 1957: 621), bound into a plain cover and still featured on most of the pages "a single column of basically uninterrupted type, broken only occasionally by a large capital letter and a small headline." (Abramson 2010: 59) This suggests that the communicative conventions, i.e. established communication forms and genres, of 19th century academic journal publishing still depicted a strong influence. However, the fact that quite a number of pages employ embedded patterns of ADVERTISEMENT-genres typical of *commercial* press communication indicates that the magazine had already begun targeting wider *popular* audiences with a science journalism that was "light and entertaining" (Lutz & Collins 1993: 22).

It was an interplay of such inspirations from the contemporary medial landscape, esp. journalistic practices of other popular magazines, e.g., *Harper's* or *Century* (Lutz & Collins 1993: 22), and coincidence, that eventually led to an increase in photographs as part of *Feature Articles*. Editor Grosvenor reports in retrospection: "By sheer chance I received in the mail 50 beautiful photographs of Lhasa, [...] on the very day that I urgently needed 11 pages of material for the January, 1905, issue. [...] So I filled the entire 11 pages with the photographs, raiding the Society's slim treasury to make the plates" (NGM 1963/Oct: 565). In the April 1905 issue, Grosvenor decided to print 138 photographs of the Philippines. Despite the high production costs, the incorporation of photographs still seemed to outweigh the expenses. As readers stopped him in the street to express their appreciation, as second printings of issues had to be ordered, and as membership "soared from 3,662 in January 1905 to 11,479 by the end of the year" (Johnson & Prijatel 1999: 67), the new multimodal communicative practices stabilized over time due to commercial success.

By 1915, the affordances for photographic reproduction were used extensively; photography had become "chief among National Geographic's strategies for 'diffusing' global geographic knowledge" (Hawkins 2010: 76). My analysis shows that most of the double-pages included both text and image. The mean number of images published as part of features, which extended over 32.6 pages on average, was 29.20 (i.e., 0.91 images per page). Even though color reproduction had been possible for over 50 years, and despite the fact that the National Geographic was the first to run a "true color photograph" in the previous year (Johnson & Prijatel 1999: 67; Mott 1957: 626), all 146 images in my 1915 corpus were black and white half-tones. It seems that there was no need to invest in significantly more expensive color reproductions, if the readers' thirst for images could be quenched by monochromes. Based on these findings, Figure 2 visualizes a prototypical multimodal macro-structure of the genre *Feature Article* by the example of "Glimpses of Holland". It also suggests that photographs typically covered large parts of a page, but never extended into the margins, even though material-technical constellations would have afforded it.

Figure 2: Multimodal Macro-structure of "Glimpses of Holland," NGM (1915/Jan)

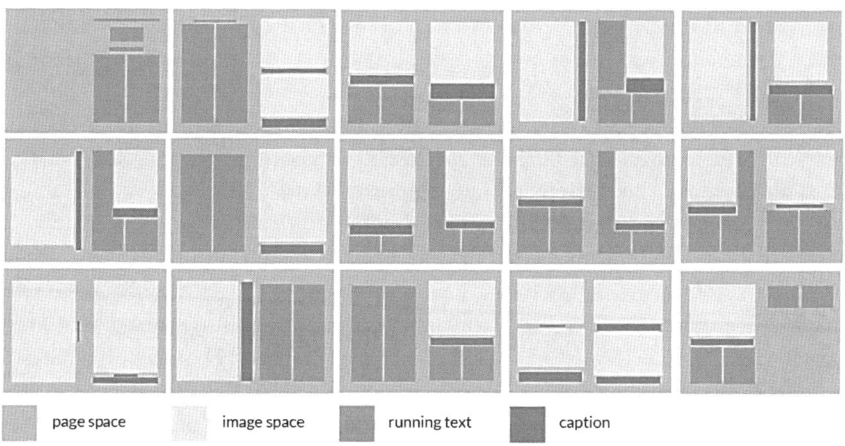

Mean values and averages, however, conceal that communicative practices vary visibly with regard to some of the genre's features: While image captions comprised 59.89 tokens on average, they ranged from 195 to 3 word-forms. Similarly, a typical *Feature Article*-exemplar extended over 32.6 pages on mean average, but exemplars ranged from 53 to 25 pages. This indicates that *potentials* within the realms of this specific genre were explored extensively at a time when the magazine was still trying to find its own path.

Figure 3: Genre Profiles of 1915 Issues of the 'National Geographic' Magazine

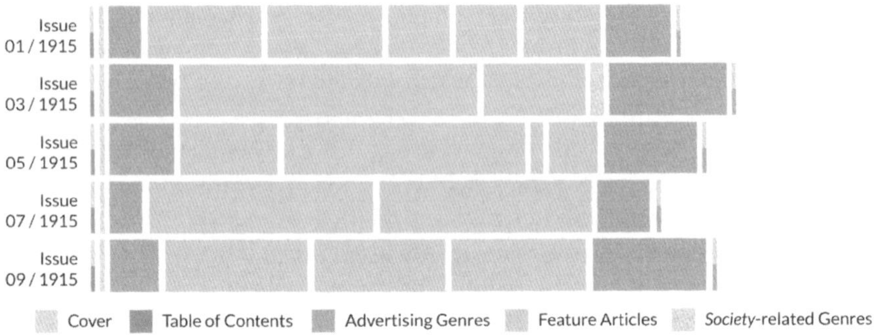

The text exemplars are similar enough to still be grouped under the genre-label *Feature Article* and show that a wide range of *potentials* afforded by the given medial setting and contoured by the established communication form MAGAZINE ARTICLE is only used to a small extent after all. In the March 1915 issue, Grosvenor writes that "the Magazine can point to many years in which not a single article has appeared which was not absolutely accurate" (NGM 1915/Mar: 319). Looking at concrete communicative practice in the 1915 data set, (MAGAZINE) ARTICLE refers to a mean average of 3.2 exemplars of the genre *Feature Article*. For the moment, a high degree of pattern variation points to journalistic practices that explored the realms of the genre while slowly stabilizing a *feature article*-pattern. As I have tried to show, three main mechanisms of making *concrete* communicative choices from vast *potentials* can be identified:

Firstly, even though the *Society* is a non-profit organization in a strict sense, they are a commercially operating institution looking to run the magazine self-sufficiently, and invest any revenue into new equipment as well as research on and off the field (cf., e.g., NGM 1913/Feb: 256). Therefore, in making choices on what gets published and how, costs play a decisive role. Even though Gilbert Grosvenor took financial risks, benefits were believed to outweigh unusually high expenses. Editor Gilbert Grosvenor identified or even projected general trends and progressions in the communicative practices magazine readers preferred. This, secondly, illustrates that changes are not necessarily induced by large and diffuse groups of people, but may go back to smaller editorial teams and individual decision-makers. Thirdly, the anecdote of Grosvenor who, looking to fill a dozen pages at the last minute, spontaneously published eleven photographs he had been sent by an acquaintance on the previous day, reveals that coincidence as well factors into exploring communicative *potentials* in unforeseen ways.

3.2. 2015: Visual Ventures into the Margins

Medial Foundations, Communicative Potentials

During the second half of the 20th century, a number of technological developments commenced, that eventually led to readjustments of the material-technical basis for producing the *National Geographic* magazine. The *National Geographic Society* had long been working with the Washington-based publisher *Judd & Detweiler*, who printed the magazine by means of large letterpresses. Even though these machines were able to produce "letterpress printing of the highest quality, work from these ponderous sheet-fed machines was not commercially salable" (Judd & Detweiler 1968). With 2.25 million members in the mid-1950s and a projection for an increase up to 4 million by the early 1960s, the *National Geographic Society* opted for the Chicago-based *RR Donelly* as a new publisher from May 1959 onwards. In spacious printing facilities, they operated heat-set high-speed web cylinder letterpresses in combination with newly developed heatable ink, which significantly reduced the production time, and hence costs. Although even cheaper printing methods were developed in the 1950s and 1960s, letterpress printing remained the preferred option until the 1970s. The reasons for this lay in a more profitable cost-benefit ratio: Letterpress plates were able to keep up with the growing circulation numbers; the higher production costs outweighed the multiple plate changes necessary in offset printing. Offset, however, was used for pages with region-specific advertisements that were printed in smaller quantities (Zimmermann 2013).

Also, photographic equipment was continuously improved "until a stage was reached which enabled them [i.e., photographers, J.P.] to record practically everything the human eye can see" (Tausk 1988: 231). Film cameras were more widely used by professional photographers to conduct field work (Bendavid-Val [1994]2008: 36; Tausk 1988: 147). Photographic lenses were perfected (Tausk 1988: 147), the sensitivity of the material to light improved, and the problems with exposure could be reduced on the basis of photo-electronic light meters which helped to estimate exposure and aperture times (Newhall 1989: 291). In photographic reproduction, the separation of colors, which had long remained technically challenging and resulted in the impression of a dirty palette until the late 1960s (Zimmermann 2013), could eventually be solved.

As the influence of the rival publisher *WF Hall* grew and the rotogravure printing technology they employed became a considerable alternative, *National Geographic* ended their contract with *RR Donelly* in 1977/78 and, with this, their 90-year history of letterpress printing. The new printing presses afforded a particularly high amount of ink transference onto the paper. Even though half-tone plates are still used to print the image spaces, and "the shadows have to have a dot for the cylinders to hold ink, the sheer amount of pigment going down yields terrific blacks" (Zimmermann 2013) and the typical dot pattern has almost disappeared. Even though publishing companies have changed a number of times over the past 40 years, rotogravure printing has ever since formed a stable medial basis for the *National Geographic*'s popular science journalism and the high quality reproduction of photographs it is famous for today.

Improved printing quality was paralleled by an increase in the quantity of photographs that could be more easily produced and chosen by increasingly professionalized freelance photojournalists. Bendavid-Val (2008: 33) recapitulates the process of photo selection at the *National Geographic* headquarters in the mid-1990s as follows:

> A dozen photographers crowded into a room [...]. Most employees had gone home, [...] a few people working against deadlines, and the group of photographers with their trays of slides. They gathered in a windowless projection room. The photographers [...] settled in for [...] a 'tray party.' You bring your tray of 35-mm slides and, if you want, a bottle of wine. Someone turned on a projector and switched off the overhead lights. [...] They were showing what they had shot. [...] Depending on the assignment, photographers can come back with 600 to 800 rolls of film – about 20,000 to 30,000 frames. But pictures are not of 20,000 different subjects. Photographers think ahead to the editing process, which reduces the number of pictures to a single slide tray – 80 slots.

With the advent and spread of computer technology, many magazines took steps to adapt to the *potentials* the changing media landscape offered. In the mid-1990s, publishers began to explore the possibilities of processing all information digitally (Johnson & Prijatel 1999: 71), and later virtually via the Internet. While the principle "computer-to-plate" is still in application today, the means to accomplish it have been improved decisively: *National Geographic* magazine staff works with desktop publishing software by *Adobe* (Adobe TV 2016), especially *InDesign* used for composing the layout of single pages as well as compiling individual sets of pages to a ready-to-print magazine design, *Photoshop* for the post-production of now typically digital photography, and *Illustrator* for creating vector-based pictorial elements such as graphics or infographics. Vector-based digital processing also afforded new dimensions of setting headlines, captions, and running text, with hundreds of fonts at hand which are scalable and movable within the layout space. Apart from technological advancements for composition as such, it is the *affordance* to create and re-use stylesheets and pre-composed page layouts which has optimized the production flow further.

Over the course of the 20th century, paper-making, photography and photographic reproduction by means of half-tones, and printing technology were developed further with the intention to inscribe affordances into a medial basis that would allow producing text exemplars of the highest possible quality at costs that are reasonable in the light of a non-profit organization's expenses.

Communicative Use

In comparison to 1915 genre-exemplars, feature articles have become much more centered around the visual by 2015 (see Figure 4). Having grown into a "mainstay and distinguishing feature of the magazine" (Lutz & Collins 1993: 27), both material-technical equipment and the institutional development was geared towards delivering high quality photographic reproduction (Bendavid-Val [1994] 2008: 50). Dot patterns are now invisible to the unaided eye as cyan, magenta, yellow and black ink merge on the 60 lbs. coated paper of 2015 issues (Zimmermann 2013). Even though the mean number of images published as part of a feature decreased to 14 images, i.e. 0.53 per page, the layout space taken up by images is extensive. In most cases, they bleed into the margins of the page and cover the entire double-page. Easily afforded by graphic software, captions have been moved into the image space. While, in 1915, pattern variation was considerably wider with respect to article and caption length, 100 years later those features have evidently stabilized. 2015 feature articles typically extend over 26.4 pages, with 20 pages for the shortest and 30 pages for the longest exemplar. Images were typically accompanied by a caption of 29.26 token on average. In contrast to highly diverse caption lengths in 1915, 2015 captions only varied between 22 and 69 words, with 69 as an extreme outlier.

Figure 4: Multimodal Macro-structure of "The First Year", NGM (2015/Jan)

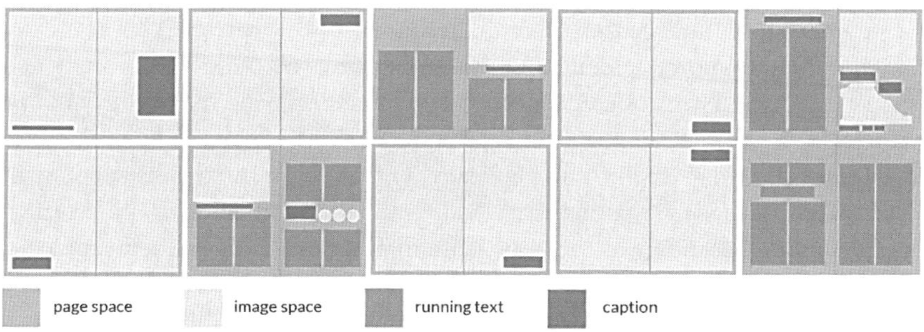

As the genre *feature article* stabilized on the page, and hence in the minds of text producers and recipients, the communication form MAGAZINE ARTICLE began to experience sub-differentiation. When *National Geographic* magazine editors realized that "our readers had less leisure time to spend on reading magazines" (Ryan & Conover 2004: 506), they opted for "creat[ing] more immediate, accessible sections allowing the reader additional entry points for browsing" (Ryan & Conover 2004: 505) through the issues. As Figure 5 suggests, the magazine's genre repertoire became more diverse with smaller, highly attention-grabbing genres.

Figure 5: Genre Profiles of 2015 Issues of the 'National Geographic' Magazine

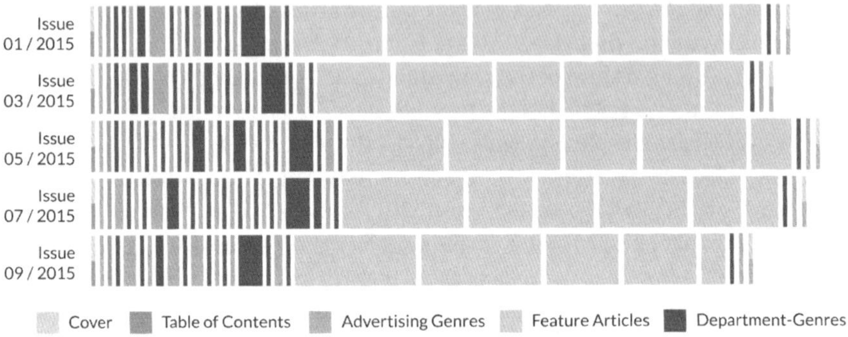

Browsing through the pages of 2015 issues, we encounter smaller self-contained multimodal texts in the department-section. They recur in all five issues of my data set and have come to bear genre labels such as *Your Shot* or *Visions of Earth*. The repertoire of these less extensive texts is diverse and has changed decisively ever since their successive introduction in the 1980s. The January 2005 issue, for instance, contained an even broader selection of genres, namely *OnScreen & Online, Behind the Scenes, Visions of Earth, Geographica, My Seven, On Assignment, Who Knew?, Final Edit, Do It Yourself*, and *Flashback*.

In 2015, all of these genres, including *Feature Article*, share the characteristics of being mainly monologic, institutionally situated, periodical, temporally and spatially indirect forms of contact between participants, who may or may not be familiar with one another. Realized in print media, MAGAZINE ARTICLE allows for communication via visually (and haptically) perceivable text exemplars, and typically makes use of the verbal and visual codes with a growing emphasis on the latter. In 1915, *Feature Article* was the only genre that the magazine's editors employed as MAGAZINE ARTICLE, the communication form has become more complex at a genre-level. While the general characteristics are still valid, the differences between genres have become more diverse on the genre-level and lie in specific topical choices and the details of the multimodal macro-structure as well as language and image use.

Most of these developments ought to be explained on the basis of, first, technological progress and institutional re-organization fueled by the intention to achieve a healthy cost-benefit ratio by optimizing medial affordances, and hence the production flow on all levels. Secondly, even though the *National Geographic* magazine has been remarkably avant-garde in many respects throughout its publishing history, its successful economic management – like that of most other popular commercial press publications – is inextricably linked with building on established conventions. Communicative patterns that turn out to be appreciated by large parts of the audience naturally contribute to the likelihood of pattern recurrence. Third, communicative patterns that gain prominence in other spheres of a contemporary medial landscape, and therefore render visible more general communicative trends, can be of interest for mass-market publications. Picture galleries, typical of online communication, that have come to be incorporated into print versions of newspapers exemplify processes of pattern embedding. The segmentation of information (cf. Bucher 1996) that has become apparent in 2015 issues of the magazine could be regarded as another example.

4. Conclusion & Outlook

In this contribution, I drew on the notion *communication form* to trace its diachronic sub-differentiation at a genre-level for the example of 1915 and 2015 issues of the *National Geographic*. According to my empirical investigations, five prominent factors seem to guide text producers in choosing from the *potentials* available by a medium's affordances, communication forms, and genres at a certain point in time, and result in pattern stability and change from a diachronic perspective:

1) **Costs** | Although the *National Geographic Society* has always been a non-profit organization, they have been commercial in the sense that expenses for operating and maintaining the medial basis, actual text production, and funding activities need to be compensated. As a general principle for *commercial* press communication, a healthy cost-benefit ratio always rules out at least a fair share of communicative potentials.
2) **Individual Decisions & Coincidence** | Gilbert Grosvenor's decision to fill space by publishing eleven large photographs he had been sent coincidentally on the previous day meant taking commercial risks. It exemplifies, however,

how an individual's decisions can lead to exploring the potentials of a medium and thereby initiating pattern change.

3) **Commercial Success** | Commercial success is something that typically stabilizes patterns in retrospect. Much more common than at the beginning of the 20th century, market research staff is typically employed today to estimate the likelihood of a pattern's commercial success.
4) **Convention & Pattern Stability** | A certain degree of preserving communicative patterns is evidently needed to ensure successful exchanges between members of a social community. However, given that editors of post-modern counter-culture magazines such as *Emigre* produced extremely diverging text exemplars (cf. Ryan & Conover 2004: 472) while using more or less the same medial basis, the communication forms the *National Geographic* magazine drew on remained comparatively stable. Former editor Connie Phelps points out that "we have to be deliberate and discreet in any changes we make" (Ryan & Conover 2004: 505).
5) **Innovation & Pattern Change** | Against the background of changing socio-historical and technological contexts, however, magazine editors need to explore the untrodden paths of a medium's affordances, or more specifically, communication forms and genres. Such explorative ventures might first and foremost result in moderate adjustments as in a 'more-or-less'-realization of genre features. However, a general trend towards visualizing information is also likely to have spurred the emergence (or *genrefication*) of the image-centric genre *Visions of Earth* in 2004 (cf. Pflaeging 2016). Furthermore, magazine editors might also consider the embedding of patterns that have proven zeitgeisty *elsewhere* an option.

As 100 years ago, "increase[ing] and diffuse[ing] geographic knowledge" (NGM 1888/Oct: i) is still the pronounced goal of the *National Geographic Society*. The means to pursue it have changed visibly in the light of the mechanisms described. Not only has the communication form MAGAZINE ARTICLE experienced sub-differentiation over the past 100 years into a diverse repertoire of genres within the realms of a medium's affordances. These socio-cognitive devices have also migrated to online environments where *feature articles*, for instance, show stability with respect to some of their genre features but change with respect to others. What we *perceive* to be a sweeping revolution of contemporary medial surroundings, however, actually necessitates more evolutionary developments since successful communication subsists on shared knowledge of communicative *practices*. It will, therefore, be interesting to see where we will be 100 years from *now* – in terms of communicative *practices*, in terms of socio-cognitive and medial *potentiality*, and the linguistic description of them.

Acknowledgements

I would like to thank Alexander Brock and Peter Schildhauer for making valuable comments on earlier versions of this manuscript.

Corpus

Issues and Feature Articles of the *National Geographic* magazine:

1915 | Issue: *January* | Feature Article: "Glimpses of Holland"

1915 | Issue: *March* | Feature Article: "Impressions of Palestine"

1915 | Issue: *May* | Feature Article: "Constantinople and Sancta Sophia"

1915 | Issue: *July* | Feature Article: "The Wonderland of California"

1915 | Issue: *September* | Feature Article: "London"

2015 | Issue: *January* | Feature Article: "The First Year of Life"

2015 | Issue: *March* | Feature Article: "Fleeing Terror, Finding Refuge"

2015 | Issue: *May* | Feature Article: "It's Time for a Conversation"

2015 | Issue: *July* | Feature Article: "Stalking a Killer"

2015 | Issue: *September* | Feature Article: "Point of no Return"

References

Abramson, Howard S.: *National Geographic. Behind America's Lens on the World.* iUniverse: Bloomington 2010.

Adamzik, Kirsten: *Textsorten, Texttypologie. Eine kommentierte Bibliographie.* Nodus: Münster 1995.

Adamzik, Kirsten: *Textlinguistik. Eine einführende Darstellung.* Niemeyer: Tübingen 2004.

Adobe TV: *National Geographic Explores New Frontiers. Adobe Systems Incorporated*, retrieved 17.09.2016, from http://tv.adobe.com/watch/digital-publishing-customer-showcase/national-geographic/, 2016.

Askehave, Inger & Swales, John M.: "Genre Identification and Communicative Purpose. A Problem and a Possible Solution". *Applied Linguistics* 22(2), 2001, 195–212.

Bateman, John A.: "Genre in the Age of Multimodality. Some Conceptual Refinements for Practical Analysis". In: Evangelisti Allori, Paola et al. (eds.):

Evolution in Genre. Emergence, Variation, Multimodality. Peter Lang: Bern 2014, 237–269.

Bateman, John A.: "Methodological and Theoretical Issues in Multimodality". In: Klug, Nina-Maria & Stöckl, Hartmut (eds.): *Sprache im multimodalen Kontext*. de Gruyter: Berlin, Boston 2016, 36–74.

Bendavid-Val, Leah: *National Geographic. The Photographs*. National Geographic Society: Washington [1994] 2008.

Bittner, Johannes: *Digitalität, Sprache, Kommunikation. Eine Untersuchung zur Medialität von digitalen Kommunikationsformen und Textsorten und deren varietätenlinguistischer Modellierung*. Erich Schmidt Verlag: Berlin 2003.

Brinker, Klaus et al.: *Linguistische Textanalyse. Eine Einführung in Grundbegriffe und Methoden*. Erich Schmidt Verlag: Berlin 2014.

Brock, Alexander & Schildhauer, Peter: "Communication Form. A Concept Revisited". In: Brock, Alexander & Schildhauer, Peter (eds.): *Communication Forms and Communicative Practices. New Perspectives on Communication Forms, Affordances, and What Users Make of Them*. Peter Lang: Berlin, this volume 13–43.

Bucher, Hans-Jürgen: „Textdesign – Zaubermittel der Verständlichkeit? Die Tageszeitung auf dem Weg zum interaktiven Medium". In: Hess-Lüttich, Ernest W.B. et al. (eds.): *Textstrukturen im Medienwandel*. Peter Lang: Frankfurt am Main et al. 1996, 31–60.

Burger, Harald & Luginbühl, Martin: *Mediensprache. Eine Einführung in Sprache und Kommunikationsformen der Massenmedien*. de Gruyter: Berlin & Boston 2014.

Davis, Melissa: *More Than a Name. An Introduction to Branding*. AVA: Lausanne 2005.

Diewald, Gabriele: *Deixis und Textsorten im Deutschen*. Niemeyer: Tübingen 1991.

Dimter, Matthias: *Textklassenkonzepte heutiger Alltagssprache. Kommunikationssituation, Textfunktion, Textinhalt als Kategorien alltagssprachlicher Textklassifikation*. Niemeyer: Tübingen 1981.

Domke, Christine: „Texte im öffentlichen Raum. Formen medienvermittelter Kommunikation auf Bahnhöfen". In: Bucher, Hans-Jürgen et al. (eds.): *Neue Medien, neue Formate. Ausdifferenzierung und Konvergenz in der Medienkommunikation*. Campus Verlag: Frankfurt am Main 2010, 257–281.

Domke, Christine: *Die Betextung des öffentlichen Raumes. Eine Studie zur Spezifik von Meso-Kommunikation am Beispiel von Bahnhöfen, Innenstädten und Flughäfen*. Winter: Heidelberg 2014.

Dürscheid, Christa: „Medien, Kommunikationsformen, kommunikative Gattungen". *Linguistik Online* 22(1), 2005, 3–16.

Dürscheid, Christa: „E-Mail: Eine neue Kommunikationsform?“ In: Moraldo, Sandro M. (ed.): *Internet.Kom. Neue Sprach- und Kommunikationsformen im WorldWideWeb.* AracneEditrice: Roma 2009, 39–70.

Eisenlauer, Volker: „Facebook als multimodaler Gesamttext“. In: Klug, Nina-Maria Klug & Stöckl, Hartmut (eds.): *Sprache im multimodalen Kontext.* de Gruyter: Berlin & Boston 2016, 437–454.

Ermert, Karl: *Briefsorten. Untersuchungen zu Theorie und Empirie der Textklassifikation.* Niemeyer: Tübingen 1979.

Foster, Beth: *Evolution of National Geographic Magazine. National Geographic Society*, retrieved 23.09.2016, from http://press.nationalgeographic.com/files/2012/05/NGM-History-10-12.pdf, 2012.

Gibson, James J.: *The Ecological Approach to Visual Perception.* Houghton Mifflin: Boston 1979.

Grint, Keith & Woolgar, Steve: *The Machine at Work. Technology, Work, and Organization.* Blackwell: Malden 1997.

Gülich, Elisabeth & Raible, Wolfgang (eds.). *Textsorten. Differenzierungskriterien aus linguistischer Sicht.* Athenäum: Frankfurt am Main 1972.

Hawkins, Stephanie L.: *American Iconographic. National Geographic, Global Culture, and the Visual Imagination.* University of Virginia Press: Charlottesville 2010.

Holly, Werner: „Zur Rolle von Sprache in den Medien. Semiotische und kommunikationsstrukturelle Grundlagen“. *Muttersprache* 107, 1997, 64–75.

Holly, Werner: „Was sind ‚Neue Medien' – Was sollen ‚Neue Medien' sein?“. In: Voss, G. Günter et al. (eds.): *Neue Medien im Alltag. Begriffsbestimmungen eines interdisziplinären Forschungsfeldes.* Leske + Budrich: Opladen 2000, 79–106.

Holly, Werner: „Medien, Kommunikationsformen, Textsortenfamilien“. In: Habscheid, Stephan (ed.): *Textsorten, Handlungsmuster, Oberflächen. Linguistische Typologien der Kommunikation.* de Gruyter: Berlin 2011, 144–163.

Hutchby, Ian: “Technologies, Texts and Affordances”. *Sociology* 35(2), 2001, 441–456.

Johnson, Sammye & Prijatel, Patricia: *The Magazine from Cover to Cover. Inside a Dynamic Industry.* NTC Publishing Group: Lincolnwood 1999.

Judd & Detweiler. *The First 100 Years of Judd & Detweiler.* Judd & Detweiler: Washington 1968.

Kress, Gunther R. & van Leeuwen, Theo: *Multimodal Discourse. The Modes and Media of Contemporary Communication.* Arnold & Oxford University Press: London & New York 2001.

Lomborg, Stine: *Social Media, Social Genres. Making Sense of the Ordinary*. Routledge: New York, London 2014.

Luginbühl, Martin. *Medienkultur und Medienlinguistik. Komparative Textsortengeschichte(n) der amerikanischen „CBS Evening News" und der Schweizer „Tagesschau"*. Peter Lang: Bern 2014.

Luginbühl, Martin: "Media Linguistics. On Mediality and Culturality". *10plus1 | Living Linguistics* 1, 2015, 9–26.

Luginbühl, Martin & Perrin, Daniel: „„das, was wir in der Tagesschau den Rausschmeißer nennen'. Altro- und Ethno-Kategorisierung von Textsorten im Handlungsfeld journalistischer Fernsehnachrichten". In: Habscheid, Stephan (ed.). *Textsorten, Handlungsmuster, Oberflächen. Linguistische Typologien der Kommunikation*. de Gruyter: Berlin 2011, 577–596.

Lutz, Catherine A. & Collins, Jane L.: *Reading National Geographic*. University of Chicago Press: Chicago 1993.

Miller, Carolyn R.: "Genre as Social Action". *Quarterly Journal of Speech* 70, 1984, 151–167.

Mott, Frank Luther: *A History of American Magazines. 1885–1905*. Harvard University Press: Cambridge, Mass 1957.

NGM Media Kit: *NGM Media Kit 2016. National Geographic Magazine*, retrieved 17.09.2016, from http://www.nationalgeographic.com/mediakit/pdf/ng-magazine/ NGM_Media_Kit_2016.pdf, 2016.

National Geographic Magazine: "Announcement". *National Geographic Society*, Oct. 1888, i-ii.

National Geographic Magazine: "The Progress of the National Geographic Society". *National Geographic Society*, Feb. 1913, 251–256.

National Geographic Magazine: "Report of the Director and Editor of the National Geographic Society for the Year 1914". *National Geographic Society*, Mar. 1915, 318–320.

National Geographic Magazine: "The Romance of the Geographic. National Geographic Magazine Observes its Diamond Anniversary". *National Geographic Society*, Oct. 1963, 516–585.

National Geographic Magazine: *National Geographic Society*, Apr. 1915.

National Geographic Magazine. *National Geographic Society*, Jan. 2005.

Newhall, Beaumont: *Geschichte der Photographie*. Schirmer-Mosel: München 1989.

Pentzold, Christian et al.: „Online-mediale Texte. Kommunikationsformen, Affordanzen, Interfaces". *Zeitschrift für Germanistische Linguistik* 41(1), 2013, 81–101.

Pflaeging, Jana: "Re-Negotiating the Storytelling Space. Tracing the Narrativization of the Genre 'Feature Article' in the Light of Changing Media Landscapes". *Discourse, Context and Media*, forthcoming.

Pflaeging, Jana: "'Things that Matter, Pass them on': ListSite as Viral Online Genre". *10plus1 / Living Linguistics* 1, 2015, 156–181.

Pflaeging, Jana: "On the Emergence of Image-Nuclear News Stories in the National Geographic Magazine". Conference Talk at Salzburg University. European Systemic Functional Linguistics Conference 2016. Salzburg, 15.07.2016.

Posner, Roland. „Nonverbale Zeichen in öffentlicher Kommunikation". *Zeitschrift für Semiotik* 7(3), 1985, 235–271.

Ryan, William E. & Conover, Theodore E.: *Graphic Communications Today*. Thomson & Delmar Learning: Clifton Park, NY 2004.

Sandig, Barbara: „Text als prototypisches Konstrukt". In: Mangasser-Wahl, Martina (ed.): *Prototypentheorie in der Linguistik. Anwendungsbeispiele – Methodenreflexion – Perspektiven*. Stauffenburg: Tübingen 2000, 93–112.

Schildhauer, Peter: *Textsorten im Internet zwischen Wandel und Konstanz. Eine diachrone Analyse der Textsorte Personal Weblog*. PhD Dissertation. Martin-Luther-Universität Halle-Wittenberg, 2014.

Schildhauer, Peter: *The Personal Weblog. A Linguistic History*. Peter Lang: Frankfurt am Main 2016.

Schmitz, Ulrich: *Sprache in modernen Medien. Einführung in Tatsachen und Theorien, Themen und Thesen*. Erich Schmidt Verlag, Berlin 2004.

Spitzmüller, Jürgen: „Chat-Kommunikation. Interaktion im virtuellen Raum als multidisziplinäres Forschungsfeld". In: Moraldo, Sandro M. (ed.): *Internet.Kom. Neue Sprach- und Kommunikationsformen im WorldWideWeb*. AracneEditrice: Roma 2009, 71–107.

Stöckl, Hartmut: „Medienlinguistik. Zu Status und Methodik eines (noch) emergenten Forschungsfeldes". In: Grösslinger, Christian et al. (eds.): *Pressetextsorten jenseits der ‚News'*. Peter Lang: Frankfurt am Main 2012, 13–34.

Stöckl, Hartmut: „Multimodalität. Semiotische und textlinguistische Grundlagen". In: Klug, Nina-Maria & Stöckl, Hartmut (eds.): *Sprache im multimodalen Kontext*. de Gruyter: Berlin, Boston 2016, 3–35.

Swales, John M.: *Genre Analysis. English in Academic and Research Settings*. CUP: Cambridge 1990.

Tausk, Petr: *A Short History of Press Photography*. The International Organization of Journalists: Prague 1988.

Wilson, Christopher. "The Rhetoric of Consumption. Mass-Market Magazines and the Demise of the Gentle Reader, 1880–1920". In: Fox, Richard & Lears,

Jackson (eds.): *The Culture of Consumption. Critical Essays in American History, 1860–1960.* Pantheon Books: New York 1983, 39–64.

Ziegler, Arne: „E-Mail – Textsorte oder Kommunikationsform? Eine textlinguistische Annäherung". In: Ziegler, Arne & Dürscheid, Christa (eds.): *Kommunikationsform E-Mail.* Stauffenburg: Tübingen 2002, 9–32.

Zimmermann, Philipp: *Four-color Letterpress Printing of the National Geographic Magazine in the Nineteen Fifties and Sixties*, retrieved 23.09.2016, from https://vimeo.com/78230375, 2013.

Hallesche Sprach- und Textforschung
Language and Text Studies
Recherches linguistiques et textuelles

Herausgegeben von / Edited by / Dirigée par Alexander Brock und Annette Schiller

Band 1 Annette Schiller: Die présentatifs im heutigen Französisch. Eine funktionale Studie ihrer Vielfalt. 1992.

Band 2 Gertrud Bense (Hrsg.): Diachronie – Kontinuität – Impulse. Sprachwissenschaftliches Kolloquium Halle 1992. 1994.

Band 3 Wolfgang Boeck (Hrsg.): Sprache, Literatur und Landeskunde slavischer Völker. Funktionale Aspekte in der Beschreibung und Didaktik. 1994.

Band 4 Gertrud Bense (Hrsg.): Kommunikation und Grammatik. 1996.

Band 5 Gisela Hermann-Brennecke / Dietmar Schneider (Hrsg.): Dona Anglica. 120 Jahre Anglistik in Halle. 1997.

Band 6 Max Hans-Jürgen Mattusch: Vielsprachigkeit: Fluch oder Segen für die Menschheit? Zu Fragen einer europäischen und globalen Fremdsprachenpolitik. 1999.

Band 7 Christiane Schiller: Bilinguismus. Zur Darstellung eines soziolinguistischen Phänomens in der Literatur. Dargestellt an Beispielen der regionalen Literatur Preußisch-Litauens: Hermann Sudermann *Litauische Geschichten*, Ieva Simonaityte *Vilius Karalius*. 2000.

Band 8 Gertrud Bense: „Giedojam taw – Wir singen dir". Zur Textgeschichte der preußisch-litauischen Gesangbücher im 18. Jahrhundert. Mit besonderer Berücksichtigung der Liedersammlung von Fabian Ulrich Glaser (1688–1747) und ihrem Umfeld. 2001.

Band 9 Gertrud Bense / Gerhard Meiser / Edeltraud Werner (Hrsg.): August Friedrich Pott. Beiträge der Halleschen Tagung anlässlich des zweihundertsten Geburtstages von August Friedrich Pott (1802–1887). 2005.

Band 10 Julia Balakina: Anglicisms in Russian and German Blogs. A Comparative Analysis. 2011.

Band 11 Thomas Bremer /Annette Schiller (Hrsg.): Dialekt und Standardsprache in Italien und Europa. Edeltraud Werner zum 60. Geburtstag. 2012.

Band 12 Anne Ammermann / Alexander Brock / Jana Pflaeging / Peter Schildhauer (eds.): Facets of Linguistics. Proceedings of the 14th Norddeutsches Linguistisches Kolloquium 2013 in Halle an der Saale. 2013.

Band 13 Anja Neuber: Perspektiven des Friaulischen. Eine soziolinguistische Untersuchung am Beispiel junger Erwachsener. 2015.

Band 14 Peter Schildhauer: The Personal Weblog. A Linguistic History. 2016.

Band 15 Alexander Brock / Peter Schildhauer (eds.): Communication Forms and Communicative Practices. New Perspectives on Communication Forms, Affordances and What Users Make of Them. 2017.

www.peterlang.com